I0071477

GettingtoWOWbook.com

"After many conversations with Christoff, and after reading through the pages of **Getting to WOW!** it is clear to me that he truly gets what is needed to be successful in the service industry. It is hard to find words to describe the inner-workings of the psyche that need to be in place for you to do the job well and, at the same time, enjoy every bit of the experience as a FOH professional, but he has done just that. His tone throughout this book bodes well for those who are actually working in the field and will give them a leg up in regards to doing the job correctly.

Even those of us that are seasoned veterans in the industry need to take a look at things needed to **WOW!** the customer experience every once in a while. This book is truly a **MUST READ** for anyone who wants to be the very best they can be. In my opinion, this map to success should be read by anyone dealing with people in any line of work.
As one who feels that customer service is the most important part of everything we do on a daily basis, Mr. Weihman hits points that are very important in the foundation of a successful career. I highly recommend that **Getting to WOW!** be part of your library."
-        Shaun Daugherty - Author of Extra Dry, with a Twist: An Insider's Guide to Bartending

"Guests today demand more for their dollars spent in restaurants. Service industry professionals are no longer expected to just serve food; they are expected to create experiences. **Getting to WOW!** educates the service professional on those fundamentals to achieve this.
Getting to WOW! equips a service professional to enhance and grow their skillset by teaching the fundamentals of service, and critical thought elements, that are not otherwise taught in the restaurant environment. These skills are invaluable in the service professional's career to execute a superior guest experience. The elements described in this book are what enable a service professional to craft and create a superior guest experience. These elements are what the novice server lack that separates them from the most seasoned veteran. This content within this book contains the fundamentals that can drastically excel a service professional's career."
-Michael Balabon, Bottega Louie- Los Angeles, California

Getting to
WOW!

Everybody WINS with 5 Star Service

CHRISTOFF J. WEIHMAN

ASPIRE ENTERPRISES-PUBLISHING
LAS VEGAS, NEVADA
2014

Printed in the United States of America

First Printing, 2014

ISBN-13: 978-0692359198
ISBN-10: 0692359192

ASPIRE Enterprises-Publishing
Las Vegas, NV 89117

GettingtoWOWbook.com

To the Love of my life-my Amazing wife, Michelle-I choose you. Thank you for saying "Yes" and for being my partner in life. I am blessed beyond words.

To my Mom, Margaret Hanselman-who lives a life of service and gives to our family, the Lord and others. You were the first person to ever model service for me

To my Daughter, Kimberly Grace, who serves selflessly as a teacher, giving of herself, with no fanfare. She is a blessing to the young lives that she touches.

To my Son, Josiah Christopher, who bravely and proudly, serves our country in the United States Air Force

To all Service & Hospitality Professionals who have ever carried a tray, greeted a guest, taken an order, served a meal, poured a drink, or bussed a table-what you do, is so much more than that. You are the unsung heroes of the industry. Now, it's time that you be sung.

Table of Contents
Preface
Acknowledgements
Introduction-What is WOW!?

1.	Getting a MAP for Your Journey	01
2.	Getting in the Flow of Positive Energy	19
3.	Getting a Servant Heart	26
4.	Getting a Sense of Pride	31
5.	Getting NOT "Good Enough"	35
6.	Getting the Book Out of the Back of Your Pants!	40
7.	Getting Back to the Basics	50
8.	Getting Knowledgeable	66
9.	Getting Ready for the Show-It is a Show, You Know	83
10.	Getting the First Kiss	93
11.	Getting to Know Your Guests	105
12.	Getting Beyond "I'll Be Your Server Tonight"	119
13.	Getting Focused on the Details	129
14.	Getting Enticing	136
15.	Getting Clarity, Confirmation & Understanding	149
16.	Getting the Balance Between TMA & TLA	157
17.	Getting Restaurant Eyes	164
18.	Getting Competent & Consistent	172
19.	Getting in Sync (FOH & BOH)	181
20.	Getting Them to Get Tiramisu	191
21.	Getting Them Where They Need to Go	200
22.	Getting Past the Soupfly	203
23.	Getting the Recovery	220
24.	Getting Anchored	227
25.	Getting the Encore	233
26.	Welcome to WOW!	239

Acknowledgements

"So understand, sincere acknowledgements nigh, harken always about remembrances"
Old English-Anonymous

Writing this book has been a journey of more than 6 years. Actually, that's not true, it's been much longer than that, because the principles in this book, I began to learn many years ago, when I first started working in restaurants. There have been so many people who have contributed to this end product-many directly, others indirectly, some of them knowingly and others-like many of my mentors-really have no clue that their work has impacted or influenced me to put these ideas and concepts on paper. The point is-there are so many that I am grateful to and for, who have assisted me in some way, in bringing my vision of making **Getting to WOW!** a reality.

First, I want to thank my wife, Michelle, for her love, encouragement, sacrifice and faith in me. And for being my main editor and sounding board. She has been with me during the final stages (2 years) of bringing Getting to WOW! to fruition. In many ways it almost seems like she has been with me from the beginning -6 plus years ago. However, at that point, our paths had not crossed yet. I thank her for all her input, suggestions, corrections, etc. Any mistakes in the manuscript though-that credit goes to me, as the author.

I want to thank all the restaurants, hotels, and catering companies that I have worked at over the years. Some of them showed me great examples of what *WOW!* service is, while others modeled what not to do and what *WOW!* service is NOT. I am grateful for all those experiences-for I learned from them all. Two places in particular where I worked that truly exemplified Service Excellence are Wolfgang Puck Catering and Events at Hollywood and Highland in Hollywood and Vin de Set Restaurant in St. Louis, Missouri. Although, I've worked at many, many restaurants in many cities and even in Guam and Saipan, it was those two that I really learned to develop *WOW!* service. I want to thank Ivy Magruder, executive chef at Vin de Set, at the time I worked there-as he was the very first person that I interviewed for **Getting to WOW!** more than 5 years ago.

In preparing for this book, I have observed, listened to, conversed with countless individuals who work in the Service and Hospitality industry. Their ideas, insights and suggestions have informed me as I wrote this book. I simply cannot cite all of their names here and truth be told, I couldn't even begin to remember all of them. But I do thank you all.

There are quite a few, that I have actually sat down with, notes, questions in hand, voice recorder turned on and we had a legitimate interview. Some of these individuals were server/bartenders, others were owners and managers. Many of them are quoted in **Getting to WOW!**-either directly or paraphrased. If the quote is not accurate, please forgive me. Much of the information and the thoughts that they shared with me, corroborated my own ideas and thoughts and therefore, I may not have actually quoted or credited them per se. But please know, that they all were very instrumental in the creation and completion of this book. Thank you all for your generous gift of your time, your input and for being ones who truly care about the Service side of the industry.

The following are Service and Hospitality Professionals who shared their wisdom and insights with me during one on one interviews:

Ivy Magruder Executive Chef-now, at Panorama Restaurant in the St. Louis Art Museum; **Adam Gnau**- Executive Chef of Acero Restaurant in St. Louis, Missouri; **Olivier de Roany**- Assistant General Manager at MIX in the Delano Hotel in Las Vegas;
Alex Stratta-James Beard Award Winning Chef and Restaurateur in Las Vegas; **Mitchell Sjevern**-owner of Bouchon of Santa Barbara; **Jim Edwards**-owner Next Door Food & Drink in Loveland, Colorado; **Sydney Nelson**-Server/Bartender at Next Door Food & Drink in Loveland, Colorado; **Christopher "Mo" Moore**-Server/Trainer at Kona Grill in Las Vegas; **Joe Cortes**- Assistant General Manager at Honey Salt in Las Vegas; **Mandy Monreal**-former Corporate Hostess Trainer for all Wolfgang Puck Restaurants in Las Vegas; **Greg DaLuz**-Server at Giada in Las Vegas; **Theo Van Soest**-Server at Yellowtail in the Bellagio in Las Vegas; **Michael Skurow**- CIA alum and wine distributor representative in Las Vegas.

I also would like to acknowledge and thank the following, for their participation and contribution:
Michael Balabon-founder/owner of Bottega Louie in Los Angeles and Echo & Rig in Las Vegas; Sheri Holliday of the Mirage in Las Vegas; **Kim Canteenwalla**-owner/partner of Blau & Associates in Las Vegas.

A special thank you to my long-time friend, **Marlo Boutte** who is an NLP practitioner and hypnotherapist, for her contribution to the chapter-Getting Anchored. I also, want to thank my friend,
Hanna Redi-who carries the same credentials, for sharing her expertise in the same chapter. Thank you Marlo and Hanna for making the topic very layman friendly.

A special Thank you to **Megan Birnstein**, who conceived & designed the original concept for the book's cover. Great vision!

I want to thank **all my Soupfly readers** from 50 plus countries from around the world for your support.

I am a lover of books and I have always dreamt of being an author, myself. There are many authors whose work has had a profound impact on me over the years. Each one has positively affected me in some way-many of them I have actually quoted in **Getting to WOW!**

My debts of gratitude goes out to:
Napoleon Hill-his book, Think and Grow Rich, was the genesis of my paradigm shift and an epiphany. My way of thinking has never been the same since.
Jack Canfield-his book, The Success Principles, has been a volume that I've returned to over and over again along my journey. His story of how he, and Mark Victor Hansen brought Chicken Soup for the Soul, from concept to worldwide multi-million dollars best seller, is a constant motivation and inspiration for any author of any level, including me.
Mark Victor Hansen, years ago, when I first moved to St. Louis, I listened to a CD series by him entitled, Dreams Don't Have Deadlines. No, they don't. Mark famously tells people-"You have a book inside of you." I've always known that I did and reading his books-any and all of them, and listening to him, has been high octane fuel for my motivation tank while on this book-writing-expedition of mine.
Marshall Sylver-whose book, Passion, Profit and Power is one of my favorite. I read it many years ago and then sort of lost track of it. Then about 6 years ago, I rediscovered it and it still has a positive impact on my daily life and the thoughts I think.

Dr. Wayne Dyer, he is such a prolific writer that I won't even attempt to list all of his works that have influenced me. Suffice to say, that in addition to being a man of great wisdom and insight, he is a wonderful writer, and reading his words has continued to fan the flame inside of me of wanting to one day be an author myself.

Rhonda Byrne-The author of The Secret-A worldwide phenomenon that took such classic works like Think and Grow Rich and As a Man Thinketh, and others, and brought the concept of the Law of Attraction to modern day readers in an easy and approachable manner. She also introduced me and many of us, to great teachers and writers who have made a positive impact.

These include: **Dr. Joe Vitale, John Assaraf, & Bob Proctor.**

Other authors whom I have been influenced by and most of them I have quoted here in **Getting to WOW!** If I have not quoted them, still their work has been important to me and my life and career in some manner:

Anthony Robbins-I have learned so much from his teaching tapes and his books. He is so much more than just a "motivational speaker". He understands people and what drives them. He has helped me to think big and really get out of my comfort zone. His passion for life is contagious. I always am mindful of his advice to "Take Massive Immediate Action" and I adopt it as my personal mantra.

Jeffery Gitomer-he is the author of the The Sales Bible and The Little Red Book of Sales. I've learned more about sales from him than from anyone else.

T Harv Eker-author of The Secrets of the Millionaire Mind, and the creator of The Millionaire Mind Intensive Seminar (MM). It was while I was at the MMI in San Diego, California-two plus years ago, when another epiphany happened for me. From that moment on, everything in my life began to really come together. **Adam Markel** was the trainer at that particular seminar-it was a life-changing, break- thru for me. It was not just one idea or concept that did it for me, but rather the whole weekend seminar. To say it was 'life-changing' is not an exaggeration. "Clarity is Power." Although it took two more years, I needed to attend that MMI in order for me to complete this book. Thank you Harv and Adam.

Jeff Olson, I first was introduced to him when I worked as an independent representative for Pre-paid Legal, (now Legal Shield). He spoke at the National Convention in Oklahoma City and I was lit up. I bought his amazing book-The Slight Edge, which I quote in **Getting to WOW!** His philosophy and teaching inform my choices daily. Thank you, Jeff.

David Siteman Garland-author of Smarter, Faster, Cheaper. I believe he is the first author, I met live and in person. Actually, I knew him before he got his book deal. I used to watch his show, The Rise to the Top, when I lived in St. Louis, Missouri. He has always been a champion of entrepreneurs and teaching others to get their message out there. Although I don't quote his book in **Getting to WOW!** I do count him as a mentor.

John Maxwell, Joel Osteen, and **Patrick Lencioni**, are a few other authors whose work I appreciate and avidly read and follow.

Recently, I discovered two more author/speakers who have become my newest mentors-**Brendon Burchard**, author of The Motivation Manifesto, and **Grant Cardone**, author of IF YOU'RE NOT FIRST, YOU'RE LAST, amongst others. Both of these guys are at the top of their game, they have amazing valuable content and I read and listen to anything and everything I can by them. Thank you Brendon and Grant. I look forward to meeting you both someday.

My sincerest thanks to **Gerry Robert**, founder and president of Black Card Books and the Publish a Book and Grow Rich Seminar. You provided the final 'umph' I needed to complete the manuscript. The resources that Black Card Books have provided me are invaluable. You helped me say, "I am an author." Thank you.

A big thank you to **Rosalyn Poon**, whom I met at the Publish a Book and Grow Rich Seminar, for her creative input on my subtitle-it was originally something different-that had less impact. Rosalyn got me thinking in the direction of where we ended up-Everybody WINS with 5 Star Service. Also, thank you for your input on one of the main graphs that I've included in the book.

I am truly grateful for **all the guests, diners, customers that I've had the opportunity to serve over the years**. I have worked in this industry in the following places: Ottawa, Illinois; Saipan; Guam; Los Angeles, California; Orange County, California; St. Louis, Missouri. Service is non-existent if there are no guests to serve. I thank you all, and believe me I know that I wasn't always a great example of **WOW!** service. I know that I didn't have a great attitude all the time. I know that I didn't get your order right all the time. I know that I didn't always do my best. But as I learned and developed my skills, my passion for the business and my mindset, I know that I did do better. Thank you all for allowing me the privilege of serving you.

I want to especially thank **the guests and the regulars at Paul Mineo's Trattoria in St. Louis, where I served for 3 plus years.** Many of you became my friends, and although we don't keep in touch, please know that I was blessed to be able to serve you for those 3 years. Whether you came in once, or I served you every week, I thank you. It was truly a joy to serve you. With that in mind,

I would like to acknowledge and thank my friends, **Apollo and Amanda Carey,** who were regulars and who I served about 2-3 times a month there. Thank you for being so encouraging whenever I would share with you about the book. And thank you for your comments and insights from the diner's perspective.

Another one of those regulars is **Attorney Rudy Beck**. I had the pleasure of serving him on numerous occasions over the course of my tenure at Paul Mineo's. I used to talk with him about my book, this book. Originally I was using the working title of How to **WOW!** or The Power of WOW!-both which I thought were very viable titles. Well, one day, Rudy came in and he suggested I title it-Getting to

WOW! and guess what? Well, look at the cover. Thanks Rudy!

I want to give special recognition to the late **Paul Mineo**-who hired me as a server when he opened his namesake restaurant in Westport Plaza in St. Louis. After a few short months, he promoted me, well, he never used the word 'promotion', rather, he gave me more responsibility. He gave me the opportunity to be the catering and event sales manager. That added responsibility told me that Paul saw some positive qualities in me and it was a great honor to represent him and his restaurant to the business community.

I learned a great deal during that time and I earned a great deal during that time. Paul passed away while I was working there, in July of 2009. I will be forever grateful to Paul for the opportunity he gave me. It was during my time at Paul Mineo's that I first began thinking about this book and putting notes on paper. His widow, **Brigitte**, continues on Paul's legacy, owning and operating Paul Mineo's Trattoria.

I'm sure there are other people who have been a part of my life, have influenced, encouraged, supported and motivated me along the way as I've been working on this book. If I have not mentioned you specifically, I still thank you for being a part of my life, for your faith in me and knowing that I would reach this goal. I thank you all.

Preface

"Ask yourself whether anyone has delivered you a truly "wow" experience within the last 90 days. I expect the answer from most of you will be no. People today are so accustomed to poor or mediocre service-both before and after the sale-that when they get something a few notches above mediocre, they are certain to notice the difference. It's very rare for people to deliver at levels that really create an exceptional experience or positive impression. Ask yourself what percentage of the time you even remember the person who served you. If you did remember them, what percentage of the time did you remember them because they "sucked"? I would expect that you don't remember more often than not-and when you do, it's because it was a bad experience, not a good one."

Grant Cardone, IF YOU'RE NOT FIRST, YOU'RE LAST

So, let's get right to it... Who am I? And what, if anything, qualifies me to write a book about 'First Class Restaurant Service'? **'Getting to *WOW!*'**?? Really? Are you serious? Well, on the one hand, I'm the average person who enjoys dining out-and has very rarely been "Wowed" in my dining experiences. I am more often 'wowed' it seems, when I am watching an episode of Top Chef or Iron Chef America. Did they really create that dish? That looks amazing. But really, how amazing- I think to myself, if it were served in a beautiful restaurant in – name your place- and the ambience, service and total experience was as fantastic as the creativity, effort, energy and process that was involved in making said dish. –

Yes, it is true that I am very rarely 'Wowed' when I dine out-and it is my contention-call it a thesis, that you, the reader, the guest, are also-similarly-rarely 'Wowed'. And so, I pose the same question to you. How often are you...or more specifically- WHEN was the last time you were 'Wowed' from beginning to end, in your dining experience or any other service related event?

Yes, perhaps, it could be that I've not gone to the right places, be it here in St. Louis, or elsewhere. Granted, there's a long, yes, long list of places, restaurants, new and old that I've yet to visit and therefore, my perspective and dining experience is limited. However, I have lived and worked in quite a few places, not only here in the United States, but overseas as well. And to be quite honest-and anybody who knows me-knows I hardly ever use that phrase- to be quite straightforward-I'm so amazed-I'm so often 'Wowed' in the other direction, as to how difficult it seems to be to find the **WOW!** in dining experiences these days.

I may be completely all alone in this matter, in a category all by myself. ...Or, is it possible that actually the art of service has somehow, somewhere, gotten lost along the way? If, so... if, indeed that may be the case then we must embark on a journey to find out what it takes, what is entailed in "**Getting to WOW!**" And when I say-"**Getting to WOW!**"- I'm not talking about "Wow, let's get out of here". But rather as in "Wow, that was a wonderful experience. And I can't wait to tell others, how great it was." So, here's my question to you-What does "**Getting to WOW!**" really mean? And how do you "get" there?

Currently, I live in St. Louis, Missouri-which certainly is not known as a culinary destination, per se. Well, don't tell the people in St. Louis that. However, there are numerous cutting edge-nouveau cuisine -Chef/owned restaurants. In fact, most types of international cuisine can be found here, although certainly not in the abundance and variety as in New York, Los Angeles, Chicago or Las Vegas.

New restaurants are opening up all the time. Millions of dollars are spent in renovating old historic buildings, transforming them into beautiful ambient spaces. At the same time, untold dollars are spent on up and coming, trendsetting chefs, menus, bars and all the accoutrements. And yet, when it comes to the service staff-be it the bartenders or the wait staff-it seems to me, that oftentimes, it is the last aspect to be considered or covered. It is the one area that seems to be given the least amount of time, energy, effort and preparation.

"Hey we are opening this beautiful new restaurant in the newly renovated downtown district- It's called 'Fennel'. The chef was trained at CIA, he's worked in Vegas and New York. The food is superb, creative, crisp, clean flavors, the chef's passion really shines through. There's a classy brass and tile mosaic on the wall near the chic and trendy bar. The ambience of the whole place says class.
We're opening in a week. Oh, and by the way-we need to hire some servers. What? Training? Of course, we'll be going over the menu with them. Make sure we hire servers that have experience. Okay, great we're all set."

Service, I believe, in so many establishments is A BIG AFTERTHOUGHT. Why? Why is that so frequently the case? I'm not quite sure, but I have some ideas that I'd like to share with you.
So, what qualifies me to write this book? First, I have knowledge gained from experience both as an industry professional- and as one -who like many of you- enjoys dining out. I am the target demographic, I'm my own market research. Although, what is set forth in this book is not merely my own ideas. I have consulted with other like-minded individuals and I've interviewed people from all sides of the service experience- the diners themselves-call them foodies if you like; the chefs and owners and people on the management side and the servers- the ones in the trenches-from all levels of service.

Also, I have some authority to write this because I, too, am a service professional. I have a passion for excellence for creating and providing an exceptional dining experience all the time, every time for everyone that I have the privilege of serving.

Another reason that I believe I am qualified to bring these thoughts forth on paper-is not only my experience, knowledge and passion- but also my frustration. I don't want to be the one who sits around complaining. You know they say that if you don't vote, then you've got no reason to complain about the government. Well, I registered, I voted and now I'm speaking out- not about the government, but about the restaurant industry.

You might ask me 'what is the purpose of this book?' Well, first and foremost, I am addressing my colleagues in the service industry. I would like to be a beacon of light of sorts. I want to pass on to you some thoughts about how to improve your game. Think of me as your service coach. My goal is not to bash you over the head and make you feel bad. I'm not here to just point out what is wrong.
Rather, I want to provide tools and information that can help us all raise the bar of restaurant service in the industry. I believe that if you approach this book with an open heart and open mind, then you may greatly benefit from reading this, that is, if you apply what you learn here.

We, in the service industry live off of tips, paid to us by our guests/diners that we serve. Yes, we are paid a minimum wage, that is a pittance-in St. Louis it is only $3.25 per hour(-in California it is $5.75 and it varies around the country) but we never really see it because that just barely, covers the taxes on the tips we receive. So truly, our income is only the tips we receive. The advantage or positive aspect of this is that we often make and take cash home every night.

The obvious drawback is that our income is so irregular and undependable. We are at the mercy of the season, the busy-ness of the restaurant, the amount of tables we get and what type of patrons and how many we serve on each day or night. So, since there are so many uncontrollable variables that affect your/our income- wouldn't you agree that it makes absolute total sense to improve the only aspect that you can effect control over-that is your service skills? I hope you begin to see the value in this.

Many servers calculate their expected tips based upon the sales they've rung.

Example: A couple comes in for a nice romantic dinner which ends up costing them $125.00. The server automatically, mentally calculates $25.00 as his expected tip. "I'll get 25 bucks from them." he says to himself. He drops the check and they leave him 15 dollars. He picks up the checkbook, sees the 15 dollars cash and immediately is upset and frustrated. "Cheap skates" he mumbles.

Why did the couple leave him such a small tip? Industry standard accepted tip is 20% or at the least 18%. So why the small tip? It certainly could be for any number of reasons. Maybe they didn't expect the cost of the dinner to be so high-they ordered a special but did not ask the server how much it cost and were therefore, surprised at the bill. Maybe, they were foreigners-foreigners are not known as generous tippers. They don't understand the concept of tipping in America because in most European countries servers make a pretty decent wage.

Now, if in fact they were foreigners- the server in our above example, would have recognized that they were and rather than just calling them "cheap" he would most likely, have commented on the fact that they were foreign. He probably would have been upset, but not surprised by the low tip. So, again, I ask, why the low tip? Could the answer be that the guests did not deem the service to be worth a higher tip? In their mind the service was not on par with the ambience of the place and the food.

Just because a dinner cost $125.00 that doesn't mean that the service provided automatically merited a 20% tip. But if one is working in a restaurant that offers entrees in the 25-40 dollar range, ought the staff be trained in providing a level and standard of service that equals such level? Ought they? I would say 'yes'. But are they always? From my experience, I would say no, not often enough. Many servers have not been taught or trained how to provide such level of service. So, maybe it's not really their fault. Then who is to blame? We'll delve into that later as the book unfolds.

Let me just say this- one of my main premises is: It takes so little. It takes so little to provide **WOW!** service. It takes so little to keep a new customer. It takes very little to make them a happy and satisfied customer. I don't believe most customers, guests, diners, are looking for unreasonable expectations to be met. They just want a little bit more. A little more care, a little more concern, a little more attention to detail. And conversely, I believe it takes so little to mess it up- a crappy attitude, a short rude answer to a guest's question, a nonchalant air about you. Little things effect a huge impact in my book.

Who am I? I'm someone who knows a little bit about what I'm talking about here. I'm 47 years old now and have quite a few years of experience in the hotel and restaurant industry, as well as in sales and service. In fact, that's about all I've ever done in one way or another since I was 15 years old, with the exception of the years I was a missionary in Asia. Yet, even during those years-I was doing ministry- and what is ministry if not to serve? Jesus, himself said, "He that is great in my kingdom is the one who is the servant of all" So, in my humble opinion, I certainly do have the qualifications and the authority to write such a book as **Getting to WOW!**

Currently, I work as an event coordinator/banquet sales manager and server, for a family owned Italian restaurant in St. Louis, Missouri.

Previously, I worked for 3 years in Los Angeles for Wolfgang Puck Catering and Events. I had the privilege of serving the Governor's Ball (the celebrity dinner party after the Academy Awards) 3 years in a row. This event hosts high profile actors, directors, producers, et al for an exquisite dinner that cost $900.00 per person. That's right-NINE HUNDRED DOLLARS PER PERSON! And believe me, we absolutely learned how to and were expected to provide top notch, excellent service *WOW!* service.

Now, as much as I enjoyed the opportunity to serve celebrities and high profile people-Wolfgang Puck is known for catering such events on a regular basis, not just during award season-it really matters not to me whom I am serving. It could be Adam Sandler at his wedding-I did; or the mayor of Los Angeles, yes, also, or President Bill Clinton-woo-how lucky, or my friends Apollo and Amanda Carey or some guy who walks into the restaurant wearing sweats, flip-flops and a t-shirt, my attitude, my focus, energy and actions and desire are always the same-to create and provide an exceptional dining experience all the time, everywhere no matter who it is that I'm serving. And that is what this is about-First Class Restaurant Service. So, I invite you to come with me through these pages and let's discover together what is involved in providing that exceptional service in **Getting to WOW!**-First Class Restaurant Service.

Update: The above preface I wrote over 4 years ago. I was, as I mentioned, living in St. Louis, Missouri at the time. I am no longer working as a Server, Banquet Coordinator/Event Sales Manager. Recently, I moved to Las Vegas which is, by many people's estimation, the Mecca of the restaurant world, at least here in the United States.

I have been privileged to work in many capacities in the Service and Hospitality industry, as well as a volunteer missionary overseas. When I lived in St. Louis, I guess I had a biased perspective thinking that mediocre standards for service was just a common thing there.

I had moved to St. Louis from Los Angeles where for 3 years, I was blessed to work for Wolfgang Puck Catering and Events. Wolfgang Puck is known in the industry as being synonymous with Excellence-not only his cuisine but definitely his Service as well.

When I was living in L.A. I didn't really dine out that much-ok-pretty much never. So, I now realize that I was living in a bubble. I experienced Service Excellence as a person on the inside-the one serving. When I moved to St. Louis and began dining out often, I would always compare the service I received there with what I know we, at least endeavored to deliver at Wolfgang Puck. I knew that Service Excellence was very achievable. I just didn't see it often enough when I dined out. In fact, I did work for at least one restaurant that I felt really took this Service and Hospitality thing seriously.

The idea for this book, **Getting to WOW!** grew out of my frustration and the gap I saw between what I know is possible-that is, the ability to provide Excellence in Service, and what I perceived as the lack of care or concern for it. I wanted to share with others about Service Excellence. Since I've been living in Las Vegas and as I've been traveling the country the past few years-I have experienced all levels of service at all different types of restaurants. I now know that there are restaurants that have poor, good and great service EVERYWHERE in the country.

Sorry, St. Louis, for it taking me this long to realize that. But certainly the ones that are excellent are much fewer than the ones that provide average or mediocre service.

Originally, the subtitle of this book was, First Class Restaurant Service, and although that is what **Getting to WOW!** is about-in many ways, these principles and concepts, can be applied to any service industry. Certainly you don't need to know how to carry a tray filled with drinks, or how to present and pour wine if you are working as a receptionist at a car dealership. However, the majority of the principles are applicable whether you're dealing with clients, customers in retail, or guests. If you work in any such industry, then you are in Service and Hospitality. What about Sales? Well, Service is Sales and Sales is Service and you can't really excel at one without employing success principles in the other. If you are a Service Professional then you are in Sales as well. Conversely, if you are a Salesperson, Service is a vital element to your success.

For all the above reasons, as I was nearing the end of writing, nearly 6 ½ years of time-I was inspired to change the subtitle to: Everybody WINS with 5 Star Service. I don't think that phrase really needs any explanation.

Earlier this year, I began my blog on the same topic, entitled, Soupfly. If you have not yet been introduced to it, I invite you to visit it: www.Soupfly.net
I am quite happy and proud to say that in less than 6 months Soupfly has traveled the globe and we have readers from over 50 countries!!

A couple of the chapters in **Getting to WOW***!* Everybody WINS with 5 Star Service, actually came from Soupfly, and have been reprinted the way they appeared in the blog, minus the pictures.

I have recently started ASPIRE Enterprises, a Service and Hospitality Training and Consulting company. Simply stated the acronym for ASPIRE explains our focus:
Advancing Service Performance, Inspiring Restaurant Excellence
I have given myself the moniker of SERVICE ELEVATER. For that truly is my goal-to help elevate the level of service and hospitality in the industry, by raising the standard for what is expected, providing coaching, training and tools and equipping Service Professionals to up their game.

I have a very simple philosophy which is proven over and over again in this industry. A restaurant that provides excellent service and hospitality to its clientele will be more likely to succeed than one that pays no mind or attention to the quality and level of Service they provide. Poor service will result in bad reviews, decline in customers-both new and old and ultimately a decline in revenue and profits. In turn, you will have low-paid, dissatisfied, unfulfilled employees. The quality of Service and Hospitality that your establishment provides it's guests is directly tied to the overall success or failure of your business.

This is a wonderful and exciting business/industry. The people who work in it are, for the most part, very committed individuals. Those who work on the service side, are the true unsung heroes of the business. I appreciate and applaud the amazing work that Chefs do. I, in no way wish to diminish the importance that they play in this industry. I have many friends who are Chefs and they themselves, also concur that it is the Service and Hospitality Professionals that are under-acknowledged and under-appreciated players on the team.

Now, it's the Service Professionals turn to Shine. My desire is to help them be the best that they can be at this game called Service and Hospitality.

It is my hope and prayer that this book, **Getting to WOW!** Everybody WINS with 5 Star Service will serve you in that mission. Here's to you, the Service Professional!

Cheers and God Bless,
Christoff J. Weihman
Summerlin, Nevada
December 5, 2014

Introduction

What is *WOW!?*

What is WOW!? Let's ponder for a moment. When, if ever, have you found yourself saying "WOW!"? When was the last time you were 'WOWed?' When you say or think of the word doesn't it evoke thoughts of something unbelievable, unimaginable-even inexplicable? Something beyond the ordinary, the mundane, the expected? When was the last time you said "Wow"?

Maybe you were in Las Vegas, watching Cirque du Soleil's water show called 'O'. You were transfixed as you took in the amazing spectacle on the stage before you, and you exclaimed aloud to your friend seated beside you, "Did you see that? Wow-that was amazing!" There was exclamation in your voice. You were drawn in-mesmerized. Or perhaps, still in Las Vegas, you were front and center for Criss Angel's show. There you sat as he performed an impossible, fantastic, mind- blowing feat. A MindFreak! And you shouted "Wow!" "Unbelievable!"

Or maybe you got your credit card statement in the mail after going on a Caribbean vacation and you said "Wow- we spent that much?" In that case your expression of 'wow' certainly was one of disbelief. Or it could be that your boyfriend or girlfriend-whom you lived with for the past 5 years, one day, suddenly, tells you it's over. You are shocked, caught off-guard, blindsided. And your immediate heart-wrenching response is "Wow, are you kidding me? This can't really be happening."

I mention the above examples to point out what I'm sure to many of you is already obvious-that is, that the concept of 'WOW!' is not necessarily always, only associated with something good. However, for the most part, and certainly for our purposes-when I speak of 'WOW!' here in **Getting to *WOW!*** it is to the positive end of the scale, to which I am referring.

Here's a thought, an idea-next time you go into a restaurant or any kind of establishment where you are going to pay for/ receive a service of any sort-that could be not only a restaurant, but a hotel, a spa, a winery, a bank, a grocery store, a hair salon, doesn't matter-I recommend that you rate it. Rate it in your own mind. Don't do this aloud. Rate it's decor, it's staff, the food or product, the service, etc. and ask yourself...How does it rate on a scale of '1 to WOW!'? Now that scale could be infinite. You set the standard in your own mind. And then once you've considered the question, answer it. How does this place rate on a scale of 1 to WOW!?
And in order to answer that, one has to answer the first question I posed above...What is **'*WOW!*?'**

Certainly, for one thing I would think it must be the unexpected. Is it not? I don't think anyone would sincerely be 'WOWed' by something they already knew was coming or by something they were expecting. Except maybe the birth of a child- but even then, it was only the birth of the child that was expected, not what kind of awe-inspiring experience it would be. So, in talking about what ***WOW!*** is, maybe we could agree for one that it would be meeting or exceeding the 'unexpectations' of someone. Would you agree?

In my humble opinion, I find it quite disheartening that many words in our English language which, once upon a time, held such weight and were pregnant with meaning, have since been stripped away of their original definition by the nonchalant, colloquial over-usage of them. For example; how often do we hear people-especially the younger generation, using the word 'awesome' to mean something that's kind of neat and cool, but clearly (at least in my opinion) not 'awesome'. "How was the movie you saw last night?" "It was awesome!"
"Did you see the game last night?" "Yeah, man, it was awesome!"

And when I hear such repartee, I say to myself or perhaps on occasion aloud- "Really? Was it really 'awe-some'; full of awe; awe-inspiring?" What a waste of a word. It's been dumbed down.

Very few things in life are Awe-Some. Bearing witness to the birth of your child - 'awe-some'. Perfecting the latest skateboard trick-not Awe-Some.
Beholding the Grand Canyon in all it's glory and wonder- perhaps- 'Awe-Some'.
 In my mind "WOW!" has to be somewhere on a scale between 1 and what awesome used to mean. Of course, it is probably true that "WOW!" is in the eyes of the beholder, the experiencer of the event. Thankfully, from my perception, the word "WOW!" is still one that has not yet been dumbed down. I think we all can agree when something is "WOW!". Not sure. I may be completely wrong.
WOW!, then, must be something that one was or is not expecting. It certainly has to do with a standard of excellence, but I believe it's so much more than that.

Oftentimes, when someone is WOWed, they may not be able to actually accurately describe just what was it that WOWed them. And that is because it is often something intangible. In a dining experience, it isn't necessarily any one "*WOW!* experiences". It's not a specific act. Instead it is an experience, an event in it's entirety. As Chef Alex Stratta said to me, "My WOW! is when somebody leaves your place and they don't know what hit them."
I think Chef Stratta has a very apt description of what WOW! is all about. We want our guests to feel WOWed by our service and hospitality. But if that guest can't really put into words why or how they were WOWed, then that's maybe a pretty good sign that we've exceeded their expectations and delivered an amazing experience for them.

That is my premise. So let's embark on this journey together, and see what
Getting to *Wow!* Everybody WINS with 5 Star Service, is all about.

Chapter 1

GETTING A MAP FOR THE JOURNEY

"All you need is the plan, the road map and the courage to press on to your destination."
Earl Nightingale

"True navigation begins in the human heart. It's the most important map of all."
Elizabeth Kapu'uwailani Lindsey

In order to get where we're going-wherever that may be, we need to have an idea of how to get there. We must have a destination in mind and a plan for our travel. An essential tool for any journey is a map. On our journey of **Getting to WOW!** in the Service and Hospitality that we provide to our guests, there is a special MAP that I would like to offer. This MAP is not a diagram that was created by a cartographer. Nor is it tangible, having physical geographic locations and directions on it. Rather, this MAP is something that is internal. But just like any other map, this MAP will guide you to your destination.

When I speak of a MAP, I'm referring to 3 foundational traits that will prepare us to be successful on our journey. These 3 traits are the right MINDSET, a positive ATTITUDE and a PASSION for this industry. Without these 3 traits, it is my firm conviction, that though you may attempt to come along, you will never truly arrive-at that level of providing a **WOW!** dining experience for your guests. Try as you may, you will always be lacking, missing some key ingredients. You may be extremely effective in your skills and technique, very adept at your knowledge but if you are one who does not possess this MAP, you will always be one step away- And a Giant step at that, from **Getting to WOW!**

The MAP

MINDSET

How you think about yourself, what you think of this industry and profession and how you think specifically about your job as a server, bartender, busser, host or any other service position will have a direct effect upon how you relate to others and how they relate and respond to you.

So, at the very outset, I want to dispel and vanquish this notion that being a server or working in the service industry is a less than type of line of work. To be a server, waiter, waitress, butler, (whatever term you choose to use) is a noble thing. I am well aware that not everybody gets that but it is my desire that by the time you finish reading this book, that you will not only be better equipped in your skills and ability but also that you will have a different sense about yourself and the service that you provide. What you do is so much more than what is apparent on the surface. How you interact with guests will either positively or negatively affect them and their day. Your actions and attitude wield such great influence over your clientele. So before we can talk about your influence upon others, we must first look inward.

Our mindset affects everything we do. What we think we become. Napoleon Hill, many years ago, penned in his classic book-Think and Grow Rich-that "Thoughts are things."

Thoughts are things. It bears repeating and pondering. It absolutely is true. And not only is that true but "Thoughts become things" is absolutely true as well.

If you are one of those people working in this industry who think and even say out loud occasionally, or on a regular basis, "I'm just a server, right now." Or "I'm doing this until I get a real job." Or any of the myriad of ways of saying that this is not a real job and that this job is really below you, then I want to encourage you to begin to think differently. Your Mindset affects everything you do. Your thoughts affect your emotions, your actions and your behavior. If you are of the

Mindset that you are ashamed of being a server, or that people will think less of you if you're still working as a server at_ age, then it's going to show up in your work. If you don't take pride in what you do now, if you think of this as just a fill in, passing the time-kind of job, then you will not be motivated to be excellent at it. You probably just try to do the bare minimum. But let me ask you, let's say you are "just a server" until you finish college, get a degree, pass the boards, or the bar or until you get hired at a "real job", what makes you think that you will put your all into it once you're at that other job, position, profession?

If you don't aspire to excellence where you are now, there is no guarantee that you will when you get to that next place. Is there a magic switch that you will turn on at that time and cause you to go from being mediocre and not fully engaged to someone who is truly committed wholeheartedly giving of one's self to their career? I am going to say "No". That doesn't happen. I've heard it said that-

"How you do anything is how you do everything."
(Adam Markel/T. Harv Eker-MMI)

Now, you may not agree with that statement but I think if you really are honest with yourself-you will admit that at the very least, there is some truth to that.

In order to really be great at this business, indeed at any business, job, profession or endeavor in life-you must have a positive Mindset. If you focus on the negative-guess what you'll get more of? The negative.

As you begin to take a sense of pride in yourself and what you do, the service you provide-you will want to excel. It's only natural. There is already so much mediocrity in this world, why would you want to be a part of that? I know that you don't. The fact that you are holding this book in your hand or that you're reading this on your tablet or mobile device, tells me that you want more. You are one of those people that wants to excel at everything in your life. I know we are already a few pages in, so now, at this moment, I want to thank you and congratulate you for wanting to learn and to better yourself and to become more effective at this business of Service and Hospitality. The fact that you have the desire to improve will help ensure that you will.

ATTITUDE
Attitude Affects Outcome

"Whistle while you work"
The Seven Dwarfs, in Snow White

Certainly there are many ways to convey the above statement-to phrase, rephrase or paraphrase it. "You get what you expect", "What you focus on expands" "Whistle while you work".
Anyone working in this industry knows you never know what to expect. At least that's truly the conventional wisdom. Feast or famine. Or phantom, perhaps. - Not sure what that meant. But most servers talk about busy days/nights, up seasons and down seasons, busy shifts, slow shifts, etc. At the end of a busy night you all sit around, count your tips, smile to yourself, maybe even boast amongst yourselves (with your co-workers) bragging about who did better-that is- made more money. Or if the night wasn't so good-as

in-you weren't completely overjoyed with the amount of tips you made-then, if you are like many in this business-you sit around and complain about the shift that just ended. So, bear with me, there is a point to all of this...

Let's imagine that you had a fantastic night.
Great guests=great tips =great amount of money for you =great mood. And so? Well your great night put you in a great mood and well... and everything is GREAT!

Then there's another way to look at it. What if I suggest that you consider that to the contrary, the above example is not great? Yes, you had a great night. You had great guests. They left great tips. You made great money. That put you in a great mood. You went home in a great mood. What's wrong with that??
Question: What made it a 'great night'?

If you agree with the above scenario and see yourself there, then there might be a problem.
"Why?" you say. So, if the tips are good-then the night was good. Right? At least that seems to be the general consensus in the industry.
But here's my question... What or who determines if the tips are good?
You say..."Well, every night is different. I can't control how much money my customers tip me. It's a crapshoot. Some nights are good..."
And my response is ... "Well, Yes and no."

Yes, every day is different in that no two days are exactly the same. No two days have the exact same guests, type of guests, number of guests, etc. Some days you ring more sales than others. Some days it rains. Some days it's too hot to sit on the patio. Some days there is live music at your restaurant. Some days you have corporate parties. Some days are busy, some days are slow.

Okay, well what if the night is slow? Do you mean to tell me, that in one of the most unpredictable businesses in the United States, that you're going to allow how you respond to it to be determined by how the day/night's business is? Does that really make sense to you?

So what if the night was slow? "I only had 4 tables", you say.

Okay. So, you only had a few tables. And how do you respond to that? You moan and whine and say "This sucks"?

I, personally have had nights when I only had 4 tables and because I only had 4 tables I was able to give more time and attention to each one. I've had nights when I only had 4 tables but I made $150.00.

How about you, what Attitude and approach do you take?

What if you did an experiment and kept track of how often you say to yourself or your co-workers, "This sucks" and also keep track of how many nights you had low tips? Is there a correlation? So which came first, the bad tips or the "this sucks attitude"?

I put forth here my very simple thesis...

"What you think and say-belies your attitude. Your attitude affects your actions which in turn, creates your outcome."

Plain and simple **"What you think about, you bring about"**. That's really what it is.

So-what one thinks and says creates their attitude? Does that mean we are supposed to be phony and say "Oh this is great! Yahoo, I only had 3 tables tonight-hooray!!?"

NO, not exactly. But what I am saying is what I've said earlier and that is:

ATTITUDE AFFECTS OUTCOME

Here's a pretty good (I used to say 'perfect'-but no example is really perfect) example of something I've experienced that illustrates my point:

Some time ago, I worked at a newly opened, popular Irish pub/restaurant, (a former hat factory in the early 1900s) in the center of the newly renovated downtown St. Louis. The food was typical Irish fare not amazing but good. The bar, however, was the main attraction-it was huge. Also, above the bar was a large, beautiful, brass, automated, calibrated liquor dispensing system which guaranteed the accuracy of a perfect pour every time. Great for liquor inventory but not great for a 'stiff drink' or a 'strong pour'. Regardless, it was quite the attraction. The bar was always full and it was, like most Irish bars, a really fun place to have a pint. Or two.

Every weekend they had live bands and the place was always packed. The tables were big, dark wooden benches-typical décor for a large Irish pub in a rehabbed old building. You get the picture.

Now, here comes St. Patrick's Day. This is the 4th of July or New Year's Eve for an Irish bar. We were informed by management that we would be mega-super busy all day and all night. There was a parade that would pass very close to the bar-about two blocks away, early in the morning. In addition to the large main bar, which had 6-8 bartenders working it, there was a bar located around the perimeter and in the main dining room.

We definitely were prepared for the business that we were expecting and anticipating. There also was a full wait staff- I don't remember how many but something like instead of the normal 10 or so servers, we had about 15-18 scheduled. All of us reported in at 7:30 am. Normally, we didn't even open until 10:30 am.

So, we were all there setting up and prepping for an early 9 am opening. And we were all expected to be prepared to work about 12 to 15 hours.

'Wow, this is going to be great', I thought to myself. I was already anticipating a big money day, this is going to be a great day. I set my expectations high and my attitude was one of eagerness, expectancy and wanting to serve.

From the moment the doors opened at 7:30 am, we were immediately busy. The St. Patrick's Day partiers and revelers came in droves. Many converged on the bar. Within minutes, all the barstools around the entire perimeter of the bar were occupied. And then lines began to form in front of every bartender. Four and five deep at a time.

We, servers, of course, only were allowed to serve those seated at tables. And even in a place as huge as this, there were really not that many tables. So, come to think of it, because management wanted to be prepared for whatever the day may bring- we were completely overstaffed. And as I mentioned, we had almost twice as many servers as are normally scheduled on a typical weekend. As the bar was being overwhelmed with partiers and drinkers- we could hear the constant cha-ching emanating from the bar area as drinks were continuously flowing.

We, the servers, however, were not being overwhelmed. We actually each had fewer tables per server than we would on a normal busy day. Instead of the normal 8, we each only had 5. Yes, we filled up quickly. But many of the tables were filled, not with guests who were there for an early lunch and would then move onto another location for the afternoon. No, on the contrary, our tables and booths were filled almost entirely with "campers". I'm not talking about wilderness-lovers or outdoorsy types. No, "campers" are restaurant patrons known for securing a prime location, staking out their spot and 'camping out'. Maybe they'll order a full meal. Maybe not. Typically they'll order less than a full meal, nurse a drink or two and stay for extended periods of time. Often they'll stay for hours. Hours and hours.

Now, all of us servers' tables and booths filled up immediately. And most of us had 'campers' at our tables. How could we tell so early on? Well, by the way they spread out in the booths. Booths that were meant to accommodate up to 8 would have only 3 or 4 people seated at them. Some even brought games with them-chess and other board games. Yes, board games! They clearly were here for the long haul.

As I observed the situation, I thought to myself, I could take the attitude of 'This sucks. These people are going to be here all day and I'm not going to make any money because they're really not ordering or drinking much.' And that is exactly what the normal, natural expected way to think, feel and respond would be. Maybe I really couldn't be blamed if I adopted that attitude. But I was there to make money and to serve my guests. I didn't wake up early and come in at 7 a.m. just for the heck of it.

So, what did I do? I committed in my mind to have a good, positive attitude for the entire day, regardless of the situation or what I perceive it to be. I set it in my mind that I was going to earn at the very least $200.00 that day. Which, for a very long day like that, was not very much money. But I decided if I walked with 200, I'd have met my goal. And I determined to be happy from the outset.

As the day wore on I listened to my server colleagues talking to me and amongst themselves and invariably, the majority of them all seemed to have the same attitude: "This Sucks!" They were so focused on the negative situation which they deemed to be so unfair that they were exuding negative energy and hostility. They were so jealous of the bartenders because they were being slammed and making money hand over fist.
I'd ask some of my co-servers, "How are you doing?"

Answer: "This sucks. I'm not making any money. I don't even know why I'm here."
They would in turn ask me, "How's it going? How are your tables- are you making any money?"
To which I'd always answer, "I'm doing great. I sure am."

I had determined in my mind that I was not going to allow myself to become a victim of circumstance. I was going to have a good, positive and upbeat attitude. I was going to be in control of my situation or at least how I respond to it. And do you know what? At the end of the day, I made way more than all of my co- servers. I earned close to $300.00. I am convinced it was because I wasn't walking around sending negative energy to my guests. I wasn't constantly in my mind, and aloud saying, "This is terrible. This is unfair. I'm not going to make any money today." My colleagues' outcome had become their own self-fulfilling prophecies.

I've seen it happen over and over again. Your attitude absolutely affects your outcome. Many people whom I've met and worked with in the service industry over the years are like feathers floating in the wind. If money is flowing, they're on top of the world, flying high. If tips are low, then, so, too is their demeanor. But they've got it all backwards and upside down to how it should be. Don't be a feather-allowing your attitude to rise and fall with the wind of circumstance. You may not be able to control the circumstances, however, how you approach and respond (your attitude) to the circumstances around you will often, ultimately have an effect upon them. So keeping a positive attitude at all times is a must, especially in this business.

PASSION

"You must have passion in order to succeed. If success is to be yours, it will be yours while you are following your passion. You won't succeed doing something you despise, you won't even succeed doing something that you like doing, you will succeed when you do what you love, what you're passionate about."
Michael Jordan

So, what in the world does Michael Jordan have to do with Excellence in Service? One word-PASSION. What does it take to be an Exceptional Server? What does it mean to be the Best? At the Top...The Cream of the Crop? (First of all-I don't know what "Crop" people are talking about when they say that. Corn? Beans? Okra? I don't know. Ok. Disregard that.)

NBA great, Michael Jordan, was the Best. I know some of you will dispute this and say "No, Kobe Bryant is. Or Lebron James is." I know some say Lebron is king but that must be with a small "k" because everybody knows that Elvis is the King. Again, yes, a digression.

Well, according to Wikipedia: "Many of Jordan's contemporaries label Jordan as the greatest basketball player of all time. An ESPN survey of journalists, athletes and other sports figures ranked Jordan the greatest North American athlete of the 20th century, above icons such as Babe Ruth and Muhammad Ali. Jordan placed second to Babe Ruth in the Associated Press's list of 20th century athletes. In addition, the Associated Press voted him as the basketball player of the 20th century. Jordan has also appeared on the front cover of Sports Illustrated a record 50 times. In the September 1996 issue of Sport, which was the publication's 50th anniversary issue, Jordan was named the greatest athlete of the past 50 years."

I think most people will agree that Michael Jordan was indeed one of best athletes of all time. How long has it been since he's played? Nearly 20 years and yet to this day-he is the Standard by which other basketball players are judged. You may think Kobe is better than Jordan was or that Lebron is better than Jordan was. But the fact remains-Jordan is the one that everyone is compared to. No one else. The question is always, "Is he (fill in the blank) as good as Jordan was?"

Although there are many factors, I believe one key ingredient that anyone, who wants to be at the top of their game, must have is Passion. Or as Jordan called it "A love for the game." Jordan not only had it. He exuded it. He lived it. He breathed it. While he certainly had natural ability when it came to sports and specifically basketball-that alone was not enough to ensure him success. In fact, when he tried out for the varsity basketball team in high school as a Sophomore- he did not make the team. So what did he do? Did he quit? No. He played on the Junior Varsity team and became the star of the squad. And during the summer he trained rigorously. He became a student of the game. He earned a spot on the Varsity squad the next year and the rest is- well, you know...
Love what you do and do what you love.

"Is the life you live the life you love?" "Do what you love and the money will follow." These are pretty well known phrases and philosophies. But does this mentality only apply to a sport, the arts or some other such pursuit? Surely one can have passion for a sport, or for music but what about for Service?

As I've been interviewing various individuals-from Servers and Bartenders, to Chefs, Restaurateurs and others for this book- **Getting to *WOW!* Everybody WINS with 5 Star Service**-there is one recurring theme that always comes out-Passion. It's stated in many different ways by these individuals but every single one of them in some way echoes what Michael Skurow told me,
"As I was at culinary school, I really enjoyed the creativity I was able to express through food but when I began working in the Front of the House-the dining room, I really fell in love with the Service side of the business."

Or as Olivier de Roany stated,
"In order to be successful in this industry you really have to have a Passion for people and for caring about their dining experience."

I completely agree with them.

The actual original definition of "passion" is "to suffer". So, being passionate about something means "to be willing to suffer for what you love". (From the book, Aspire, by Kevin Hall)

If you are in this business-the Food and Hospitality World and you don't love it- you ultimately will not be successful at it. This is a really tough business in so many ways. It is super high stress. There are often long hours required. Your life schedule becomes topsy-turvy. You don't have control of your nights and your weekends.

But on the flip side-if you do enjoy it and if you can find your passion in providing exceptional service and in creating memorable dining experiences for your guests- then the rewards you receive will be manifold. Yes, you can make fantastic money working as a Server or Bartender but I'm not talking just about the money.

I'm talking about the satisfaction, the gratification, the feeling of fulfillment when you bring happiness to someone. When a group of guests walk into your restaurant and maybe they have an idea of what to expect, or maybe they don't, but after 1 1/2 or 2 hours or more of being your dining guests, they walk out not just fully satiated but completely content beaming with happiness and gratitude. It's really an amazing feeling to experience that.

It's really pretty easy to tell if a person-a Server, is doing this just for the money or if they truly have a Passion for this business. It's evident to you, if you're their co- worker and their only focus is seeing how much money they can squeeze out of/make off each guest. If they have a guest who is ordering the bare minimum- maybe a glass of wine rather than a bottle, an entree but no appetizer- no salad, does that Server's attitude and focus and level of attention begin to slide because they know they are not going to make a big tip off that table?

The guest certainly becomes aware of it as well. Was there a pleasant happy greeting by the Server to the table of 6 but all of sudden the original, upbeat, positive attitude turns sour when all but 2 of the 6 guests say, "I'll just have water."? What happened to that cheerful guy who said he was here to "take care of us"?

We know that sometimes there will be guests that don't tip well, don't order much for a meal and maybe don't know what it means to dine out or to have a dining experience. And there will be some people who just cannot be satisfied no matter what is done for them. But those guests are few and far between. Most people that come to your dining establishment, wherever that may be, want to be your guests and want to experience the great food and ambience and service that you and your establishment have to offer.

I interviewed a friend of mine yesterday, Greg DaLuz who currently works at the newest restaurant on the Las Vegas Strip-Giada-the namesake of Celebrity Chef- Giada De Laurentiis.
He told me that he considers himself more than a Server and in fact he views his job description as to *"Host your dinner party"* at Giada. He says he is a *"Dining Experience Coordinator"* I love that phrase that he coined. But more important than the phrase, is the attitude behind what is said. That makes me want to take my wife out to dinner at Giada all the more. Frankly, it's not Giada's-the restaurant itself that I am excited about per se. Rather, it is the opportunity to be "hosted" by Greg, wherever he is working and in whatever capacity-as he has worked both as manager and as server at various places.

My wife and I just know that it's going to be great, because Greg is there. Greg's Passion for this business is clearly evident. Not only that, but he has a genuine care and concern for his guests. His enthusiasm is uncontainable when he talks about food and wine-whether he's serving his guests or he is recounting his own experience of enjoying being a guest himself.

When one has Passion or "a Love for the Game", to quote Jordan, it will lead to becoming a student of the game. If you are in this Food and Hospitality Industry, are you a student of your game, your craft, and your industry? Do you study and practice your craft? Or do you just show up for your shift each day hoping that the day or the night goes well for you? Have you been in this business for so long that you feel that there really is nothing left for you to learn or to practice?

Anyone who wants to excel and be their best will be willing to do whatever it takes to reach that level. Yes, your management should provide ongoing training and education for you but if they don't, you should take it upon yourself to study and learn more. The more knowledgeable you become the more helpful you can be for your guests. I'm not talking about knocking your guests over the head touting your superior food and wine knowledge. But being able to share insights and information with them at the appropriate time is often welcomed.

The more you learn about this industry, the food and wine that you serve and develop the skills of great service and hospitality-the better you will feel about your job. And that, in turn will rub off, resonate or vibrate with your guests in a positive manner, causing them to be happy and have a more enjoyable dining experience. They, in turn, will compensate you with a more generous tip (most of the time)

(*PLEASE NOTE-THIS IS NOT A GUARANTEE-THERE ACTUALLY WILL BE TIMES WHEN YOU PROVIDE OUTSTANDING SERVICE AND YOUR GUESTS, FOR WHATEVER REASON, WILL NOT PERCEIVE IT AS SUCH OR WILL, BUT JUST WON'T TIP YOU ACCORDINGLY. Please do not hold me responsible.) They will also, often, commend you to your management and recommend you to their friends and family to ask for you when they come in. In due time they could become your regulars. Not a bad cycle to begin, right?

Am I saying that everyone who works in this business must have a burning passion for the Food and Hospitality industry from day one? No, not at all. And yes it is true-every manager, owner, chef and restaurateur that I have interviewed has told me- "I can teach and educate my staff on points of service, on the food, the wine, etc., but one thing I can't teach them is how to truly, genuinely care for their guests."

Passion cannot be taught nor bought. But I do believe it can be caught.
If you surround yourself with people that have that burning desire, that passion, then either you'll catch what they're sending out or you will not want to be around them anymore. So take heart, if you don't yet have a passion for this business and you are just biding your time until you're finished with college or until you get what you consider " a real job" I would recommend that you connect with someone who does have the Passion and ask them what is it about this business that they love so much. And maybe you too will catch the flame.

Michael Jordan said he had "a love for the game". To me that means exactly that- the game. I don't know if he loved practicing hundreds of free-throws every day, or doing wind sprints or other conditioning exercises. He didn't say he loved the "Practice". But one has to go through the hours and days of the tough stuff, the grueling practices to get to "The Game"/Game Day. That's where "being willing to suffer for what you love" comes into play.

Likewise, in this business, I'm not sure if my friend Greg "loves" polishing silverware, or wine glasses or folding hundreds of napkins or doing any number of the myriad of "practice activities'/sidework that is required and must be done every day in every restaurant. But they are necessary for the restaurant's success. But his passion for this industry/love for the game is unmistakable.

I used to do some acting when I lived in LA a few years back. I have a friend, Carey Dunn who writes, directs and produces his own plays. He has a Passion for theater. He'd do it if he made money or not. How do I know this? Well, because sometimes he made money and sometimes he didn't. But regardless, he still always put his heart and soul into it-the writing, directing, producing, and acting. All of it.

Am I saying that my friend Carey is the absolute best at those disciplines? No, that's not what's important. He is good. He's very good, but he's not the best. I'm sure he will say the same. But I would always take the opportunity to see or be in anything that he produces because he has passion and that speaks way more than amazing raw talent absent the passion.

When I was doing plays back then with Carey, I don't recall any of my co-actors saying how much they "love" memorizing lines over and over again. They have a Passion for acting-a love of the game. But in order to be ready for the stage, one has to spend hours practicing their craft, honing their skill, sharpening their reflexes. Memorizing with your scene partner and by yourself and then rehearsing with the entire cast. You have to put in the work, they say.

But finally, after all the memorizing and getting into character, after all the free- throws and strength conditioning, after all the side work and silverware polishing, and wine learning and tasting, now comes Game Day. Now, comes the Performance. Up goes the curtain and Dinner Service begins. The guests are your fans, your audience. And your role tonight is that of a Dining Experience Coordinator, The Director of an Exceptional Dining Experience, for your guests.

So, you have set out on a journey of **Getting to *WOW!*** in your Service and Hospitality. You must always remember to keep this MAP on you at all times for without it you may be led astray and get lost in the wilderness of Negative Poor Attitude and Passionlessness.

These 3 traits; of Mindset, Attitude and Passion will act as a MAP-to guide you on this journey to becoming an exceptional Service and Hospitality Professional. This MAP is essential to keep with you and to use daily to help you in Getting to Wow!

Chapter 2

Getting in the Flow of Positive Energy

"The predominant thought or the mental attitude is the magnet, and the law is that 'like attracts like', consequently, the mental attitude will invariably attract such conditions as correspond to its nature."
Charles Haanel (1866-1949)

In the last chapter, we discussed the importance of our Mindset, our Attitude and having a Passion for this business. I stated that these three things are foundational to us achieving our goal of **Getting to WOW!** I also, mentioned that our attitude affects our outcome. I know a lot of people really don't believe that but it absolutely is true. So, you might be wondering, "Is it really that simple and why is this true?" Yes and one word-ENERGY.

This is not a new idea. It has been taught for centuries. I first learned of this principle when I lived on Guam in 1995 and I was introduced to the book, Think and Grow Rich by Napoleon Hill. The very first chapter of Think and Grow Rich states that "Thoughts are Things". What does that mean? Literally, and yes, I do mean, literally, our thoughts have power. They have power because they emit energy. That's right- energy. Everything is energy. Everything, including our attitudes, thoughts and emotions carry a vibration. And because we are energetic beings, other people-including your guests- can read your attitude. Your attitude sends out a vibration that is picked up by those who are receiving it.
When I began to ponder and realize the meaning of that statement the light bulb came on for me. Thoughts truly are things. Not only that, but:
"Thoughts become things."

There are so many authors and books that I've read over the years that explain and expound upon this concept. Marshall Sylver, the famous hypnotist, author, speaker and success mentor, in his book, Passion, Profit and Power, simply states it this way:

"What you think about, you bring about."

A few years ago a book and a movie of the same name became a world-wide phenomenon. The movie was seen by over 300 million people. It was called-The Secret. Rhonda Byrne is the author of The Secret, but she collaborated with many, many others like Bob Proctor, John Assaraf, Jack Canfield, Dr. Joe Vitale and others. The basic premise of the secret is that we are vibrational beings and we send out energy. That energy attracts to us people, things and events that resonate with or are vibrational matches to what we send out. We are like human tuning forks. The book says that the Secret is The Law of Attraction!

John Assaraf says,

"The simplest way for me to look at the law of attraction is if I think of myself as a magnet, and I know that a magnet will attract to itself."

So the energy or vibration that we send out to others is acting like a magnet.

"Everything that's coming into your life you are attracting into your life. And it's attracted to you by virtue of the images you're holding in your mind. It's what you're thinking. Whatever is going on in your mind you are attracting to you. Every thought of yours is a real thing-a force."

Prentice Mulford (1834-1891)

So, how does this energy, our energy via the law of attraction, work for us or against us in a practical way? Well, consider this.

We all know people who put on fake smiles and charming voices when they greet their guests. But people can see right through them. If you are able to tell when your co-workers are being phony, don't you think the guests can also? Of course they can.

Maybe this may all seem elementary or you may say it's not really that simple. There's so much more involved. But let me give you an example that I know we've all either witnessed or personally experienced.

You have a group of guests that you are serving. You do absolutely everything correctly (on the outside-that is in appearance). You greeted them with a smile (a fake one). You told them about the specials with accurate descriptive words (but had no enthusiasm-lacking positive energy). You presented and properly opened and poured the wine they ordered. You brought their food out in a timely manner, etc., etc.

Even though you seemingly, did everything correctly in outward appearances, the energy that emanated from you, loudly and clearly said that you did not want to be here. Everything on the outside was correct. But on the inside, the unseen, invisible part was wrong and negative. Wrong attitude. Negative emotion. Wrong energy and wrong vibration.

Later, as the guests are leaving you pick up the check after they've paid and you see they left you the bare minimum tip-whatever that may be. You name it. Perhaps they gave 10%, 12%, whatever. As the guests are out of earshot you either mumble to yourself or loudly proclaim to your co-workers, "Tightwads" or "Cheapskates" or whatever your favorite descriptive derogatory word of choice may be.

Let's be honest, though...you know in your heart that you really got what you deserved. They were tight with their tip because you were tight with your energy. There was no **WOW!** service involved.

People can read and sense our energy. This includes your guests. If you are walking around with negative energy or a negative attitude-it is often readily apparent. And then it just becomes one seemingly, unending, vicious cycle:

You have negative energy-your guests sense it. Then they send negative energy back to you and this usually comes in their responses to you. So, you give less focus, care and attention to this particular table of guests. They, then express their dissatisfaction of your service in the form of low tips. This in turn, causes you to be upset, so you continue to curse your "cheap customers/guests" and throughout your entire day you get nothing but more "cheap customers/guests".

Jack Canfield, Co-creator of the Chicken Soup for the Soul book series has a formula in his book The Success Principles that he calls **E+R=O**, which explains this very well.

E+R=O
(Event+Response+Outcome)

He says that,

"Every outcome you experience in life (whether positive or negative, success or failure, wealth or poverty, joy or frustration etc.) is the result of how you have responded to an earlier event in your life."

He says that if you are not happy with the outcome that you are experiencing that there are two choices one can make.

1.   You can be upset and blame the event (E) for the lack of or unsatisfying results/outcome (O).

2.   You can change your responses (R) to the events (E) –the way things are- until you get the outcomes (O) that you want.

So, in the example we discussed above, you can blame the event (E)-the interaction with your guests for the lack of positive outcome (O)-satisfactory tips.

Or, you can change your response (R) to the way your guests are treating you/the way the service is going-the event-(E) until the outcome (O) becomes what you want-a satisfied guest and a proper/satisfactory tip.

E+R=O is a very simple formula but once you understand and realize that you are not a victim of circumstance and that you have great power and authority over the situation then, your outcomes will be begin to change and be more in your favor.   The cycle has to stop and it's incumbent upon you to do it.

Jack Canfield, in the same book, The Success Principles, encourages us all to be individuals who take full responsibility for the results in our lives. It really is up to us to achieve the outcomes that we desire.

Many of the Service and Hospitality Professionals that I spoke with or interviewed for this book, including Theo Van Soest, and Greg DaLuz, said that they don't even bother counting their tips throughout their shift. Theo says *"Just count your money at the end of the night, and shrug off the negative comments or not so great tips."* I'm paraphrasing him.

It All Averages Out

Also, Greg told me that it all averages out. Sometimes you get guests that no matter what you do, how amazing a dining experience that you provide for them, they're never going to tip anyone more than percentage.   That could be12%, 15%, whatever. Maybe even only 10%. But then, right after that, or the next day, you serve a party of 8 whose automatic gratuity on the bill is already is $175.00, and on top of that the host hands you two 100 dollar bills as he leaves. Is that fantastic? Yes! But did you really earn that entire tip? No way. So complaining about poor tips is really in the grand scheme of things completely unwarranted and pointless.

Change the Cycle

Let's look at it in a different way. Rather than you faking it and putting on a phony smile (because the inauthenticity of that is also easily sensed), and instead of wishing you weren't here working at this restaurant today, instead of having an attitude that these people are imposing upon you today, why not take a more positive approach?

Put yourself in their shoes. These people, your guests, are coming into your place of business for   ? Fill in the blank. A quick lunch, a business dinner with an important client, a romantic evening, a family celebration-there's a myriad of possible reasons. Whatever the occasion may be, I guarantee you that they do not ever expect to be met with your lousy attitude. What if they had a stressful, rough morning at the office and they just need a quick bite and a few moments to relax their brain?

So, they come in, they're seated, they meet you, order their food and eat their lunch. But they get so much more. You greet them with a smile (genuine one) and an upbeat attitude which emanates a positive vibration. Your positivity is like a gentle massage for their stressed out mind. Next, you not only greet them with a smile, you take notice of something that they are wearing and pay them a compliment. Immediately, the burden of the office is lifted, at least temporarily.

As they enjoy their lunch you stop by a few times to check on them and you crack a joke and together you all enjoy a laugh. Whatever was stressing them out when they came in is at least for this

moment, forgotten. You are the breath of fresh air that they needed. And in return, they keep mirroring back to you the same positive energy that you are sending to them.
How's that for a different type of cycle?

What happened here? You've set the tone from the outset, not just for them, but for yourself as well. You've sent out positive energy and they've barely sat down but already they are feeling good. They have a feeling that this is going to be a good lunch and they may not even really know why. They have a great lunch and it goes by so quickly. You feel good, even better than when they first walked in and so do they! As your guests are leaving they thank you and say they'll definitely ask for you when they come next time.

You have a great feeling of contentment. You know you put a smile and a bit of joy into their day. And this was not just at this one table, but you repeated and duplicated the process at all your tables throughout your shift. You think to yourself, "What great customers I have today". Your customers think, "Wow, what a great server we had today."

Oh and by the way, that first table left you a 25% tip. Not bad. Good feeling. Good energy. Good job!

Understanding the effect that our mindset, attitude, emotions and energy has upon other people and circumstances, will greatly improve our success in **Getting to *WOW!*** And we'll achieve success, not only in our Service and Hospitality, but in every other area of our lives as well.

Even with the MAP for your journey and Getting in the Flow of Positive Energy, there is yet another very important internal piece we need in order to become successful in this business of Service and Hospitality. I'll give you a hint.
Service isn't, without it...

Chapter 3

Getting a Servant Heart

"Service which is rendered without joy helps neither the servant nor the served. But all other pleasures and possessions pale into nothingness before service which is rendered in a spirit of joy."
Mahatma Gandhi

I take issue with this whole notion of "I'm your server not your servant", which is a very common attitude amongst some servers today. While it's true that servers are not servants as in waiting hand and foot on someone or being a slave. However, Service Professionals who actually excel at and are successful in their job, by and large, are people with a "Servant heart". That goes for Management as well. Successful Leaders are always Servant Leaders first. One leads successfully through influence not through exerting authority by virtue of his or her title or position. James Beard award winning, Chef Alex Stratta, who has had two extremely successful restaurants at the Wynn in Las Vegas, and has multiple restaurants in the works currently, says that, "Humility is key."

When I say having a "Servant Heart", what exactly am I talking about? First, having a Servant Heart, means serving because you enjoy it, gain pleasure from giving to others. Because at the very core of 'Serving' is the act of giving. When you serve-you give of your time, effort, energy, etc. to others. To have a Servant Heart, is to put the other person's needs above your own. Jesus said, "To be great in God's kingdom is to be the Servant of all."
One can always tell when someone in this industry truly has a Servant Heart. They exude cheerfulness and joy. They do not have an attitude that they feel they are being treated poorly.

All too often, I meet servers who, in my opinion, really shouldn't be in this business. They mumble and complain and say either to their co-workers or to themselves, things like, "I'm your server, not your servant." Or "You want what?

I'm not your slave" and other similar type phrases. That is not someone who has a Servant Heart. That is someone who is here because they think they can make good money with little work involved. Well, instead of having that mindset or **heartset**, what if you approached your guests with an "It would be my pleasure" attitude? This is the Service industry. That means that you serve others

Having a Servant Heart, does not mean that you are fair game to be belittled, ridiculed or treated or considered as "less than". On the contrary, those who have a Servant Heart, actually are ones who can and do exert great influence on their guests. As we mentioned in the previous chapter, when we discussed energy-our thoughts and emotions carry a vibration, and whatever we send out- that is what we attract more of. We are lightning rods to the thoughts and energy that we project and are focused on. Those that have the attitude of "I'm not your servant", are also the ones that complain about guests that seemingly, treat them poorly. They believe that their guests are being too demanding or trying to take advantage of them. They become their own self-fulfilling prophecy of a self-perpetuating cycle.

We know that sometimes there are guests that are unaware, un-enlightened, rude and just plain jerks. We have to learn how to deal with or put up with these types. And sometimes, they may need to be put in their place on occasion-but not by you. However, this is the rare occurrence. If you can get to the point where you actually find joy in serving, I guarantee that you will begin to see and respond to things, people and events in a very different way.

Servers are like Nurses

My wife, Michelle, is a registered nurse and works in the ICU of a major hospital in Las Vegas. She has more than 20 years of experience as a nurse. Although she has never taken an order or carried a tray, or ever done anything in the service industry-that is, she's never worked in a restaurant-we both agree that our two industries are so very similar. When I think of a person with a Servant Heart, I would say that Michelle definitely fits the description. In fact, she epitomizes it. Yes, I'm biased but I know I'm right on this one.

Nurses are to the medical field what servers are to the Service and Hospitality industry. Nurses do all the dirty work, so to speak, and oftentimes, literally and the doctors get all the praise and glory. Servers, similarly, are on the front lines in the front of the house, but the Chefs get all the accolades. In both industries there are tasks that are vital to the operation/success of the business yet not desirable by those who must perform them.

Although, there is a lot of technical and medical knowledge that nurses must call upon from their training, on a daily basis to care for their patients-as in checking and recording vitals, communicating medical information to them and their families, administering medicine and a myriad of other things, they also do many other non-glamorous things for their patients like-feeding and bathing them, propping them up in their beds, moving them, helping them use the bathroom, emptying bedpans, etc.

These other tasks are equally as vital to the patient's care, comfort, and well- being as the former ones are. And Michelle, truly has a calling to care for and serve people. We all know that nurses do command a very good income and rightfully so. But although, I know Michelle is very happy and grateful for her compensation, her primary motivation is not the money. She cares for the people. That is what God has called her to do. And gifted her to do.

In the same way, I am saying that if you want to be, believe you are to be, in this business of Service and Hospitality, in whatever capacity, somehow, someway, you must develop a Servant Heart. If you don't enjoy serving others but you just love the money and the flexibility of schedule-you will not be truly successful. In fact, deep down you will be miserable.

Giving and Receiving

The Bible says that it is more blessed to give than to receive. Years ago, when I first heard that, I thought, that doesn't make sense. How can it be more of a blessing to give than to receive? I didn't really understand it back then. For if one is giving to someone else, wouldn't the person receiving the thing (time, money, tangible item, assistance etc.,) from the first person giving it, be more blessed than the person giving the thing away? Since now the receiver has the thing that the giver just gave.

Well, it wasn't until I had the opportunity to serve as a volunteer missionary that I began to understand this. I worked as a volunteer for a Christian mission organization for about 10 years in the Philippines. I assisted in feeding programs, medical outreaches, taught Bible studies, taught literacy and other types of ministry. I felt a calling to go 'help' the less fortunate. At first that's what I thought I was doing. Me, helping them. But anyone who has ever volunteered anywhere-soup kitchen, Salvation Army, homeless shelter, wherever, they will tell you that they (the volunteer) walked away being more blessed than the one that they were helping.

I, too, in my years in the Philippines, as a volunteer missionary, experienced the same. No matter how much of myself, my time, my effort, my energy, my years of commitment that I gave (by the way-volunteer, as you know, means "no pay") I, in return, received so much more than a huge salary could ever afford. I not only received the sense of fulfillment, of being blessed, but I also received a wealth of life experience, deep relationships, perspective and education that I could never gain from a higher learning establishment.

A Divine Principle

The word 'ministry' literally means "to serve". Other definitions are: to look after, care for, treat, nurse, attend to, assist, and help. My point is that those that have a Servant Heart and who joyfully serve others-they themselves will be blessed in a way that is immeasurable. It's a law of the universe. To be blessed is to have God's favor or fortune. So it is a matter of divine principle that in your giving/serving that you are more blessed than the one you are giving to/serving. There is no way around it.

When we approach this business of being Service Professionals with a Servant Heart, we see the people that come into our place of business in a whole new light. When you begin to realize that you are doing so much more than serving them food and drink, that you are actually doing more than creating a great dining experience for them but that you are actually ministering to them, then you will realize what having a Servant Heart is all about.

You, with your joyful attitude, your positive energy, your charming personality and your servant heart are administering refreshing nourishment to this person's spirit. I know that that's what my wife as a nurse, realizes that she does every day. So, why are you, as a server any different?

I'll bet you never considered or were ever told that what you actually do has a powerful spiritual component to it. Pretty exciting isn't it? So, now what do you think about getting a Servant Heart? Are you in?

Chapter 4

Getting a Sense of Pride

"Pleasure in the job puts perfection in the work."
Aristotle

As a server it's important for you to see yourself as more than someone who explains the specials, takes the order and brings the food. To the uninitiated diner, that may seem like the complete job description of a server. However, we, who know, realize that this job entails so much more. If you approach your job with the mentality that you are just an order taker, then indeed, that is what you will be and nothing more.

I have met so many of my peers in this industry who, when asked what they do, respond by saying, "I'm just a server." or "I just wait tables right now."

My friend, let me speak to you from the heart here. Whenever I hear that response I sense that there is some shame in the position. They kind of hang their head and mumble, "I'm just a waiter."
When I hear someone say that to me, I try to encourage them.

There is absolutely no reason to be ashamed of your job. There is great dignity in what you do. And you will take on the energy of the mentality that you hold about your job. Granted, as mentioned before, this may only be a temporary position for you-until you get your degree, finish school or find another job. Or it may be at this moment your means of bringing in a second income. Regardless of the reason you are here-you have made this choice. You are not compelled to be a server. So, since you are here now, it would benefit you greatly if you began to take pride in your job.

Pearl S. Buck, the popular novelist of the 1930's, says it like this, *"The secret of joy in work is contained in one word-Excellence. To know how to do something well is to enjoy it."*

Whether you are a service professional-yes, (I did say "Professional"), whether this is your career path or you are here temporarily, in order for you to excel, you must find a way to take pride in what you do.

Oftentimes when someone is working in the industry but this is not their intended career path, they approach the job with a half-hearted attitude. My friend, Michael Skurow, who has worked as a restaurant General Manager, an apprentice pastry chef and now is a wine consultant for a major beverage distributor, says that regardless of why someone is working in the industry they need to:

"Put their whole heart into it. A person's pride in their work is evident in their work habits. If you show up 5 minutes early to work, you're already late."

What Michael is speaking of is about being accountable, taking responsibility, and realizing that what you do, matters.
Having a sense of pride, in other words. Whatever your job is-server, hostess, busser, dishwasher, cook, food runner or manager-every position is necessary and vital to the effective smooth flow of service in the restaurant. Yes it may seem that especially with the rise of celebrity chefs and the proliferation of television shows that celebrate them and what they do, it's easy for the rest of us to feel like that's the only important job in the operation of a restaurant. It is not.

Be Your Own Standard of Excellence

I encourage you to develop a standard of excellence for yourself. So many times I hear people make excuses for themselves as to why they don't put their heart into their work or take pride in their job.

Their feeble explanations usually go something like, "I'm just here to make money. I really have no need to learn how to be a great server. That's fine for you, but I'm in school and I'm getting a degree in International Business." It always amuses me when I hear such ridiculous reasoning for a person's current standard of mediocrity in their work.

That, to me, is very faulty thinking. So, what you're saying is that because being a server is not your long term career path and you are only here because you know you can have a flexible schedule and make "decent money", that you somehow can be excused from doing things properly or in an excellent manner. Right? And once you graduate and get a degree and get hired at a "real job", then you will automatically change your mindset and attitude and become a person of excellence? Well, I'm not buying it. I've said it before, you are here now, so focus on where you are now, learn the job, put your whole heart into it and do it well.

"Doing your best at this moment puts you in the best place for the next moment."
-Oprah Winfrey

Even if your "next moment" isn't until 4 years from now, do yourself a favor and see what a valuable opportunity you have here. Also, realize that if you are even slightly proficient at this service and hospitality thing, thank your lucky stars, because not everybody can do this-be a server. There's a multitude of reasons why most people can't make it as a server. If you are making it, then you have something special. Use it, cultivate it and do your best while you are here.

Play Sports and Work in a Restaurant

I've worked in restaurants on and off ever since I was 14 or 15 years old. Paul McGann, who owned SilverFross Drive-thru and Restaurant in Ottawa, Illinois, where I worked during my 4 years of high school, believed that working in the restaurant business helps build character in a young person. He only hired high school students and only ones that were involved in sports or some other extra-curricular activity. At the time I didn't really get his philosophy but now I do.

There is much value that comes from both playing high school sports and working in a restaurant. Both teach values like teamwork, discipline, following directions, respect for authority and taking pride in what one does. I am thankful that my parents allowed me to do both as a teenager. As a result, early on, I began to learn to have a standard of excellence for myself.   I hope the same for you, as well.

The fact that you've picked up this book-(and I must commend you on doing so), shows that you have some degree of care, concern and pride in what you do. Perhaps you do want to improve your skills and excel at this current job. The mere fact that you are reading, even browsing through this book, tells me that you see yourself as one who can excel in whatever you do.

I encourage you to set yourself apart from those servers who do not take the job seriously and really don't care about anything beyond the amount they "walk with" each night. Those people never really examine what they are doing right or wrong, and never consider ways of improving themselves and their service skills and abilities.

Be proud of what you do. Take pride in yourself and your work. As you take pride in your work and pleasure in what you do, it may lead you to actually doing the job well and striving for excellence.

Getting a Sense of Pride is a great stepping stone to not only a job done well, but also to a life of excellence.
You, my friend are clearly on the right path.
Now, it's time to start thinking about...

Chapter 5

Getting NOT "Good Enough"

"The quality of a person's life is in direct proportion to their commitment to excellence, regardless of their chosen field of endeavor"
-Vince Lombardi

Are you still with me? I am happy that you're joining me on this journey of **Getting to WOW!** Remember, we really do have a specific destination in mind that we are moving towards. And all that I am sharing with you here is for a reason.

My wife, Michelle and I, were reading this morning from Joel Osteen's latest book, YOU CAN, YOU WILL. He was talking about mediocrity and how being mediocre is not honoring to God. I completely agree with him. We all have something that we are excellent at. Many of us are gifted in multiple areas. But if we are not using our gifts, then they are being wasted.

- **Your Gift is NOT For You**

Similarly, if we don't make a conscious decision to be excellent and to do excellent-that is, do things in an excellent manner, then we are cheats. We are cheating others of the quality work we should be doing. We are cheating others of our great talents, wonderful personalities, great senses of humor, extensive knowledge, amazing insights and kindheartedness. Whatever your gift or calling is-it is your responsibility to do that to the best of your ability. Why? Because your gift is not for you. What? I'll say it again. Your Gift Is Not For You. Yes, that's exactly true.

I learned this from T. Harv Eker. He wrote a life-changing book called Secrets of the Millionaire Mind. When I attended his seminar two years ago and I first heard that statement, I thought, "That's crazy". My thinking was, "Of course my gifts are for me. They're My gifts and talents. That doesn't make sense. If they're not mine, then whose are they?"

Answer: Your gifts are for everyone else. Your gifts, your talents, your passion, though they may be things that give you joy, happiness and satisfaction-you are supposed to be a blessing to others via those gifts. They're not just for you. So, guess what? If you are not sharing your gifts, then you are depriving others who are meant to be beneficiaries of them. And you probably never considered yourself a selfish person. Right? But if you are withholding them, you actually are blocking the flow. And I know you don't want to be a flow blocker. Keep the energy, the blessing flowing.

What does all of this have to do with Service and Hospitality? Just, Everything. If you are coming to work every day and just being there but not really Being there, if you are not giving your all every day in every way-then, You are Mediocre. Who really wants to live a mediocre life? When one looks around, it seems a lot of people must want to. Mediocrity is in. Everybody's doing it. But it's really not ok.

Choose Excellence

What about Excellence? You will never be successful if you don't have Excellence as a primary objective, motivation and standard. I encourage you to strive for excellence in your work, your job, your relationships, your personal life. I'm guessing that you've all heard of The Law of Attraction, which states that "Like Attracts Like". That means whatever you send out, you attract back to you. If you settle for mediocrity in your life that is what you will get more of.

When you greet your guests, do you always have a smile and a cheerful attitude? Or, just sometimes? When a guest has a complaint-do you have a positive mindset and true willingness to turn the situation around, or do you then go and complain to your co-workers about the guest that's complaining? That's not being very congruent. Do you make a conscious effort to always give the very best service that you possibly can, to every single guest? Or is it just a crap shoot?

Some days you're on your game, you're loving life and as a result, the guests that have the pleasure of being served by you benefit. But other days, you really just don't care and you just do the bare minimum.

Be Better than "Good Enough"

The problem with mediocrity is-it's not good but it's not really bad. It's just so, so. What a pathetic way to be. If you as an individual, are okay with "just okay" and there's many like you at your establishment, and I'm betting that there are-then the whole place becomes infected with an "It's good enough" mentality. When you think and say, "it's good enough", usually, it's not. You're just settling. So, I ask you, Good enough for who? You're supposed to be providing a service. Is "good enough" really what your guests or customers want, expect and appreciate? I think not.

If you make a decision to Be and Do Excellent-that is what will return to you. You get what you expect.

When you arrive at work each day, do you set an intention in your heart and mind that this is going to be an amazing day? Or do you just wait and see what happens? If you're waiting to see how the day goes, see what comes up, see how you're treated, then you're not taking responsibility for your results. You reap what you sow. You get what you give. How about focusing on EXCELLENCE and giving that to every one of your guests, customers, clients today? My bet is that if you do-you will be amazed at the results. You will begin to see Excellence show up in other areas of your life as well.

As T. Harv Eker says,
"How you do anything, is how you do everything."

Come on. Stop being okay with "Good Enough", because it's really NOT. Give Excellence a shot. What do you have to lose?
Answer: Mediocrity

So, here's my question for you. Is all, or any of this, resonating with you? Remember energy and The Law of Attraction? You know, "Like attracts like". If your answer is "yes" then repeat after me, "Mediocrity is NOT for me."

If this is true for you and you truly want to learn how to up your game and you're ready to begin, then let's jump in and get serious.
It's time to get down to business and take action...
You can start by...

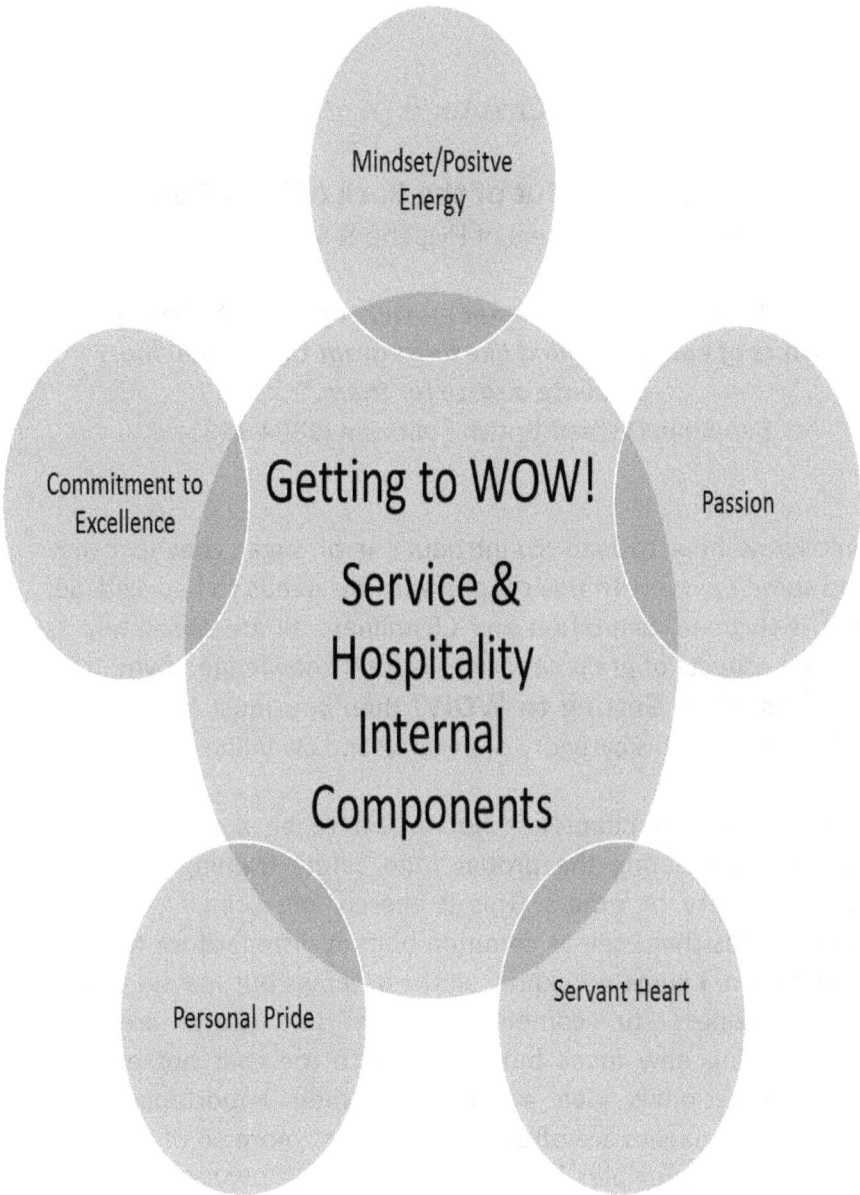

Mindset/Positve
Energy

Commitment to
Excellence

Getting to WOW!

Passion

Service &
Hospitality
Internal
Components

Personal Pride

Servant Heart

Chapter 6

Getting the Book Out of the Back of Your Pants!
(And Other Matters of Hygiene & Sanitation)

"Cleanliness and order are not matters of instinct; they are matters of education, and like most great things, you must cultivate a taste for them."
Benjamin Disraeli-British Politician (1804-1881)

I don't know how to lead in, introduce it or sugar coat it. I may offend some of you with this chapter but this needs to bed said. So, here it is-Hygiene, Sanitation and Cleanliness all are absolutely as important aspects of great service as is food knowledge. If you truly are committed to **Getting to *WOW!*** then you must be on point when it comes to this category of hygiene and cleanliness.

**Please Note, this chapter is not meant to be a substitute for taking and completing the proper food safety training programs such as SafeServ or others. This is merely me bringing to your attention areas that I see as common blatant disregard for hygiene and sanitation. I know you know all these things but maybe you've just let laziness or complacency set in. These are not groundbreaking new ideas but it seems to me that not enough Service Professionals give attention to their importance. And owners and managers are often as guilty if not more so of violating these very basic principles.

TOUCHING ONE'S FACE/HAIR, EYES, NOSE, MOUTH, EARS, BALD HEAD, ETC. –PLEASE DO NOT DO IT!!

A server, bartender, busser or anyone handling or serving food or drink, should not EVER put, place or raise their hands above their shoulders except to carry a tray or to pull something down from or place something onto a high shelf.

I've worked in and dined in many restaurants where the servers were constantly wiping their brow with their hand, coughing into their hand, scratching their face, rubbing their nose, running their fingers through their hair etc., etc.

Not only are these actions not creating a **WOW!** experience for the diners who view them.   But they are absolutely not acceptable at all-anytime-anywhere.   I don't care what level of restaurant I'm in- it is not acceptable-ever! It is not sanitary. If you are doing that in my view-God only knows what you're doing when you're out of sight.

My wife and I dined recently at a James Beard Award Winning restaurant in Kansas City recently, and while every other aspect of our dining experience was exceptional, the Sommelier constantly was stroking his beard as he was surveying the dining room. I was quite surprised that he was so unaware of his own body gestures. He should absolutely know better.

Of course-I don't know how many times or how often you wash your hands throughout your shift. I'm hoping and assuming that you do often and that when you are serving my food that your hands are clean. We, the dining public really have no way of knowing- so I guess in that regard there is a great deal of trust.

I know many people who say-"I don't want to know what is done in the kitchen-as long as the food tastes good, don't tell me anything else." But that's not me. And I think people say that because they truly don't want to know, which tells me that they really don't think very highly of the sanitation practices of most of those working in the food and service industry. And that is a shame.

I want to believe, no-I want to KNOW, that at the bare minimum that your hands are clean.

Be Courteous-Announce Your Exit to Wash Your Hands

If you are sneezing, hacking and coughing in front of me-whether right at my table or just in my view-you should make a point of saying –"Excuse me, I've got to go wash my hands." Believe me that goes a long way in putting guests at ease. At least you're conveying that you care about cleanliness.

If You are Sick, Go Home or Stay Home

If the server is actually sick-as in having a serious cold or flu, something more than just a minor cough or throat irritation or an occasional sneeze-(sometimes I sneeze a lot-but it is usually a reaction to something in the environment, like some chemical or an overabundance of perfume that someone sprayed-it's loud and dramatic but I'm not sneezing all night and my nose dripping all over the place), then said server should not even be at work.

I know that being sick when you work as a server is very difficult, because many restaurants don't provide health insurance for their servers, unless they are part of the union, as they are in Las Vegas. If we don't work-we don't make any money at all. This industry is different than all others, in that we are around food, beverages and people all the time and there is a very high risk of spreading our germs, contamination to the very ones that we are seeking to serve. Therefore, I say, "If you are sick-Go Home!" Better yet, don't even come in for work. Stay home and get well and keep your germs to yourself.

Truly, I state my point here, you cannot provide and deliver an exceptional dining experience unless you have a clean manner about you.

Know Thyself-Become Aware of Your Nervous Habits

That being said, sometimes the server is not sick, they just may have a nervous tick of scratching their neck or they, unconsciously, constantly run their fingers through their hair or wipe their bald head with their bare hands. Whatever it may be-these, too, are very unsanitary practices. And nobody wants you handling their food or even the plate that it comes on after you've been touching your face or hair. I suggest you become more aware of yourself, your body and what you are doing with your hands from moment to moment.

Using the Restroom

I hope it goes without saying that you absolutely must thoroughly and properly wash your hands after using the restroom. However, I have noticed that many servers and even many managers don't seem to be aware of the importance of removing their apron before even entering the restroom. You should absolutely never use the toilet facilities with your apron with you. Even if you take it off before you use the toilet and hang it on the door that is not a sanitary practice. Remove it and set it aside somewhere before you enter and use the facilities. If you forget, you must toss that apron in the dirty linen and get a clean one.

Book in the Pants

If you are one of those servers who's too cool for school to wear an apron-and put your server book in the pocket and instead you just stick it in the back of your pants

STOP IT!!! Stop it Now!! Cease and Desist!!

You may think it looks cool and hip. But every time I see that I cringe. You have that book in the back of your pants-I don't care if it's touching your skin, your underwear or what.

If you stop and think about it, surely you will realize and agree with me that it is

ABSOLUTELY NOT SANITARY IN THE LEAST.

I want to start a campaign in all restaurants all across America to ban the sticking of the server books in the back of the pants. Maybe even a song ala "The Pants on the Ground". "Looking like a fool with your book in your pants". If you're not familiar with it, look it up.

I know some people will ask or wonder what the big deal is? Ok, I'll tell you. The server uses that book in the back of their pants to write their orders on. But think about it. They touch that book that's been back there-wherever and then they pull it out to see who's ordered what while they're serving your food and then they touch your plates and cutlery and glasses and wine bottles with the same hands that touched that book that's been stuck 'back there'.

NOT SANITARY. PLEASE STOP DOING IT. IT'S NOT CLEAN. IT'S NOT COOL AND IT'S NOT CLASSY. IT'S TACKY LOOKING AND IT IS NOT PART OF A *WOW!* EXPERIENCE IN THE LEAST EXCEPT MAYBE AS IN "WOW THAT IS DISGUSTING!!"
And that my friend, is NOT *WOW!* service.

Bottle Opener in the Back of the Pants
Lady Bartenders, this goes the same for you. I know it's supposed to be cool and look sexy for you to have your bottle opener lodged partially into the side or the back of your pants but **IT IS NOT SANITARY.   Don't do it. It's certainly not classy either.**

The Last (dirty) Straw

A short word here on...you guessed it, straws. A straw is used for drinking and therefore there's almost a one hundred percent chance that it's going to be placed in the diner's mouth. Or at the very least the straw will be put in the glass of the beverage that your guest is going to drink. So, it will still technically be in contact with the liquid that they are going to imbibe. To me, a straw is no different in its functionality than any other utensil with which a guest is going to use to partake of their meal. Meaning, there's a pretty high probability that it is going to go into the guest's mouth.

I know that you would never, (I hope) hand a guest a fork with your grimy hands (I still say grimy-even if you just washed them) holding it by the tines. So, why, oh why, I lament, is it so common for a server or bartender to touch, handle, paw, or fondle the instrument that I'm going to be drinking with?!?   And especially in my view?

I've heard some servers/bartenders say in jest, "Well, if there are any germs on my hands transferred to the straw, the alcohol in the drink will kill it".

Is this really the justification for not taking time and care and concern for your guests? Some of you may think that I'm a Howie-Mandel-like-certified-germaphobe.   Memories of Howard Hughes. I can assure you that I am not. I believe that it's important to be clean and sanitary always when I am handling and serving other people food and drink. To me it shows care, concern and respect and it is part of providing an exceptional and safe dining experience for them.   Actually, that's not exceptional-it's really pretty basic.

So, what do I do? Well, there are many approaches to this. There are basically two types of straws.   Sleeved, either in paper or plastic, and unsleeved/unwrapped.

For the paper sleeved straws, I recommend tearing all the paper off except for a small maybe 1 ½ -2 inch portion at the top and placing the unwrapped portion in the drink. This way you accomplish putting the straw in the drink without touching the straw itself and leaving the small tip to be unwrapped by your guest.

Now, of course one really has no way of knowing if the unwrapped portion was touched by the server but if the tip is left wrapped, I'm going to assume that he held the straw by the wrapped portion to place it in my drink.

Another option is to bring the straw and present it/hand it to your guest while it's still completely wrapped. The problem that I see with doing this is that it doesn't really look very elegant. That's kind of what you would expect if you're eating at an all-night diner. Or an all-day diner. Sure, the straws are still sealed and clean but reaching in your apron pocket and pulling out a straw to hand to a guest each time isn't really **WOW!** service.

One other way is to present the unwrapped straw to the guest is on a napkin. That's if you don't have multiple drinks needing straws to be served at the same time. Again, if the straw is unwrapped, I have no way of knowing that it was not touched by the server's hand as he unwrapped it or pulled it out of the dispenser/receptacle at the bar and then placed it on a napkin. However, I think that the implied intent here is the concern for the guest's awareness that you're making every effort to be hygienic in your service.

Here's another little **WOW!** tip for you regarding straws. If you have a tray of glasses of soda and you place straws in the glasses they will have a tendency to float. If there is a fan blowing in the restaurant the straws may fly out of the glasses as you walk through the restaurant on the way to your guests table. This is even more likely if the glass has no ice in it. So be aware.

Exceptional **WOW!** service is in the details. If you do what your guests don't expect I promise you it will not go unnoticed.

Do you want to make a lasting positive impression? How difficult is it to be cognizant of this? If your goal is the same as my premise in this book to create and provide a WOW!/exceptional dining experience all the time, everywhere for everyone, then, no detail-no matter how small-that's what details are-ought to slip your notice. And no detail is too insignificant to give attention to.

Remember that game we used to play as kids - The Last Straw that Broke the Camel's Back? Each player places one straw- (yes I know it was straw as in hay rather than ones used for drinking but I still think it's an apropos illustration) on the camel's back and the weight of each straw becomes increasingly and incrementally, slightly greater until the placement of one final straw causes the camel's back to break.

What a great metaphor. Don't let something so small and seemingly insignificant negatively affect the level of service that you provide. This is not about sweating the small stuff. Don't sweat it, just pay attention to it and do it. It's about paying attention to detail in order to provide a great dining experience.

It's really no different than a chef neglecting to put some seemingly small, insignificant ingredient in a dish such as saffron or a dash of vanilla. If it calls for it-it's not insignificant. Even though an ingredient may be small it can have a great impact on the taste and flavor of the dish. It's not sweating the small stuff. Rather, it's just being aware of what is required to make that dish great. The same goes for you as a server-even with straws.

Since we're talking about small things let's delve into another related topic:

Beverage Garnishes

Many drinks, cocktails and even some beers are prepared and finished with a garnish of some sort. Vodka and gin drinks often are paired with olives or onions or limes, whiskey and bourbon drinks with cherries or limes and some beers like wheat beers are often garnished with citrus-lemon or oranges. Now with the increasing popularity of mixology type bars there's no limit to what creative types of garnishes are being used-from all sorts of herbs to exotic fruits.

There have been so many times when I've ordered one of the above drinks and the bartender or server neglected to put the proper or any garnish in my drink. So, I request the server or bartender to fix it and they come out with the piece of lime in their hands or on a plastic sword and they hand it to me like that. That, is not **WOW!** service. There are a few options that are more acceptable ways of bringing a lost and lonely garnish to the guest to be united with it's drink partner:

1.   Put it on a beverage napkin
2.   Skewered with a plastic sword and on a beverage napkin
3.   Skewered with a plastic sword in a shot glass, on a saucer or some other receptacle

A garnish should never be simply handed to the guest.

How about when the bartender is making my drink at the bar? Why are they compelled, it seems, to fondle, hold, handle or paw the lemons, limes, olives and other garnishes with their grimy hands? They shouldn't. That is not exceptional or **WOW!** service. And please make sure that you wash the citrus before it is cut and served as garnishes.

These may seem like simple, basic principles and they are. The problem is that most of the time bartenders do not take the time and care to bother doing it the right way. I could have a fantastic cocktail made by you but if you take such care to craft this wonderful drink, why undermine your hard work by being careless about my straw or my garnish? Also, bartender, please wash your hands. Often, please.

Now, how about a nice very dry martini with extra olives. And please use the tongs. Cheers!
Now that we are all on the same page in regards to sanitation, cleanliness, and hygiene-
it's time to focus on...

Chapter 7

Getting Back to the Basics

"Gentlemen, this is the football."
Legendary Football Coach, Vince Lombardi, standing before his
players, at the start of every football season

If it was good enough for Green Bay Packers Coach, Vince Lombardi to focus on something as simple and basic as showing what a football is to his players, then I see no reason why we, as Service Professionals ought not to start at the very same place. Okay. So, this is a tray.

One thing that Lombardi knew and instilled into his players, season after season, is that excellence comes from first mastering the basics. If we don't perfect our technique, our knowledge and understanding of the basics, then all the advanced enological and culinary education will be for naught. You can accurately identify and describe the nuanced flavors and aromas of a Chateau Margeaux, but you can't balance a tray of four wine glasses? Something is really wrong here. Oh, you're a Sommelier, and you don't have to know how to carry a tray? That doesn't seem right. Lombardi's Packers won a lot of championships and a large part of that was due to their focused dedication to the basics.

So, now let us begin:
A Manicure, Please- por la Mesa
It may be a humdrum, boring topic to read about, and partially, I apologize. Yet, I'm covering this because, I believe it's so often overlooked and missed completely even at many high end restaurants, and I am always flabbergasted that it is. Yes, I know that we've been instructed by Richard Carlson, that we ought not to 'Sweat the Small Stuff' and yes, crumbs certainly are small, but that doesn't mean that they should be considered small stuff.

I'll state it here, plain and simple-ANYTHING THAT IS NOT BEING USED, OR IS NOT GOING TO BE USED ON THE TABLE, NEEDS TO AT THE PROPER TIME-BE REMOVED, CLEARED, DISCARDED, TAKEN OUT OF SIGHT OF THE PATRON.

I don't mean if there's a ketchup and mustard caddy on the table as part of the table setting that you should remove it if your guest is not going to use it. Nor do I mean removing the salt and pepper shakers. What I'm talking about is anything that is used, soiled, dirty, trash etc. Yes they are small things but what a big impact and impression such simple attention to detail will achieve for you. I promise you, it will leave lasting impression upon your guest.

This is called manicuring the table and it is to be done throughout the entire meal. This includes a whole myriad of things; empty sugar or artificial sweetener packets strewn on the table or tucked neatly under or beside a saucer. Please, my friend, think about it; if your guest has gone to the trouble of folding and tucking said wrappers, obviously they care about neatness and such. The least you could do and the best you could do, is to remove them, kindly please. They may have only crumbled them and tossed them-not so neatly, aside. Obviously, they're not using them. So tell me, aside from laziness, why would you leave them on the table?

I've been to many restaurants and seen tables beautifully cleared, nicely manicured-nothing left on the table, in front of the guest save for a teaspoon, as they might still want to order coffee, and a glass of whatever they are still drinking-beverage, or water or both and yet, the sweetener packets will still be lying there like tiny fallen paper soldiers waiting for a proper burial.
I've known many guests to ask a server to 'please take these plates, utensils, etc., we're done with them.' Yet, I've never known or seen anyone say, "Hey can you please take these empty sweetener packets, too. I'm not using them anymore."

Why? BECAUSE THEY'RE EMPTY!! I don't get it, why would you clear everything except a sweetener packet?! Why is that any different than a dirty plate? It's NOT!!!

I originally titled this chapter, Are You Finished with these Crumbs, Sir? because of the ridiculousness of it.
Scenario- Your guests just enjoyed a fantastic dinner-you explained the specials with enthusiasm and made great suggestions. You were attentive to their needs and even anticipated what they might need. You've built great rapport and now the table is cleared and your guests are now finishing their wine, a bottle of Silver Oak Cabernet, a bottle of which you suggested at 145 dollars a pop. They bought three- Nice job!

So, now, here they sit, wanting to relax, trying to enjoy the conversation and the wonderful wine but they can't completely. Why? Because, for one, on the table- (it's a 6 top) one person-the host has a ½ dollar size glob of sauce on the table cloth in front of him. And on the rest of the table in front of all most of the others-crumbs, crumbs, crumbs from the wonderful yet crumby bread.

Oh, my friend, you were batting 1000 percent until this point and it is my belief that no matter how great a dining experience it has been-it can still be ruined by the last thing(s) the guest experiences and remembers. Such as? Well, I'll get to that later.
But how about those crumbs and sauce spots. You may think to yourself, "How can people be so messy?" That's the wrong attitude my friend. Thinking like that will not serve you nor will it serve others.
Well, the crumbs, that's so simple.   All servers should be issued by management,-if they are not, they should take the responsibility and purchase for themselves- and carry with them always to be with them at work-A CRUMBER.

I have worked in restaurants where a crumber has never been seen and they're considered a foreign object or a USO-that is an unidentified server object. But to me-it's just as important as a wine opener. Here's my thinking- how can you open a bottle of wine without a wine opener? You can't. Unless it's a twist off. In the same respect, how can you complete your task/goal of providing an exceptional dining experience for your guests if you have no crumber?

Answer-YOU CANNOT.
So you've done so well thus far, batting a thousand, do not drop the ball now. I know I mixed metaphors. You must carry and use a crumber.
Why?
Well, stating the obvious-it creates a clean environment-table for your guests. Now, many times, as I'm going around with my crumber to my tables, my guest will beat me to the punch. They swish the crumbs onto the floor. Nothing I can do about that.
However, it usually provides me with an opportunity to engage my guests once more. You can't crumb a table without getting somewhat close to the table and to your guests. This shows your guests that even at the very end you care about their dining experience. And without fail it ALWAYS IMPRESSES. Every time. I guarantee it. Your guests may not expect it. So again, you are exceeding their expectations. You're going beyond and exceeding their un-expectations. If they are left on the table I'm quite sure your guest is finished with the crumbs.
A manicure, please, por la mesa-for the table.

Left, Right, Left
Do I really have to say it? One would think not. But my experience tells me otherwise. So, at the risk, once again of sounding remedial-this is really back to basics-here I go. Let me just say that if this would not even be on my mind or a consideration of a topic to cover, had I not experienced it so frequently, both, as a diner and

with co-workers whom I've worked beside in the past and even management that I've worked for. It seems that many of us have forgotten this simple yet important concept-that there actually is a right and proper way of/manner of serving and clearing a table. Food, plates of any sort should always be served to the guest on their left side with your left hand and your body open towards them.

Conversely, in the exact same manner but with the opposite hand and on the opposite side, all bussing should be done - right hand, right side. Your body open towards your guest. No elbows in faces or forearms reaching across the guest.

I have experienced and witnessed complete disregard or ignorance of this vital point of service. Does it really matter? You ask. Absolutely, without question. Okay, maybe not without question. Let's entertain the question here. Why does it matter? Well, if you think we're just being all hoity-toity about it-that is not it at all. It's the established way and it makes sense. It's established as the proper way and therefore there should be continuity from one server to the next, one restaurant to the next.

Why are forks placed on the left for table setting and knives on the right? Well, I wasn't there when it was decided but now it has been decided and it allows for continuity and consistency. Anyway, back to the left and right of service. It really makes logical sense. One, it does show a certain manner of finesse. It looks like you know what you are doing. You have a system and it's the same system that everybody follows. Second, it is a more open way of serving and clearing with your open front toward your guest rather than your side being in their face.

Reaching

Okay, maybe this topic might be a stretch. Yes, a pun. Sorry.

But I really don't think so. I've experienced this so many times that I think it's time to address it.

So, here's the usual scene: Out to dinner with my wife, the ambience is pleasant and inviting. The server has a really nice, engaging and friendly demeanor, exhibiting just the right balance of friendliness and professionalism. We're enjoying our wine and an appetizer that we are sharing. Then, invariably when it's either time to refill our wine or water glasses or to bus the appetizer plates or to serve the next course, here comes the server, the busser or sometimes even the manager with arms and elbows all aflail. No, I don't know if that's a real word but it's the best way I can describe it. Here they are reaching their arms in front of my wife's face to hand a dish to me or to refill my wine.

This is a basic fundamental of good service. This is not fine dining, hoity-toity, white glove service. If you do not get this down, you are failing at the very basic first rules of correct service.

Please, you must always serve, bus, pour, and pass etc., with your open body towards the guest. Do not put arms, elbows, wrists or hands in in front of the face of your guests. The backs of your arms, wrists and elbows should always be away from the guests. I understand that you may be thinking that you are being expedient and using good time management. Perhaps you think that as in a basketball game, it's a wise move to just remain stationary as you pivot on one foot as you reach toward each guest. This is not only NOT good service, it is actually RUDE.

Now, I know you don't mean to be but that is how it could be perceived. And I know it's just a matter of ignorance. I find that the nicest servers, who often are very proficient at most if not all of the other basics, somehow seem to fall short in this crucial element. It's really on par with pointing your finger directly at someone's face.

When serving or clearing or pouring, you must move toward each guest you are serving. Yes, of course there are times when guests are seated in booths or in long tables and it's a bit difficult to reach all the way to them. However, there's never an occasion when it's alright to put your arms or elbows right in front of someone's face.

Even when serving or clearing or reaching to serve or clear something from one of those long tables or hard-to-get-to-booths with your open body towards the guest, you must always be polite and say something like, "Please, pardon my reach, sir, ma'am." Or "Please, excuse me." Or something to that affect.
This is not being petty. This is being courteous and respectful of your guests and their personal space. By you taking the extra few seconds to walk to each guest and to serve or clear or pour in this non-intrusive manner this will contribute to making this an exceptional dining experience for your guests.
And oh, by the way, please, please serve ladies first. All the time. Must I elaborate?

Hand Me a Glass, Please
The Proper Handling & Care of Glasses & Stemware
As I write this chapter I'm sitting at a bar and grill in the Central West End of Saint Louis, on a hot summer day with a friend, enjoying the beautiful weather.

A nice, tall, cold, frosty mug of Blue Moon sounds like the perfect beverage right now. We both order the same. We wait a few minutes, anticipating that first sip of the refreshing brew. Soon, out comes the waitress carrying two, tall, frosty glasses. She places one in front of each of us. My buddy immediately grabs his and takes a quick gulp. I, however, motion to the waitress to hold on. I say to her, "This is not what I ordered".

Yes, it is true that in that glass is indeed the beer-Blue Moon, that I ordered but she carried it to me with her grimy hands palming the rim of the glass where I'm about to sip from. (See illustration) So, No, this is not what I ordered.

Am I being ridiculous? Is it too much to expect that a server know how to properly handle and serve beverages? I do understand that it's 'just a bar and grill', as my friend points out to me. Yes, I realize that. However, it's not acceptable service that a server does not know or does not seem to care how to properly carry and serve a beverage to the guest. This is so basic. And it shouldn't matter if this is a fine dining establishment or a food truck.

There is a proper way to and a way NOT to handle and carry glasses. Of course, if one has never been trained what the proper way is, if it's never been addressed-then I guess you can't expect people to know. I learned long ago,
"You can't expect what you don't inspect." But then again, this is common sense.
So here's the basics. Your hands and fingers should never be placed higher than about 1 1/2 -2 inches away from the rim of the glass-a rocks glass, a high ball, a water glass etc.
A wine or martini glass or any glass that has a stem should always and only be held by the stem. That is what it is there for.
Exception- there are now stem-less wine glasses- so in that case they should be handled the same as the aforementioned rocks, highballs etc.

"The top of the glass is for the guest. The bottom of the glass is for the server."

Wine glasses should always be clean and spotless. Sometimes I hear people say well it's just a water spot. True, but an important part of tasting wine is looking at the wine in the glass, holding it to the light and observing its characteristics. If the wine glass has water spots or worse, finger marks and smudges or God forbid, lipstick stains, it will be a big turn off to the wine drinker.   Stemware should always be polished before being set in front of a guest or being placed as part of a table setting.

Often times, when they are polished, one just uses a clean moist linen to wipe them. However, linens usually have soap residue on them and that just moves the soap around on the glass.

Rather than just wiping them with a linen, it is recommended to steam them.   Get a stainless steel solid cutlery cylinder wide enough for the bowl of a wine glass to fit inside. Fill receptacle about half way with steaming hot water. Hold your glass by the stem upside down and over the steam partially in the receptacle but not submerged in the water. Hold there for a couple seconds until the steam creates condensation on the bowl of the glass. Wipe dry with a lint free towel – preferably a microfiber one.
Stemware should always be clean, spotless and free of watermarks, fingerprints, smudges and lipstick stains.

Yes, it is simple and basic but I can't tell you the countless times I've been to a beautiful, upscale restaurant and my wine glass was not spotless. It's not that difficult to do but it does take a conscious effort and a bit of time. However, I'm quite sure that your guests will certainly appreciate you doing it and it will save you the embarrassment of your guest pointing out a dirty glass to you.

Traymanship
I know I've already spoken previously about hygiene, sanitary practices and the importance of clean hands when serving. But I feel the importance to broach another related subject here.
So, what is traymanship? It is just like it sounds-"a man with a tray on a ship". No, I'm kidding. Traymanship is a word that I coined which means the ability to use and carry a tray. How proficient you are in your traymanship will have a great effect on your overall service.

If indeed, our goal, our desire is to provide a **WOW!** experience for our guests, then the importance of serving from a tray, cannot be overstated or overemphasized.

If you have more than two drinks to carry to a table, a tray must be used. Yes, I do know servers who can carry 3 bottles in one hand and 2 rocks glasses in the other to a table and not spill a drop. That's amazing-5 drinks! But I ask you, does this really look good? Is there a grace and style in the manner of handling of beverages brought to the table in this way?

Beverage trays are in restaurants for a reason-plain and simple- to be used. And please don't tell me that you can carry more without a tray. Or some people say "It's easier not using a tray." Well, that may be true but it doesn't make it a better way. If you are not proficient in Traymanship, you must practice. A server who lacks in this area will not be successful in this industry.

Carrying more than 2 drinks to a table without a tray is tacky and not a very high level of service. Yes, there are exceptions. Beer buckets-obviously a tray is not needed. Three or more wine glasses on a wine flight carrier-no tray is needed.

Even bringing 4 or 5 empty wine glasses and an unopened wine bottle to a table - no tray is necessary. Carry the glasses by the stems, upside down, one each in between your fingers in your left hand and then hold the base of the wine bottle in the palm of the same hand. This leaves your right hand open and available to place the glasses down on the table in front of each of your guests. After placing the glasses down, with the bottle still resting in the palm of your left hand, you can now use your free right hand with the corkscrew to open the bottle.

In my mind these are the only exceptions of bringing more than 2 drinks or glasses to a table without a tray.

Sure, you can make an argument that not all restaurants are "like that".   But if your goal is to create a **WOW!** experience-to set yourself apart as a server with exceptional standards-then you must take the responsibility to do so. Whether you work at a sports bar, bar and grill, a diner or anywhere other than a fine dining restaurant you can still do better than what you've done in the past. We know that you can easily carry multiple bottles of beer, glasses, cocktails etc. But which do you think your patrons perceive as better service? Carrying with your hands or on a tray? If you stop carrying drinks with your hands, I'll bet that your guests will appreciate your traymanship.

Yes, it's true that carrying a beverage tray loaded down with drinks is not easy. It's much easier to spill a tray of drinks than when carrying them in your hand. It takes practice. You have to build up the strength in your hand and wrist and the dexterity in your fingers. But if you practice you will become good at it.

I would also suggest trying some finger, hand and wrist strengthening exercises. These will help you build up your strength as well as your manual dexterity. A few exercises that I have found extremely effective are the following:

1.   **Grip Strengthener**-This device is used by rock climbers and body builders to strengthen fore arm muscle and hand muscles. They can be found at any Target, or Walmart for $10.00-$20.00. If you use this for a few minutes each day, you will quickly build up your hand, finger and wrist strength.

2.   **Planet Waves Vari-Grip Hand Fitness tool**-These range from $9.00-$19.00. These are hand grip tools that are specifically made for Bass guitar players to build up strength in their fingers, hands and wrists. Even though it's made for guitar players, I would recommend it for anyone wanting to improve their tray holding/handling ability.

3.   Hishru/Baoding Chinese Balls-The basic exercise consists of rotating a pair of Hishru balls in the palm of the hand, ensuring even and constant contact is made between the balls. Once this has been learned, the rotation speed can be gradually increased until the balls separate in the hand. Eventually one can learn to rotate them completely without the balls making contact with each other. Exercises have been developed involving two, three, four or more balls.

In fact, it's not just the carrying of the loaded tray that presents difficulty to the uninitiated, but so, too, does the maneuvering and balancing of the tray. As you remove each glass, the weight of the tray shifts from one side to another. You then must readjust the position of your hand under the tray, creating a new center of balance. This requires poise, quick timing, balance and coordination. Do not be daunted by this. Practice and soon you'll be proficient in the skill of traymanship.

If you are a non-server reading this book and you have never worked in a restaurant as a server, or you do work in a restaurant and have never acquired or have never been required to perfect the skill of traymanship-then I highly encourage you to give it a whirl. No, not a twirl. If you give it a whirl, whether you are successful at it or not, I promise you, you will develop a healthy respect and appreciation for those in the service industry that do this and especially for those who do it well.

I have practiced for years and yes, I am very good at it. I'm confident with a tray of drinks in my hand. I wasn't always good at it though.

I can't count the times in the early days of my service career when I've dropped trays, glasses, spilled water, wine, cocktails, on myself and yes, on my guests. It does happen. It's embarrassing when it happens. Practice and you'll get better at it. The not-spilling, that is.

I don't think there's any server anywhere who can honestly say that they have absolutely never, ever spilled a drink or dropped a tray in their entire career. Just like I don't believe that there's a cook or a chef anywhere who can honestly claim to have never cut their finger or burnt a dish they were cooking. I may be wrong. But I've witnessed it countless times from my colleagues and I've been the guilty one myself, numerous times.

So, what does one do when that unfortunate, embarrassing event, occasionally happens? Hopefully, it is in your nature and goes without saying that you apologize to your guest-immediately. Offer them a clean and dry cloth napkin for them to dry off. If red wine or something similar has been spilled that has stained the guests clothing, please, quickly bring them a glass of soda water and a dry napkin-white if the stained garment is light colored, black if it's dark colored. Most people know that this is effective in lifting stains such as wine from material.

Next, communicate to your manager or owner, regardless of how slight or seemingly insignificant and small the spill was. Management must be made aware of every mishap, spill, mess up etc. They are ultimately responsible. It's not that you can't or shouldn't be trusted or that there needs to be a high level of micro-management. However, if there are repercussions either now or at a later date, it's important for them to know and be aware. So always be smart, no matter how small the problem-tell your manager.

Tell them now. Today, as soon as it happens, before the guest leaves or before the guest has a chance to preemptively get to the manager or another staff member before you do.

This gives your manager the opportunity to smooth things over, to offer to pay for dry cleaning, or offer a gift certificate, pay for their dinner or offer other compensation.

Don't Allow a Mess up to Become a Blow-up

A good manager/owner is always aware of Everything that goes on in their establishment. That's right, Everything. If you inform the manager as soon as a mess up takes place, they are equipped to be able to defuse any potential blow up from the guest-justified or not. Even if you do your best to take care of the situation, your manager has more authority to compensate the guest and ameliorate the situation.

Also, most guests won't fly off the handle if they feel that enough or adequate attention has been given to them and the unfortunate situation. An apology and acknowledgement by the manager or owner goes a long way. Even though you may have apologized, people feel better when they know that you have communicated the situation to someone in authority. A manager is able to offer more to the guest- to pay for their dry-cleaning, give a gift certificate, comp their meal, etc.

A seemingly bad situation can be turned into an opportunity for great service. Okay, so you spilled, that's clearly not good. But how you respond and the actions you do or don't take will speak loudly about you as a server and the restaurant itself. Is this a place where an apology is made and nothing else is done to compensate the guest?

Or, does everyone in the restaurant become aware? By everyone-I mean the entire staff? Does the chef now do something special for that individual, once the spill has been cleaned up? This is an opportunity to shine. Just because you spilled, that does not mean it's a forgone conclusion that the guest will not have a good dining experience from that moment onward. I'm not saying that it's going to be easy. But if it's a simple spill-glass of water or wine or other liquid- no food involved, then, you certainly should be able to regain your composure and continue.

Mistakes happen. Accidents happen. It may not have been 100% your fault. Maybe another server or busser backed or charged into you. Regardless of whose fault it may be, you still, hopefully, have an opportunity to humble yourself and to create a better experience for your guest and to re-establish rapport with them. Often the guest will now be concerned for you if you are genuinely sincere when you apologize. They may be worried about your embarrassment.

That's not to say you ought to orchestrate a spill on purpose, in order to draw attention to yourself and then to have the opportunity to apologize to the guest, thereby creating an opportunity to build a better bond with them. What I am saying is that accidents happen. Don't freak out. Don't get down on yourself. Shake it off. If you need a moment to regain your composure, once you've communicated with your manager it may be okay to take a break for a moment. But make sure that your guests' needs are being attended to first.

Next, you must assess the situation. It is entirely possible that your guests no longer wish to have you as their server. Don't take it personally. They simply do not wish to be served by you. Maybe you spilled a hot bowl of chili on them and it's not just as simple as dabbing some soda water to remove the spot or stain. Now their pants smell like chili. Chili might smell great when it's steaming hot in a bowl. But when it's warm and drying on a guest's pants-it's not the same.

They are disgusted and yet they still want to or need to stay and eat. They just do not want to have anything to do with you. At this point, you must recuse yourself (just like judges do) from the situation. Depending on how outraged your guest appears, you may or may not want to inform them yourself that another server will be taking over service of their table. Tell your manager and find another server to take over your table. Explain the situation and entrust the continuation of service to your peer.

Hopefully, for your sake, the guest does not complain too vehemently to the manager or you could end up like the Spanish busboy on Seinfeld. George told the manager that he left the napkin on the table too close to the candle and it caught on fire. That small seemingly innocent complaint by George not only cost the busboy his job but it destroyed his life, his lamp and his cat.

What to do if/when you spill something:
1.   **Remain Calm**
2.   **Apologize immediately to your guest(s)**
3.   **Tell your manager, supervisor, owner**
4.   **Help them wipe up, clean up the mess.**
5.   **Find a way to turn it into a positive situation**
6.   **Recuse yourself if the situation warrants.**
7.   **Transfer your table to another server.**
8.   **Move on**
9.   **Practice your traymanship, even at home**

What NOT to do if you spill something:
1.   **Cry**
2.   **Throw a tantrum**
3.   **Hide and pretend you don't know what happened**
4.   **Blame someone else**
6.   **Curse to high heaven**
7.   **Yell at customer & say they tripped you/made you do it.**
8.   **Quit the business. Unless of course, if the spilling and dropping things is a recurring theme for you.**

T. Harv Eker says that, **"Every Master, was once a disaster."**

I know that you are well on your way to becoming a master.
As you master the basics of Service, we can now start thinking about what other things we need to learn.
Service and Hospitality Professionals who excel in this industry understand the importance of being equipped and...

Chapter 8

Getting Knowledgeable

"Knowledge is a treasure, but practice is the key to it."
Lao Tzu

We've all heard the phrase that "Knowledge is Power", and I absolutely believe that is true. But the other part of that is that true empowerment is having the knowledge and effectively utilizing it or applying it. As Lao Tzu, the Chinese sage states, "...practice is the key to it". Having an encyclopedic wealth of knowledge in your brain on any topic, really has no value unless you use it to your advantage. On the other hand, the individual that does not have the knowledge needed to be effective in their job, whatever that may be, is ill-equipped and very weak. That is, they are powerless to be successful in their job or position.

As I write this chapter, I'm on a flight to Minnesota, sitting next to a gentleman, David, who owns a beauty school in Milwaukee. He believes that great service-great customer service is dependent upon constant training. Not just constantly training new employees joining the company, but also constantly training staff who've been on the team for years. Very specific training, in fact. He says that if management doesn't teach the staff exactly what to say, then everybody ends up winging it. And then you get a multitude of responses to the same question from various guests.

For example: What are tonight's specials? How do we handle complaints? How should everyone answer the phone? How do you greet a customer or guest that walks into your place of business?

Even amongst management there should be continuity and consistency in answering questions. Does this mean that one should be a robot and always speak in rote memorized sentences? Not necessarily-but certainly there should be a unity, a solidarity in how the company, the restaurant, whatever the business is and all its personnel, presents itself to the public.

Even something seemingly so simple as how you and your staff answer the phone at your place of business is very important. Does one person say, "Thank you for calling Johnnie's Bistro. This is Sean, how may I help you?" While another person simply says, "Hello"?

Isn't it amazing how many times when you call a business, restaurant, law firm, etc. and the person on the other end of the line answers by saying, "Hello"?
You might wonder to yourself, did I misdial and get a residence? This certainly is not the company I called, is it?
So you ask, "Is this XYZ Company?"
"Oh, yeah", comes the reply.   "What can I do for you?"

Now I'm just being petty, you might say. What about "don't sweat the small stuff"?

Well, if how someone on your staff answers the phone is small stuff, then it's no wonder why your business is sometimes up and sometimes down. Sometimes you get rave reviews from your clients/customers and other times they can't wait to go on a review website and harangue you.

Service Begins at "Hello"

You may think that how the telephone is answered has very little bearing on the level of service at a restaurant. But I disagree. I believe that the person's dining experience begins, not when the server approaches the table, nor even when the guest is greeted at the door. Rather, the dining experience begins hours, days, maybe even weeks in advance when the reservation is made.

How a person is greeted and treated on the phone when they first call in will set the tone in the mind of that guest as to how they expect their dining experience to be.

Sure, the person answering the phone may be 'just' a host or hostess (we'll address that mentality in a later chapter) but how they answer the phone is an integral part of the service and experience of the patron. In fact, it is the first point of contact between the guest and the establishment.

Here's a thought, a question to ponder. At the restaurant or establishment that you work at currently, do you ever have people that call back and cancel reservations? Of course, it happens. Some places it may happen more often than seems normal.   Why is that?

Circumstances arise that are unforeseen. Uncontrollable, even. Of course, people have the prerogative to change their mind. People get sick, flights get delayed, and there are changes of plans. They decide not to go out due to inclement weather.   There's any number of reasons why. And the guest, when pressed may or may not wish to divulge the reason for the cancellation.   Most likely, though, the reason will not be because of or due to anything that could have been changed or prevented by the restaurant. The reason, most often is not anything that the restaurant could have otherwise affected. In fact, cancellations are really, often, just postponements for a later date.

No one likes cancellations. But they are a fact of business. They happen even to the best, top notch restaurants in the industry. But thankfully, at least the patron did you the courtesy of calling to cancel. At least you know that they are no longer coming.

Now, let me ask you another question: At your current place of business, do you ever have people that have a reservation booked and they just don't show up?   Do you ever have 'no shows'?

I'm sure you'll say yes. If you say no, then you're the rare exception, or you're not being completely truthful. If you said yes-that you do indeed have no shows-my next question is-"Why?"

It may be difficult to ascertain the reason why, especially if the reservation is for a table of one to four guests, as many restaurants do not even take a phone number for small groups of less than 5. (To me that is just poor customer service and laziness on the part of the one answering the phone) Some places it's less than 6.

But let's consider this for a moment.   Why do people just not show up?

Many restaurants do require a credit card with the reservation and charge a cancellation fee for no shows. So it kind of compels the booked party to actually call and cancel. But what if yours is a restaurant that does not require credit cards for small reservations? You call the number to confirm and the person who answers says, "Oh no, we called and cancelled a few days ago." However, there is no record of the cancellation. So, what happened?

Whether it's a reservation for 2 or 12 a no show is a no show and that's lost business. It cuts into your profit, it hurts the restaurant and it certainly demoralizes the staff that were waiting and prepared and expectant of that group that evening. It is a very disheartening feeling for you as a server. You walk into work, the manager tells you your section, you check the layout and the reservation book or Open Table and see you'll be serving Johnson party of 5 at 6:30. You're happy and excited. You polish your silverware, you carefully place the polished wine glasses at each setting, anticipating selling at least 2 bottles to the group. Everything is all set to go. 6:30 comes and goes. No sign of your guests. 6:45-nothing. 7pm. still nothing. At 7:30 the manager says, "I guess they're not coming. Break it down."

And in your mind you're thinking, "Break it down? What happened?" Indeed, what happened?   How about break it down to me? Can you, Mr. Manager tell me what happened? Was this reservation confirmed?
Is it possible that something happened during the phone call when the reservation was made?

Perhaps the guest did not feel that they were warmly greeted when they called in. Maybe they were put on hold for too long while the one answering took another call and didn't even apologize or say "Thank you for your patience", when they came back on the line. Maybe they were rudely answered when they asked about the menu prices, bringing in their own wine, corkage fee, etc.

I'm not saying it's always or even most of the time due to something that transpired on the phone when the guest called in. But don't you think it could be?   And what if it is?   Or was?

Why not count the number of no shows you have in a month and consider the lost revenue both for your restaurant and for the servers involved. Is it possible that something as basic as how your staff answers the telephone could either positively or negatively affect your reservations? I say, ABSOLUTELY!   Without a doubt. Yes it can and it does.

So how important is training? Proper and ongoing continuous training is absolutely vital to the success of any restaurant.   If the staff at a restaurant is not trained in something seemingly as simple as how to properly answer the phone, what other areas are they NOT being trained on? I'm guessing pretty much everything.

Remember what we discussed before:
YOU CAN'T EXPECT WHAT YOU DON'T INSPECT-YOU CAN'T MANAGE WHAT YOU DON'T MEASURE

So if it's true about something as basic as how to answer the telephone and how something that seemingly insignificant can affect your business, wouldn't it follow that it can have the same affect if everybody on your staff is just winging it when it comes to explaining the specials-what they are and how they are prepared? Or in how they deal with or respond to a guest complaint?

There's a difference between trusting your staff (to communicate properly and accurately) once you know they have the correct knowledge and just letting them wing it.

A successful business needs to have everyone speaking the same language. It's part of having a team mentality. That's one reason why restaurants require their staff to wear a uniform, aside from the need for guests to distinguish between other guests and staff. Again, does that mean there is no room for personality or individuality? Of course, not. You need to be yourself but everyone should all be on the same page and reading from the same playbook.

Speaking of playbooks, think of professional athletes. Whatever you favorite sport may be, baseball, football, basketball, soccer or something else-do they train constantly or do they just show up on the field, the court or the stadium on game day? We all know the obvious answer. Of course, they practice and train on a daily basis. And they get continuous instruction. So why is there so little or even no training in so many establishments these days?   And I'm not just talking about the Service and Hospitality industry.

I worked for a few years in the staffing and recruiting business and the person who owned the franchise where I worked did not require his staff to go to or take any sort of training, at all. In fact, in 6 years he only once sent his staff to any kind of training. Although, he did allow me to go and go, I did, to any and every training that was available, online, local, regional and national training events, but that's because I've always been a learner.

I am well aware of how important training is and how impactful it can be. But, while I would go to training, my colleagues did not. It did not make for a very effective team. We were not all following plays from the same playbook. How effective can a recruiter or sales person or staffing team be if they are just winging it? The answer is not very.

So, if you, or your staff are always improving, it's just a matter of time before you're headed for disaster. Or at the very least, you will be less successful than you possibly could be.

So my server friend, with that in mind, what do you do if you work at an establishment where training and ongoing training is not valued highly, or worse, is completely ignored?

There's a number of possibilities:

1)   Consult with your management. I know this will take some courage but it will, hopefully, be worth it. If you understand the importance of training and you are not being equipped, then you and your guests are suffering. I guarantee that you and your colleagues are not providing exceptional service on a consistent basis. Give your management team a copy of **Getting to WOW!** and attempt to influence them about the importance of training. You can blame it on me, and tell them that this crazy author guy said that training is super important.

However your attempts may be met with resistance. You have to be prepared for that. If they've been in business this long-however long that may be, and they've not placed any or much emphasis on training, it's doubtful that they're going to see the light now. But people do have epiphanies all the time. So my advice-give them this book and pray for an epiphany.

If they do have an open mind and hopefully that will be the case, and they truly want to improve service and provide training, then perhaps they will:

A.) Purchase multiple copies of **Getting to *WOW!*** and give them to each staff member

B.) Hire ASPIRE Enterprises to conduct Service and Hospitality Training Seminars for the entire staff-including management

C.) At the very least, strongly suggest or even require all front of the house staff, both new and current team members to purchase said book, **Getting to *WOW!*** and read it.

This is not an unreasonable suggestion or request. For most restaurants require staff to purchase certain items; aprons, uniforms, you must provide your own tuxedo, pens, nonslip shoes, wine opener, crumbers etc.

Bartenders must often purchase and provide their own shakers, tumblers, strainers etc. So why not require **Getting to *WOW!*** as part of the complete tool kit for all front of the house staff?

2.) Train and Equip Yourself

• Read books on food and wine and service. Certainly, this book, **Getting to *WOW!*** is one resource for you. In addition, I strongly suggest that you get yourself a copy of both The Food Lover's Companion and The Wine Lover's Companion. These are classics and invaluable parts of any serious Food industry professional's knowledge arsenal.

There are so many resources available to you that even if your management don't really give a hoot about training and ongoing education, which, though it is a shame, it is NOT an excuse for you being less than knowledgeable about your product and how to effectively sell it.

You must educate yourself about your product-food and wine-both the raw ingredients-the produce, how and where it is sourced as well as the preparations.

- **Talk with your chef**. I don't know of any chef anywhere who does NOT want to talk about his culinary creations, especially to the staff that are selling and serving it. The more you can learn from your chef, the more knowledgeable you become and the easier it is for you to effectively communicate that information to your guests.

If you work at a restaurant where a daily line-up (pre-shift meeting) is not the norm where the chef shares about the specials and other items on the menu ask your chef if you can talk with him or her daily for a few minutes. Ask specific questions about ingredients, preparations, sourcing of product, etc. Be aware though, that your chef may not have that much time available just for you. In that case, ask if you could do it at least once a week. Hopefully as you take interest, your co-servers will follow suit and it will organically grow into a daily pre-shift meeting.

I know how frustrating it can be, as I, too, have worked in a number of restaurants where there was no training, no pre-shift meeting. The only training was done for new hires to learn the menu. After that, everybody just showed up for their shift. Everybody just kind of did their own thing. In at least one of those places, we did have daily specials which the name of it was merely written on a white board. No explanations, or descriptions and not even a short meeting to go over them. So, each server just kind of figured it out on their own what said specials were. Everybody was saying something different about the same special.

- **Watch The Food Network, The Cooking Channel & PBS-Just by watching various shows** on these networks you will learn more about food, ingredients, preparations, what goes on in a restaurant kitchen, etc.
- **The Internet**-Do I really need to explain?   Ok-Google and YouTube

- **Meet, connect and learn from and with other like-minded industry professionals**-Go out to eat together. Learn and study other restaurant's menus. Cook together, experiment and learn from others who have a passion for the industry.
- **Go to any food, beverage, wine, service, hospitality trainings, shows, conventions or seminars and Learn!**

Be the Change that you want to see at your restaurant. With all your new-found knowledge-Lead by example and encourage your co-workers to do the same.

3.) Quit working where you are and get hired at an establishment that DOES value training and encourages on- going learning.
You become like who you spend the most time with. For most in the industry, the restaurant or establishment where they work is truly their second home. You spend more time, more waking hours with your co-workers than with anyone else in your life. If you are not in an environment that promotes, encourages, provides and endorses training and ongoing education, then maybe it's time to move on. If that environment is causing more stress for you because you want to excel and others around you don't, then move on. There are endless opportunities and possibilities for anyone who is truly serious about achieving success in this industry. You just have to go out and find them. Do not allow yourself to stay stuck just because you're not willing to venture out. If the status quo is not acceptable to you DO NOT SETTLE.

In addition to being fluent in wine and cuisine speak, that is, having great food and wine knowledge, there are a number of other subjects that you, as a Service and Hospitality Professional must be equally well versed in.

Other topics you must be well versed/educated on:

1.) Safe Food Handling and Sanitation

Although the laws vary from state to state, I highly recommend that all front of the house personnel go through a Food Safety course like ServSafe.com. This course, though geared toward the kitchen staff/food handlers, is very important and covers topics that all Front of House staff must be educated on as well: Basic Food Safety, Personal Hygiene, Cross-contamination and Allergens, Time and Temperature, and Cleaning and Sanitation.

2.) Responsible Alcohol Serving

It is a well-known fact that if you are going to be in this industry, then you will be around, indeed not only around, but actually serving and selling alcohol to guests. Serving alcohol to guests has many benefits, both to the diner-that of enhancing their food and dining experience through pairing with wine, beer or a cocktail; as well as to the business, by generating increased revenue from alcohol sales.

Along with those benefits come the very serious responsibility of needing to know how to: identify signs of intoxication in a guest, how to respond to a guest that needs to be "cut off", how to prevent underage drinking and what the laws are regarding alcohol service. Just as important as proper wine knowledge and how to present and pour wine is for the service professional, so too is, the knowledge of when and how to say "You've had enough." Again, I recommend the National Restaurant Association approved course: ServSafe.com

3.)   Food Allergies

The number of food allergy related reactions that require emergency room visits each year in the United States is over 200,000. More than half of those happen outside of the home. So, translation-many of them occur while people are dining out at restaurants.

It is absolutely imperative that you understand the seriousness of this. Many people seem to think that this is just something those working in the kitchen, preparing the food must be educated on, but that is not true.

Every service professional MUST be not only aware of but also KNOWLEDGEABLE in Food Allergens as well. For example, do you know what the big 8 are? That is, the 8 most common food allergens? Do you know how to detect if a guest is possibly having an allergic reaction? And do you know what to do about it?

People with food allergies exhibit varying symptoms when having an allergic reaction. These can range from something slight and mild like having a feeling of itchiness on their tongue or mouth, to a potentially life-threatening reaction-anaphylaxis.
Every Service Professional should complete an allergy awareness course. These can be found from www.Safeserv.com or at www.foodallergy.org.

While diners certainly must do their part of calling ahead to a restaurant and finding out if their particular allergen can be avoided, as well as informing their server when they are ordering, the service professional, equally, has a responsibility to clearly inform the appropriate kitchen staff of the guest's allergy and to ensure that what they serve said guest is accurate and safe. By being well educated, conscientious and caring, you and your team should still be able to provide an amazing dining experience for your guests.

By the way, those big 8 are: Milk, eggs, wheat, soybean, peanuts, tree nuts, crustacean shellfish and fish.

4.) Dietary Restrictions

Aside from actual Food Allergies, many guests have other types of dietary restrictions. These restrictions can be for a variety of different reasons and take many forms. Some people have medical or self-imposed guidelines such as removing or reducing sodium, red meat, sugar or fat from their diet. Others like Orthodox Jews or Buddhists may have religious reasons for eating or not eating certain foods.

While still others may have other personal convictions.

For example, did you know that not all vegans are vegans for the same reason? My friend, here in Las Vegas, Paul Graham, has a written an excellent book on this subject entitled, Eating Vegan in Vegas. In it he sheds light on and discusses the 3 main reasons why a person may and in his mind, should, be a vegan. What are these three reasons? I'll let him tell you, as I highly recommend his book. Even if you are not interested in a vegan diet or lifestyle for yourself, as a Service Professional, I think it is helpful for you to be able to understand your diners that are.

Regardless of what a person's dietary restrictions are, be they self-imposed, medical, religious or personal convictions, it is not your business to interrogate them as to the reasons why. If they care to share with you, that's fine. But please don't ever press them as to why. It is your business, however, to be aware of what those restrictions and food needs or limitations may be and to honor and respect them.

In my years in the industry, I have sadly, been witness to servers as well as chefs and even managers speaking derogatorily about dining guests with said restrictions.   This is not professional and it is unacceptable.

With the growing number of people with Celiac disease, for example, the popularity of the gluten-free diet is also on the rise.

While some may be jumping on the gluten-free bandwagon as a personal preference, it is actually a real health risk to the people with the disease. People with Celiac disease cannot properly digest the compound found in gluten.

As a conscientious professional, it is vital that you are certain of what items on your menu do and do not contain gluten.   Gluten is found in wheat and many other grains. But one would think that a sauce, say a simple marinara sauce would not contain wheat. However sometimes wheat flour may be used to thicken a sauce. Also, some soy sauce, according to my friend, Sheri Holliday, actually has wheat added to it. Not all soy sauce does, typically the naturally fermented soy sauces do NOT contain wheat but the ones that are not naturally fermented DO.

Please take the time to educate yourself and if you are a manager, to educate your staff as to what items on your menu are vegan friendly, non-dairy, gluten free, etc. Is it a lot of work? Perhaps, but being a well-informed service professional helps you be more effective and helpful to your dining guests. Consider it part of your ongoing education that is required for you to be successful as a Service and Hospitality Professional.

5.) Sales

Sales? Yes, Sales! Surely not, you must be thinking. You're a service professional not a salesperson, right? Wrong!

Sales is Service is Sales. The two are interconnected. I often hear people say, "I'm in Sales, not Customer Service." So, that means you don't provide any service/customer service to your customers? Or, people will say, "I'm a Server, I'm not a Sales person." So, then I ask you, "Does that mean that you don't sell anything to your guests?" As I said,

Service is Sales is Service AND Sales is Service is Sales.

Now before you throw out your objections to me, let me just preempt some false thinking on your part. When I say you are a salesperson, I am not talking about that picture you may have of a fast-talking, shifty-eyed, greasy-haired, leisure-suit-and-gold-chain-wearing, not-to-be-trusted used car salesman.   That is not who you are nor who I would want you to be.

However, the simple fact is, that unless you are just an order taker- as in, "What'll it be?", then any service and hospitality professional IS indeed a Salesperson. You may not have realized it or never have been told it and maybe that's why your sales-the amount you ring every night sucks. And therefore your income/tips suffer. If on the other hand you learn how to be proficient at sales, automatically your income will increase.

So, if you've never picked up a book on sales, or been to a sales seminar, or ever even learned some simple Sales basics, I strongly suggest that NOW would be a great time for you to start. And if you have misconceptions about what sales is all about and how to effectively sell, then you really need to learn. If your picture of what a salesperson is even remotely resembles the one we described above, then it would be very helpful for you to pick up a book on sales. Once you learn certain principles, you can then tailor them to your personality and use them in the appropriate situation.

The fact is, and if you are honest, in any given restaurant, the person who is the most successful, makes the most tips is Always the one who can sell the best. You may have just thought that they have a great personality, and that most likely, is true.   But I guarantee you that they also are very adept at sales. It may be a very soft sell, understated approach. But they are great salespeople. I know it. And by you learning and practicing proven sales principles, you, too, will become more effective at your job.

You will most likely come to enjoy it more. Why is that? Because there are two dynamics going on-creating an exceptional dining experience for your guests while also making sales. There is a feeling of immediate gratification of knowing that you are making someone else enjoy pleasure AND at the same time you are reciprocally feeling pretty great yourself.

In the restaurant industry we are very fortunate in that, our customers are a captive audience. Once they are seated, it's pretty much a forgone conclusion that they are there to buy. That's a very strong buying signal. (Learning sales, you will know what buying signals are and how to capitalize on them) The question is, how much and what will they buy? Do you influence them or just take their order?

Another key component to effective sales, and actually the number one first step, is to Listen. If you are a good listener, and because you are a service professional, I know that you are, then as you develop that ability even more, you will become a better and more effective server-salesperson.

There are so many books on sales on the market and so many offering teaching and training on the subject. Two of my favorite sales mentors are Grant Cardone and Jeffrey Gitomer. While neither one specifically talks about sales in a restaurant setting-if you learn the principles from these two and then apply to the restaurant environment, you will stand out amongst your peers, you'll be more proficient at providing **WOW!** service and your sales, duh, will increase dramatically.

So, as you can see from the various things we've talked about in this chapter, Getting Knowledgeable is so important for you to become an exceptional Service and Hospitality Professional. In this industry, Ignorance is NOT bliss. There is no limit to the number of resources available for you to fill your arsenal with the appropriate knowledge.

I encourage you to take your profession seriously, whether this is a temporary stop for you or if this is your passion and your career path, be a learner. It's been said, that "Learners are Earners and Leaders are Readers."

Take responsibility for yourself and as you travel on this path of Getting to *WOW!* be one who leads the way. Don't say to your guests, "I don't know, let me go ask." Rather, be equipped with the knowledge and information you need.
This will enable you to be better prepared because now you'll be...

Chapter 9

Getting Ready for the Show –This is a Show, You Know
Lights, Camera, Apron!

"There is a commonality between the excitement people feel when they are seeing a show or concert, and the excitement they feel about having dinner at a new restaurant or their favorite eatery. Restaurants obviously fill the need of sustenance for guests, but most of the time they play an experiential role in the guest's life. Guests are expecting a show."
Los Angeles/ Las Vegas Restaurateur-Michael Balabon

The above quote, by my friend, Michael Balabon, a successful Los Angeles and Las Vegas restaurateur of many years who was a managing partner with Bottega Louie and Echo and Rig, describes it so eloquently. This business is very much like show business. It certainly is a cliché in Los Angeles that all servers are actors or is it that all actors are servers? Either way, the joke is when someone in Los Angeles says that they are an actor, the normal response is, "Oh, really? What restaurant do you work at?"

While that may be a slight to the actor, it truly is not to the service professional. Anyone who truly understands this business of Service and Hospitality will concur that each day or night shift that one shows up to work at a bar, a restaurant, a bistro, a diner, at a catering event, on a cruise ship or a private yacht-there is an element of performance involved. The dining floor is the stage, you the server, or bartender, are the performer.

My friend Greg DaLuz who currently works at Giada on the Strip in Las Vegas considers his pre-shift preparation of following his specific daily routine as very important. He says he makes sure that he makes sure that whatever he is doing that he gets home at the exact same time every day to get ready for work.

He eats a very similar pre-shift meal, drinks the same amount of water or coffee, and takes a shower at the same time. He takes the same route to work and talks withthe same people in the building upon his arrival. These all help get him into character-much like a Method actor.

If you are not familiar with the term Method actor, it basically means that the actor or performer remains in character all throughout the performance whether on stage or screen even between takes and breaks. They live and breathe the character. They are not portraying a character, rather, they actually embody or become the character. Jim Carey is famous for Method acting, especially when he was shooting the film Man on the Moon. He was portraying the eccentric comedian Andy Kaufman. All throughout the many months of shooting, Jim Carey WAS Andy Kaufman. He acted as Andy Kaufman. He required that everyone on set address him as "Mr. Kaufman".

When one is adept at Method acting-it can become a little surreal-because even the person's cast members begin to believe that that person actually has become the character that they are playing. When I did plays in Los Angeles with Carey Dunn-no relation to Jim Carey, I, too, did Method acting. I played an older gentleman in one of those plays and I walked with a cane and had a bent over posture. I was without a car at that time and I rode the bus to the theater. When I got on the bus in Los Feliz to for the 30 minute ride to Hollywood, I was the character. I was no longer Christoff. If the director, Carey, or one of the cast members had a question for me-when I arrived at the theater, I remained in character from the moment I arrived until I left the theater.

Every Server is a Performer

So what is the point? If you are a server, you are a performer. You have lines that you must memorize-the specials each evening. (We cover this in depth in Chapter 14 –Getting Enticing) You must know your script. You have a director-either the General Manager, the Owner or the Chef. Backstage is the back of the house. That's where all the costumes and props are-the food, the accoutrements. It is your job to create an experience for your guests. And you cannot create a great experience/performance if you are not prepared. Ivy Magruder, a former colleague of mine and a very successful Chef in St. Louis who did a stint for the Disney Corporation tells me that there they actually call their staff "Cast Members".

Every single person on your restaurant team is your co-cast member. And it takes each and every one of them, regardless of the part they are playing, to pull off a successful performance.

How does one prepare for the Show that is Service? First, it begins with a knowing, a realization that your guests are expecting a show. Now don't say "I'm just a server." Or that you aren't a performer. Sure you are. In fact, I'll venture to guess that one of the reasons that you were hired is because of how well you did in your audition. Audition? Absolutely. Even if the person who hired you didn't actually require you to perform-that is, to Serve them at a table-they certainly interviewed you and during that interview you displayed your excellent communication skills. You had the poise, the charm, the charisma, the personality and yes, even the right look. So, you got the part. Now, you must embrace it.

If you are truly committed to **Getting to *WOW!*** then you must accept that you are a performer in a show every time you come to work. Some of you are stars in a Broadway play, some are actors in a small summer stock theater, some of you are matinee idols and some of you are blockbuster movie stars. But please let's make sure that we are all past the level of a middle school or high school play.

Wherever you find yourself in this industry, realize that your guests are here for an experience. They will have a dining experience. The question is, how good or great will that be? That all depends upon you and how prepared you are for the Show.

Just as in live theater-you receive immediate feedback for your performance from your audience-your guests. The poor chefs-they have to wait to get responses from the guests. But you are there on the stage in the dining room. You definitely know (at least most of the time) if your performance is spot on or if you are bombing or dying on stage.

Service Professionals that excel at providing ***WOW!*** Service and creating ***WOW!*** dining experiences, take responsibility for themselves, their guests and what transpires during their shift.

The Dining Room is Your Stage

Theo Van Soest, a seasoned Service and Hospitality Professional and restaurant owner in Las Vegas says it like this.

> *"When you walk through those doors every day and you put on your uniform, you have to realize that you are on stage.*
> *You've got to leave your problems and your personal issues at home, focus 100% on the job at hand-the Show and put on that smile."*

Well said, Theo. Leave your problems at home, focus on the performance at hand, and put on that smile.

Once you come to the realization that you are on stage, you will begin to see the value of creating your own pre-performance ritual. Certainly becoming familiar with and memorizing the specials is a must for you. But beyond that, what else could you, should you do to ensure that you give a great show?

Know Your Script

It's absolutely vital that you know your script. What do I mean by that? In addition to knowing the specials of the day, you must know your menu-forwards and backwards. Inside and out. Not just know the words on it but become familiar with the preparations, the ingredients. Everything. Again, I go more in depth in Chapter 14 on this topic. Be well versed and able to answer questions that your guests may ask. Yes, I know that you can always go in the kitchen and ask the chef but that really kills the flow of the show. Be prepared. Be knowledgeable. Know your stuff.

Know Your Wines

One thing that Greg DaLuz does every day at Giada, is prep himself on wines that he's going to sell. The wine list at Giada boasts over 400 wines. How on earth does a server learn over 400 wines? They probably don't. But what Greg does is before his shift everyday he checks out the wines that are available and he chooses at least 3 that he's going to sell for that evening. How does he know which ones he's going to sell? Because he preps himself on them, becomes so familiar with them, that later, when a guest at his table asks for a suggestion, he describes them so well that they actually believe that he must have drank each of them hundreds of times. In reality, he may not have ever had the opportunity to try them but because his guests trust him they go with his suggestions.

He says he typically will choose one crowd pleaser, one domestic US or New World- Australia, New Zealand etc. and one French or Italian-a Brunello, a Super Tuscan etc. He doesn't pick the most expensive ones-maybe just around the $100.00 price range. So aside from being familiar with his wine lists, he has added ammunition in his arsenal which makes him a better host to his dining guests and a better salesman server. Plus, the fact that he does this every day, he is systematically learning the wine list, attacking it in 3 wine bites a day. Very smart.

You might be asking, well is that something that is required of the staff at Giada? No, it's not. You may also be wondering if all of the service staff there do this to prep for their shift. Again, the answer is NO. So why do it? Because we are talking about becoming people of excellence. That is what **Getting to WOW!** is all about.

I'll give you one other example that, depending on where you live and work, you may be able and interested in executing. One of the restaurateurs that I interviewed for **Getting to WOW!** was Mitchell Sjevern, owner of Bouchon of Santa Barbara. Being in Santa Barbara-the staff there have the unique privilege of living near Wine country. The Vineyards of Santa Ynez Valley are only a short 30 minute ride away.

Bouchon of Santa Barbara is a restaurant whose cuisine is created from "as fresh and local as possible sources" and to reflect and pair with Santa Barbara County wines. With that in mind, Sjevern not only encourages his staff to learn about and taste the local wines in order to educate themselves, but he also tells them to go to the vineyards to meet the winemakers and experience the wine in that setting. Now, how much more knowledgeable are those servers and how much more exciting is that information when they are not just sharing tasting notes that they read off of Google but they can actually tell you what the winemaker's goal or philosophy was in making a certain wine.

Know Your Vegetables

That is a level of preparedness that is uncommon and of course we are not all blessed to live close to local wineries. However, that same depth of knowledge could be acquired, say, for the produce or the meat that your restaurant sources. You could go to the local farms and meet the farmers who are raising the animals and growing the vegetables. That's exactly what Jim Edwards, owner of Next Door Food & Drink in Loveland, Colorado does. He actually takes his staff on field trips to the local farmers who grow their produce.

In fact, Sydney Nelson, one of his star server/bartenders whom I also interviewed for **Getting to WOW!** told me that from one of those field trips-her perspective on something as lowly as the zucchini suddenly changed. After meeting the farmer and seeing and picking the vegetable herself and then tasting the simple but amazingly delicious dish their chef created, she now is in love with zucchini. And that interest and passion comes through when she talks with her guests. I guarantee you that when describing a dish, for example, the lamb, she doesn't just say, "And it comes with vegetables". Oh no! She describes them making them sound delectable and exciting. Sydney knows her vegetables!

Imagine yourself doing the same-going on a field trip to the local farms and learning about where what you are serving is sourced. Now, when you have guests that are truly interested in where their food is sourced you have first-hand stories to share with them. That would really be providing **WOW!** service.

Look the Part

How else should you prepare for the Show? Let's talk about your appearance. Some servers come to work looking like they just rolled out of bed. Why? Because, they probably did. Yes, this industry does tend to have crazy hours- working until 11pm, 12am or much later. Service professionals do not have banker's hours. No, it's more like musician's hours. Coming home late at night, sleeping much of the day, even up until right before your shift, is all too common. But guess what? That is Never an excuse to come to work looking disheveled and unkempt. That is not what your character calls for.

Instead you must look good and feel good every time you get on that stage. That means smelling fresh and not like a cigarette ashtray. But also, don't be over perfumed or over-cologned. This is a very common mistake that many in the industry make. It is very important for you to realize that your guests are not coming here to smell you, good or bad. Too much cologne or perfume can adversely affect the guest's ability to adequately smell the dish you just served them. Better yet, you should just smell like you just took a shower, clean and fresh sans added aroma.

Please tuck your shirt in. Wear a belt. If you don't know how to properly tie a tie- learn. Iron your shirt, your pants or skirt. Please make sure your apron doesn't have yesterday's marinara stained on it. I know these are basics but if you can't master these-I don't care how well you deliver your lines or how great the other parts of your performance are-I -the guest-will be distracted by your uncombed hair, your smelly cigarette breath and your wrinkly slept-in white shirt. Look good and you'll feel good and then your guests can focus on the Show.

Last points to be aware of: Know your lines. But just as in theater-if you forget a line, or you mess up-just keep going. Improvise. In fact, I highly recommend that you take an improv class. Doing improv will help you improve your ability to think on your feet, be quick witted and help you with listening and timing.

This is a show. You are always on stage. Don't let them see you sweat-even when you're in the weeds. Just as any actor or artist or athlete must continually practice to become excellent, so too, must you, prepare yourself and then continually practice. There is principle of becoming excellent at something that states that it takes 10,000 hours of practice to achieve mastery. So, just keep at it and over time as you apply the principles in this book, excellence in Service and Hospitality will be second nature for you.

I want to end this chapter with the entire statement from Michael Balabon that I quoted at the beginning:

"There is a commonality between the excitement people feel when they are seeing a show or concert, and the excitement they feel about having dinner at a new restaurant or their favorite eatery. Restaurants obviously fill the need of sustenance for guests, but most of the time they play an experiential role in the guests' life. For some people this is the place you go to end your busy week on a high note. It's what you look forward to all week long. The excitement and anticipation builds and as you walk in the door your pulse races.

Guests are expecting a show. From the sights they see and the aromas they smell; to the interaction they have with other guests and the service staff, these elements all culminate as they would in any theatrical performance. There is a beautiful drama that should unfold at the table throughout the meal. The service professional has at his/her disposal, multiple opportunities to add theatrical elements. The perfectly timed arrival to the table, the culinary concept description, the ability to craft and create a culinary journey for the guest, and the manner in which they carry themselves mentally and physically throughout the meal, these all add drama to the experience.

A good drama, a show, a performance. Your guests are paying for that. It helps the food taste better and the experience be more memorable. This is not a style that should be reserved only for the most exclusive of restaurant, but a general service style backed by critical thought that can be performed at any concept level. Guests should feel as if something magical just took place and they want more of it."   Michael Balabon

When all those parts come together to create a great performance, an amazing dining experience for your guests, then, there's a much greater chance that soon you'll be...

Chapter 10

Getting the First Kiss

"Everyone knows that first impressions are key. The first 5 minutes are the most crucial in setting the tone for the entire dining experience."
Olivier De Roany, MiX Restaurant, Delano Hotel, Las Vegas Strip

In the previous chapter, Michael Balabon, talked about how providing an exceptional dining experience is akin to giving a great performance. It is a show, you know. Another friend of mine in the business, Christopher 'Mo' Moore, server and service trainer at Kona Grill in Summerlin, Las Vegas, says that it's almost like being on a first date. You, the server have to get to know your date- your guest. You want to greet them warmly, perhaps pay them a sincere compliment, set them at ease and pay attention to them.

Your date, your guest is expecting a great experience and you must deliver. But it starts from the very moment that you lay eyes on her. On a first date it may be when you pick her up at her house or when she walks into the restaurant. With the dining guest, it is when they walk in the door and up to the host stand.

Mandy Monreal, who was the corporate hostess trainer for all Wolfgang Puck restaurants in Las Vegas for 5 years, says that you must engage the guest while they're waiting for a table. All too often a guest walks to the host stand puts their name in for the wait list and then just stands around, waiting. Mandy says she would train her hostesses to mingle with their guests-find out if they're a first time diner to your location. Are they a returning regular or an out of town tourist? Is it they're first time to your city? Make your guests feel comfortable.

She says, "Unless they are a returning regular, you must realize that they are 'out of their comfort zone'. They are coming to your place, into your house. Your job is to make sure they feel welcome. As they're waiting for a table, don't just let them wait-talk to them, get to know them and make them feel special."

If you fail at the beginning, it will not bode well for you for the rest of the date. You'll never get that first kiss, let alone a second date, if you don't do everything correctly from the very start.

Similarly, if the greeting and the "very first 5 minutes", as my friend, Olivier de Roany explains, is not perfect, then that guest is not coming back. There are way too many choices of restaurants to patronize, for someone to worry about coming back to a place that didn't give them a warm welcome.

Yes, the first 5 minutes is so important, but Mitchell Sjevern, owner of Bouchon of Santa Barbara in the seaside town of Santa Barbara, California, goes even one step further. He told me,

"The first 10 seconds is critical. People have to instantly feel happy to be here. The person at that host stand has to be someone incredibly competent. That's the primary reason my wife works the front door."

Whether its 5 minutes or 10 seconds-the point is, that once a guest steps foot into your establishment, the clock on Service Excellence is ticking. You only get one chance to make a first impression and whatever that impression is, will be a lasting one for sure. Good, great, bad or mediocre-it's all up to you.

In order to create an exceptional dining experience all the time, everywhere for every guest, there are so many factors that must work in harmony with each other. Every component is so vital and so important that if even one, seemingly small part, is missing, it's like listening to the music of a beautiful orchestra with just one obo out of tune and hitting a flat note. That one part being out of sync can turn what potentially is a very wonderful experience into something less than pleasant. That one instrument, that one musician is messing up the entire concert. The very first notes of the symphony literally and otherwise, SET THE TONE for the entire experience to follow.

So it is, in the Restaurant Business. The importance of the Host, Hostess or Maître' D' (henceforth I may refer to them as HHM) performing their responsibilities in an excellent manner cannot be overstated. And yet so many times it is the one position that is so undervalued, under recognized and certainly, often under compensated in the Service Industry.
I'm sure you may have experienced something similar to the following: Upon arriving at a restaurant whether with my wife or a group of friends, we are often greeted by the Host or Hostess at a restaurant with a one word question, "Two?";

"Four?" Or if they feel like going all out they may say something to the effect of: "Is there four?" "Will there be four?"
To which I, with my bit of sarcasm-sorry-might reply; "Four what?" And to that, their response is often, "Are there four of you?" OR "Four people?"
No "Hi". NO "Hello, Good evening,"

NO "Welcome, sir, to ABC Bistro." Why, oh why, is this such a common occurrence?

Let me address all the Hosts, Hostesses and Maître' D's reading this. Your job is so very important. You may not feel like it or believe it sometimes. You may never have really been told so. But it truly is vital to the success of your establishment. The manner in which a guest is greeted as they enter a restaurant, truly Sets the Tone for their entire dining experience. We've all heard and been taught that "First impressions are lasting impressions." And "You only get one chance to create a first impression." These are not just clichés. No, they are statements that are absolutely 100% true.

When a guest walks into an establishment and they have to wait to even be greeted or acknowledged-that's not good. Or if they are only greeted with a grunt of "Two?" Or they are greeted by a host or hostess that has a less than pleasant attitude, or is chewing gum, or eating, or more focused on their cell phone than on their patrons standing in front of them-that doesn't set a great tone for how this dining experience is going to be. It doesn't set a high bar for their expectations.

A guest needs to be welcomed warmly and made to feel welcome as they enter your establishment and feel happy as they are exiting. Whether one is a "regular" at the place or a first time guest-everyone who walks in the door should be made to feel special. They need to feel like you've been expecting them all along and that you are so glad that they are here.

How do you feel when you go to your best friend's house? Or better yet, your Grandmother's house? Think back to when you were a kid and you were going to visit your Grandma. How did you feel? I'll bet pretty great, right? She always knew how to make you feel like you were the absolute most important person in the world. Right? Why is that? Well, because to your Grandma-you were. I know I was. Or at least I felt that way. Maybe some of you still are. That's how you need to make your guests feel who come into your restaurant and it begins with the Host, Hostess, Maître' D (HHM). Your position is crucial to the success of the entire operation.

Imagine this: A guest or group of guests comes to your restaurant and not only do you greet them warmly and welcome them with a pleasant smile and a cheerful upbeat-"Good evening, Welcome to ABC Bistro. How are you all this evening?", But you even go one step further and one or two of you on the HHM team actually *opens the door for the guests!* This may be perceived by some to be a very small gesture but it carries such a great impact. And what do you think might be going through the mind of those guests? Maybe something like; "**WOW!** We've barely stepped foot inside the restaurant and we already have a feeling that this is going to be a great dining experience."

Next, as the guests are being escorted to their table, the hostess is not walking twenty feet in front of them racing to put the menus down on the table. Rather, she is walking just slightly ahead of the group of guests and looking back at them engaging them in conversation. "How has your day been so far?" she asks one of the group. She says; "What are you celebrating tonight?" She then tells them that she heard in the meeting that they just got in some freshly harvested Morels and says, "I don't know if you all are fond of mushrooms but the chef has a few specials featuring fresh Morels tonight. Be sure to ask your server about them. Especially the Morel mushroom soup."

Put yourself in the place of those patrons. Now that you have been welcomed, greeted, escorted and seated by an enthusiastic, pleasant and upbeat HHM, the Tone Has Been Set. When the server arrives a few moments later at the table, you are in a pleasant mood and you are confidently expecting a wonderful dining experience. And that is all due to the HHM doing more than the all too common; "Two? Ok. Follow me. Enjoy" routine.

The Server, now picks up the baton of Excellent Service that the HHM has handed off to him. I'm not saying that the responsibility of setting the tone and setting the expectations of the guest lies solely with the HHM team. It most certainly does not. And it really is incumbent upon that server to carry on and capitalize on what was begun by the effective HHM. Heck, his job is already half done for him. (Don't tell any server, I said that.) However, you (HHM) are on the front, front lines. You are the first ones that the guests interact with. It all begins with you.

The Restaurant business is not the only industry that has HHM type positions. What we are really talking about here is any public facing, customer interacting, front lines position in any business. Whether you work as a host or hostess at a restaurant, a front desk clerk in a hotel, a receptionist at a doctor's office, law firm or car dealership, a customer service representative, or a clerk at the DMV, YOU are the one who creates the first impression and the customer perception of that business.

I once saw a plaque on a receptionist's desk at a large fortune 500 company that read: Director of First Impressions. To me, that pretty accurately describes it. You set the tone for what that guest, customer, client thinks of that business or establishment. You wield great influence. Therefore, it is mandatory that you truly take your position and that responsibility seriously.

And if ever the misfortune of a Soupfly does happen, there is a greater chance of a strong and positive recovery happening because then it's just a mistake that can be remedied because the Director of First Impressions (YOU) did their job properly and effectively.

De Roany stated it like this, *"If you are careful to set the tone right at the beginning and you actually host your guest, then even if you mess up, it's easily forgiven because you set the stage."*

I do agree with him and I've experienced it for myself countless times. We'll talk more about what to actually do should a Soupfly occur, in a later chapter.

Although, I do believe we've clearly explained what it takes to set the tone and get the first kiss, I feel like the best way to drive this home is to share with you about my actual experience at Mix, where we, my wife, Michelle and I and her friend not only dined but were hosted by Olivier and his wonderful staff.

So, if I may I would like to share that experience with you. The following originally appeared as a post on my blog Soupfly in August 2014.

"Welcome Back to Soupfly!!
I told you that I would share with you about our Amazing dining experience at Mix on the top of Delano Hotel (Mandalay Bay property) in Las Vegas last Saturday night. Michelle and I had dined there previously and had a wonderful time. I emailed the Assistant General Manager, Olivier de Roany (whom we did not meet then) telling him that we enjoyed our experience. He promptly emailed me back asking me to inform him of the next time we'd like to come in because he would like to 'host' us. Not really sure what that meant but I assured him that we would.

In the meantime-about 3 months ago, I asked Olivier if he'd be willing to be interviewed for my book-**Getting to WOW!** Everybody WINS with 5 Star Service. He said yes and so I did. Since that time-of hearing him describe his philosophy of what exceptional hospitality/restaurant service was all about, I had really been looking forward to the next opportunity for us to dine at Mix again. And so, with Michelle's friend Lori visiting Vegas for her birthday-last weekend-it seemed like the perfect time to call Olivier and tell him we'd like to take him up on his invitation.

Setting the TONE

"Everyone knows that first impressions are key. The first 5 minutes are the most crucial in setting the tone for the entire dining experience." Olivier De Roany

From the moment we checked in at the Host stand in front of the elevator-when the Hostess told us that we were "All Set" (even though I wasn't sure what that meant) I will say it was the beginning of "**Getting to WOW!** MIX Style. Having just enjoyed a cocktail at RX Boiler Room-after taking the elevator to the 35th floor- the 3 of us decided a stop at the restroom would be in order. Why oh why-tmi- you say? Well, the reason I tell you this is that as we exited the restrooms and walked into the Mix Lounge (which one has to pass through to get to Mix Restaurant) there was Olivier standing in Mix Lounge talking with one of the hostesses. He greeted us with a sincere cheerfulness.

Was he purposely there waiting there for us? Did the hostesses downstairs radio up to him to tell him that we were on our way up? I can't say. All I know is that as Olivier escorted us into the dining room-every single staff member that we passed by smiled at us and gave some version of a cheerful "Hello or Welcome". What a friendly staff I thought.

Upon entering the dining room, Olivier told us that he has "a nice table prepared for us". I don't know if there's such a thing as a 'not nice table' in Mix. To say that Mix is an absolutely beautiful dining room is a hyperbolic understatement. It is gorgeous. With a stunning all-white decor- and a hand blown white bubble Murano glass chandelier as the hanging centerpiece it almost feels like one is inside a glass of champagne. Not a bad feeling to have.

Even though the entire dining room is beautiful, when we saw where we were being seated-(in one of only 3 pods in the entire place) we realized that-yes- Olivier did have "a nice table prepared for us". We really started to feel special. The pod that we were seated at had a fantastic view of the Las Vegas Strip. Within seconds of being seated we were greeted by Scott-our server and Franco his assistant. While there were many others who assisted the team-these two gentlemen were the primary ones creating and executing this wonderful experience.

Our dinner began with Scott offering us complimentary champagne from Alain Ducasse' (the owner of Mix and a culinary legend) own private label. Or if we didn't want champagne, Scott said he'd be happy to start our dinner with something else. "Yes, please bring on the champagne." was our reply. We're not even 5 minutes in and I know that this is going to be an Amazing dining experience.

Next, Scott gave us what I can only describe as guided tour of the menu. He so creatively described many of the dishes from the appetizers to the main entrees that he even almost made the duck sound delectable to me. Anyone who knows me knows that I only eat fish-no other animal protein. He carefully explained the lay out of the menu-one part was the traditional Alain Ducasse fare, another part a tasting menu and then the third section being a little more modern and contemporary versions.
Scott exhibited the perfect combination of professionalism but not stuffy and a truly friendly nature. There was no culinary question that stumped him and he made excellent suggestions for each of us.

We all trusted his guidance and the three of us were all thoroughly impressed and happy with our dinner choices. But oh wait, I'm getting ahead of myself.

Within a few minutes of the champagne we were greeted by Matt George, the Sommelier. He has thousands of bottles of wine to order, maintain and educate the staff on. What a great responsibility. After ascertaining the palate and wine preferences of my wife-Michelle, Lori and myself, he easily guided us to a nice bottle of Tobin James Zinfandel. It was the perfect complement to each of our entrees. Again, with such a friendly and helpful demeanor, Matt was so pleasant and his presence added to our evening.

ATTENTION TO DETAIL

Next came a refreshing amuse bouche. What looked to me like butterscotch pudding turned out to be a "lobster salad" with chopped cucumber, lobster and a cantaloupe foam (espuma). This was our first bite of food and it was scrumptious. And it did, what an amuse is supposed to do-tantalize and prime the palate or the appetite. What made it even more amazing to me-is that from our short conversation when we were discussing the menu-I mentioned to Scott-I don't eat meat and I really prefer to stay away from dairy-he took note and paid attention to details. So, when this amuse, that clearly looked like it had cream in it was placed in front of me, I was so pleasantly surprised that indeed it did not have dairy. Scott was in tune with his guests and what my/our needs were.

For our appetizer-aside from the Champagne, we shared a wonderful crab salad. I can't remember all the ingredients-I do remember it had gnocchi (potato dumplings) in it that were the lightest and fluffiest I had ever tasted. I highly recommend it.

DELECTABLE DISHES

Our entrees were excellent. My wife had one of her favorites-Roasted Duck. She orders it quite often when we dine out and Chef Bruno Riou did not disappoint. He prepares his Roasted Duck with radishes and turnips with a black olive sauce. Michelle absolutely loved it. She commented that she especially enjoyed that it was more salty and savory whereas most of the time Duck is usually prepared sweet. Scott recommended the Cod Brandade for Lori, which was prepared with lemon and capers and cooked with a brown butter sauce. I think from the picture you can see that Lori was in Cod heaven.

And me? I enjoy lobster. So the Roasted Maine Lobster "Au Curry" had my name on it. It was served with coconut basmati rice and a very mild curry or tikka masala type sauce. The flavors were perfect for me and there was so much lobster. Lobster tail, lobster claw, lobster meat everywhere. Yum. There seemed to be so much care in the preparation of each dish. (Note-the pictures do not do justice to how amazing each dish was)
"Tasting a dish should be memorable. If nothing remains in the memory of the guest, then I have made a mistake." Chef Alain Ducasse
If I may say, Chef Ducasse, you gave us great memories-No mistakes here.

TEAMWORK
Scott and his team, Franco, Alex and others whose names I did not catch, did a fantastic job of working together. The serving of the dishes, the timing of courses, the explanation of dishes, the clearing and table manicuring-everything was spot on. And yes they actually crumbed our table. Thank you. The whole dinner was a seamless production from beginning to end. No cues missed. And every member of the team seemed to care about our experience.

Also, we noticed Olivier, Sebastien, (General Manager) and other management staff, walking by periodically to observe our enjoyment of the evening. Franco, in the middle of dinner, asked to see my phone because he said he was going to take a picture for us. Well he didn't take a picture of us. Instead, he went and stood directly under the Murano glass bubble chandelier and took pictures of it for us. See picture at the top of the page. What a really cool picture. And what a thoughtful gesture. Thanks Franco. Oh and he also introduced us to General Manager Sebastien and to Chef Bruno, as we were leaving.

We concluded our dinner with two surprises- a funky, foamy, delicious pina colada and a nice dessert from the kitchen to celebrate Lori's birthday. I don't even remember what it was- something with chocolate in it. (I rarely eat dessert).
There is so much more that I can say about Mix Restaurant and even Mix Lounge. Like the view from the bathroom-when you are seated. Ahem. You must check it out.
But I will end by saying this...*WOW!* From the greeting and seating and setting the tone, to the exquisite food and the decor and the ambiance, to the amazing hospitality extended to us-truly here's **GETTING TO *WOW!***-They've really got it- THE PERFECT MIX."

That really says it all. It all begins within the first 5 minutes. That determines how the date will go, how the service will be and whether there will be a kiss at the end of the night. Well, then following through with the metaphor, from my perspective, our first date with Mix definitely merited them a second date and a first kiss, so to speak.
That's what **Getting to *WOW!*** is all about!

Chapter 11

Getting to Know Your Guests (Reading Your Guests)

"Every guest has a different agenda for their experience; some guests want recognition and attention, others are looking for a quiet romantic time, some want the foodie experience. Whatever their needs are, it is important to recognize their needs and cater to their needs. Passion and Sincerity will go a long way in our business."
Kim Canteenwalla, Blau & Associates, Las Vegas

Just as in sales- there are many types of customers, with varying needs and motivations to buy- so too, in the restaurant business/service industry- there are equally as many types of guests and reasons why people dine out. In this chapter we will discover what some of the basic types of people are and how each one ought to be approached in a manner that is most in tune with their type.

By types, I mean varying needs-or "agendas" as Kim Canteenwalla explained above. It is very important to understand that not all guests/diners have the same requirements in terms of attention required or the type of experience desired.

For example, a group of businessmen- engaged in deep conversation or important negotiations may-actually, most likely, not want to be constantly interrupted- because the restaurant is merely a location for their meeting. Their focus, will be entirely on their discussion, presentation or meeting. In this situation, it is best to inform them of the specials of the day/evening as soon as they are seated, bring their drinks to them in an expedient manner, and from that point on become a silent server.

This may be difficult for the server who mistakenly equates chattiness with good or even great service.

I remember a co-worker, let's call him John- because that's his name- who said to me and I quote, "Well, based on how long I've been talking with my people at table 24, I should get a really great tip. I've been in deep conversation with them all night."

This server, John, thought that the more often and the longer a server talks with their guest, the higher the tip will be because in his mind, that was the essence of service. Never mind that their water glasses were always empty and he had to constantly be asked to refill them, and their food was not even hot when he brought it to their table. But, by golly he sure could tell a good story! And maybe his guests enjoyed the interaction, but it is so important to let the guest lead the way.

To provide **WOW!** service is to effectively read your guests, and respond appropriately with the type of service or amount of attention they desire. But the point here in the above example is to be a silent server- unobtrusive yet aware and available throughout the entire meal.

"If I see 4 men in business suits carrying laptops come in-they want to be left alone. They want good service but they want the silent service. The family of four-they want their kids to be entertained, so I'll do the magic tricks or I'll do fun and creative things with the dessert for them. The group of older ladies my mom's age, want to hear about my son because it reminds them of their grandkids. The out of town tourists want the flair and the pizazz and the big personality. You just read your guests and give them what they want."   Christopher "Mo" Moore, Kona Grill, Las Vegas, Nevada

Another time when being a silent server may be difficult, is for the server who wants specific verbal feedback to know if each person is enjoying their food. I have been guilty of this myself, more than once. I would come up to the table and while one person is speaking and the rest of the guests are eating, and at the same time completely engrossed in the person speaking, I would politely say, "Excuse me..." or "Pardon me, how is everyone's dinner?"

Of course, it's important to check and see if all is well at the table. Certainly that is part of your job in providing excellent service. However, sometimes your guests may actually view (perceive) this as being rude, or at the very least, intrusive. So, how do we accomplish our goal-of providing great service and ascertaining if indeed, everyone is enjoying their dinner and if each one's dinner is to their liking?

Consider this, if someone is speaking or telling a story and everyone at the table is riveted by the speaker, if you ask the table "How is everyone's dinner?" do you really think that if someone has a complaint or a request, that they will actually speak up and voice their complaint in front of all of their colleagues and take more time and attention away from the person speaking? From my experience, the answer is no.

If you come and address the table as a whole, you will get a collective answer- of everything is good, great or whatever. But that will not give you the true picture. So, how do you glean the information that you need without continuing to interrupt, putting people on the spot in front of the group or taking the group's collective answer as the answer for each individual diner?

I have learned an effective way, after much trial and error, to accomplish all of the above. First I approach the table and observe everyone while standing off to the side, to make myself available for anyone who wants to catch my attention visually. Next, I make my way silently and even stealthily around the table, and I ask individuals-maybe not every single person, but I do stop at an area long enough for anyone at that side of the table to ask for something or make a complaint or tell me if something is missing. In that way I am silently available to hear them without disrupting the other guests. I speak quietly and only within earshot of the individual I'm speaking to or to them and the person seated nearby. "How is your filet, Sir?" "And you Ma'am, how is your salmon, is everything to your liking?"

Depending on how many people are at the table, you may or may not be able to ask each and every person. However, if one person is speaking at the table and all are listening, I'm guessing that it must be no bigger than a 15 top. So, you should be able to easily make your way around and make yourself available to every guest, even if you don't speak to each individual.

This, I have found to be much more effective than to stand in front of the table and ask them collectively "How is everything?" This way you will get a better read of how each one is enjoying or not enjoying their dinner. If you approach the table collectively, and the diners are listening to a person speaking, telling stories or whatever the case may be, they may actually all look up and cease talking every time you come to the table and you may think this is great.

They, however, may become perturbed at what they perceive as constant interruption by you and wish that you would just disappear. You may mistakenly think to yourself, "Wow, I really have the respect and the attention of this table. Every time I approach, they stop talking to listen to what I have to say, this is going great!" That may not actually be an accurate portrayal of what's going on. Your guests, unbeknownst to you, may begin to view you as a nuisance (p.i.t.a.). You figure it out. And they may silently be cursing you and wish that you would just leave them alone until they are done eating and meeting.

I know I've spent quite a bit of time on the above example, and I said all that to say this... It is absolutely imperative that you learn to read your guests, their needs and their desired amount of your involvement and interaction with them. Please understand me. I do not mean to convey here that those who don't welcome constant interruption or engagement by their server, deserve less attention or service. It's just that it should be a different type of service-less obtrusive, less noticeable but nonetheless, still exceptional. In fact, if they want you to be a silent server, then, you obliging them, and carrying that desire out, you will be providing exceptional service to them.

It's important for us as servers, to be self-regulating.   Try this. Watch, observe, try to mentally take a step back and see. Ask yourself. You need to be aware of the following: Does the conversation at the table seem to abruptly stop whenever you approach? Does it feel like they're being polite-a forced politeness towards you? Is there an energy of annoyance towards you? It may be subtle, but you should be able to tell the difference. Learn to read your guests, and adjust your style of service to match your guests' needs/energy.

Sometimes you don't really need to read your guests- you just need to pay attention to what they're telling you. Often, the host will tell you in advance what the situation is or will be..."We're going to be having an important meeting." If that is what is said, and only that, you should be astute enough to know that THEY DO NOT WANT TO BE BOTHERED OR INTERRUPTED DURING

THEIR DINNER. PERIOD. He's telling you without saying the words, "Please don't pester us."   Be available, but please do not interrupt every few minutes.   Be unobtrusive.   Yes it is a skill, and it is a skill that can be learned.

This is where sign language and non-verbal cues, especially by the host, play such an important role. And it is up to you to be cognizant and on your game, completely aware without having to ask too many questions. If you've poured wine and the bottle is suddenly empty, be proactive, bring another bottle and a fresh glass for the host to taste –instead of approaching, interrupting and asking the guest out loud. Make eye contact, raise the bottle and the glass and silently ask for his approval. Chances are on your side that he will appreciate your non-invasive service style and nod you-yes. You just made your host happy and added an additional 50, 70 or 100 dollars to your check.   Nice job.

Please don't come to the table and ask if people want refills on their soda, iced tea, coffee or water.   That is the lamest thing to ever ask a guest.   If their glass is empty and refills are free- (the aforementioned beverages)-why on earth would you ever ask, "Would you like a refill, sir?"??!

You should only ask if it's a not-free-refill drink-alcohol, wine, and specialty non-alcoholic drinks-espresso, cappuccino etc. However, very rarely do people ever want a refill on espresso or cappuccino.

If you are serving a group of businessmen who are engrossed in a meeting and you are attentive, unobtrusive and available, always anticipating and meeting their needs before they even have a chance to ask for something- even if you barely say two words after taking their order- they can still walk away raving about their dining experience saying "Wow that was a great dinner and great service!"

Another type of guest is what I call The High Roller, The Big Shot or The IMPRESSOR. This person may or may not really be a high roller, but in one way or another, he has made it plain to you that he expects to be treated as such. He wants, (and craves, I suppose, - please don't tell him I said that) a lot of attention. This type takes many forms. He may- and yes, I keep saying 'he' because in all my years in this business I've never really seen a woman in this position – of needing so desperately to impress his/her guests. He may be on a date and therefore, is trying to make this event a beautiful, romantic experience for him and his lady.

He may call ahead of time and request a special, quiet booth. He may drop by early, prior to the actual date time and leave flowers to be placed on the table ahead of their arrival. He may call to check on your champagne stock- to make sure you have plenty of Dom Perignon. Have you ever known anyone to order more than one or two bottles for just him and his date?

As with all guests, as I mentioned earlier, it is absolutely vital that you adjust your style and your approach to match the personality and needs or desires of your guests and to meet or exceed their expectations. Actually, you should count it as a blessing- knowing ahead of time, what kind of guests you have coming and what their expectations of their dining experience might be.

This allows you to be better prepared both logistically and mentally.

It may not be a dinner date with his wife or girlfriend but rather with a group of friends or business partners. Usually this will be someone who's already been to your establishment a few times though, not necessarily always. The point here, is this person is clearly wanting to make a big impression on his dinner guests, but he is unable to complete or fulfill his mission, without your assistance. He has enlisted you to be his partner in impressing his guests, so to speak.

So what shall I say here? If the man wants to impress his guests and he's chosen your restaurant as the location for this event, you should consider it an honor. He has given you a wonderful opportunity to pull out all the stops and Wow them!

Take it seriously and become engaged. Become as involved as possible. Of course, it depends on how many other tables you are serving. Certainly you don't want to neglect your other guests, because you have a special table. So, it becomes a balancing act at this point. Do be aware of what is going on at your other tables, but if Mr. Impressor has enlisted you for the task, do your best to give him extra focus and attention.

Perhaps. You could ask the hostess to try to seat you other guests that may not need so much attention- though that may be difficult for her to ascertain that.

It might even be helpful and fun to clue your other tables in on what's happening.
"You see that couple over in the corner? The guy really wants to impress his girlfriend. He came in earlier today and gave me flowers to put on their table and ordered champagne. He's asked me to help him make this evening extra special. She thinks they're just celebrating their 1 year of dating anniversary, but he's actually going to propose to her after dinner."

Now your other guests know what's up. In fact, even adding something like, "I just wanted to let you know in case you may at some point wonder or think I'm paying too much attention to them- that is why. But rest assured, I don't intend to neglect or ignore you."

When you let others around you know what is going on, they will be more likely to forgive the lesser amount of attention you are paying to them. In fact, some of your guests may be very interested and will probably ask you how it's going at the couple's table.

And that's all because you communicated to all of your guests what is happening.

If you hadn't told your other guests, there is a greater chance of them feeling slighted. But truly, most people are not going to begrudge you giving extra attention to a table where the gentleman is going to propose. They will most likely, ask you throughout the evening how it is all unfolding at the special table.

Now, back to the specifics of helping your guest impress his girlfriend...Use his name when addressing him-whether it be Mr. So and So, or his first name. I recommend addressing him this way unless you feel that he doesn't like it. You could even ask him, "Sir, how would you like me to address you this evening?"

Most of the time, this person has gone out of the way to make preparations for impressing his guest, date, girlfriend, business partners-whomever- but there's also the possibility that he really has no game plan at all. They've only gone as far as making the reservation, and then asking you-enlisting your help.

In this situation, there is a lot more pressure on you. He may say, "Don't worry about the money, just help me impress my guests tonight. Here's my credit card. I just want this to be super special."

If he really has no clue, this is your time to shine. Make suggestions. Even pre-select some appetizers to be brought out, soon, after they are seated. That will definitely make him look good, and make his guests think that he's planned all of this. Let him take the credit when you bring out the appetizers, and they rave about how great they are. This will set the tone for the evening, and establish him as one who is wanting to impress his guests. Set him up for success. This will translate into success for you as well. Do I even have to mention that, chances are very good that you will be nicely tipped at the end of the evening?

Also, just imagine, if the occasion happens to be that Mr. Impressor is going to propose to his girlfriend, and you make him look good and wow him and his girlfriend, it could translate into them booking the restaurant's private room for their rehearsal dinner, reception or for her bridal shower. What you do today, can definitely have an impact on your future. (If she says yes)

There are many things you can do, depending on how much communication you've had with the guest ahead of time. If your restaurant doesn't normally have wine glasses on the table as part of their setting -put them out. Or if he's ordered champagne, place the flutes on the table as part of the setting. This will set their table apart. It creates not only a romantic ambience, but it also conveys anticipation. An extra fork and knife that usually is not part of the normal setting would be nice.

A "reserved" sign, perhaps.   A small special vase with a single rose in it. These simple things will communicate more than words alone can say.

1.   It says that this table was set specifically for them and only them.

2.   It says "Welcome, we've been expecting you and we are looking forward to serving you and your guest."

3.   It says that this is going to be a special dinner. Wine glasses, champagne glasses, so many forks. WOW!

You could even go one step further and even suggest that Mr. Impressor go to the grocery store or the nearby florist and pick up a bag of rose petals that you can sprinkle on the table and the surrounding area to set the romantic mood for them. Better yet, don't ask him, you just do it. You will score points with him, and his girlfriend will be blown over because she'll think it was Mr. Impressor's idea.

Hopefully, just doing these small actions of preparedness, will cause the guest to feel special and welcomed. And they may attribute all of those little extra touches to the guest who is trying to impress. Never mind, that he didn't ask for that or even think of it. The more that you do, that he can take credit for, the more he will succeed in effecting that lasting impression for which he has enlisted your assistance. Your forethought and creativity and extra effort will go a long way to make him happy and his guest(s). Your guests will walk away saying "**WOW!** We definitely need to come back here."

I can't tell you how many times me doing these little extras have translated into hugs from guests, double tips, people wanting to be my friend and multiple return visits, with requests for me to serve them, as well as them referring their friends and family to me.

It is so important to realize that every guest or group of guests is different. You must learn how to adjust your approach and your style of service to match the type of guest you are serving, and make sure that you are on the same page as your guests. We've only covered a few different types of guests in this chapter, there are so many, many more to consider. But as you become more adept at learning and understanding who your guests are, and what kind of dining experience they are looking for and expecting, you will become more effective at creating and delivering **WOW!** dining experiences for all your guests, no matter what type they are.

Not only is reading your guests so very important, so too, is actually knowing and knowing about your guests. What do I mean by this? First, it is absolutely essential that you give recognition to regulars and repeat guests. Having a reservation system like Open Table is invaluable for this. Open Table allows you to basically build a database of your guests. When a guest has dined with your establishment once and has made a reservation, their information is stored in Open Table.

So, every time they call in, you can make notes that will be helpful and useful for providing a great dining experience for them. The type and depth of information is almost unlimited. This can be in addition to their name, family members' names, but also birthdays, anniversary, preferences where they like to sit, their favorite server or bartender, the wine they usually order, any allergies or dietary restrictions, etc.   The possibilities are endless.

Restaurants like Wolfgang Puck, where Mandy Monreal worked, will use this information very strategically. For example, if Mr. and Mrs. Smith are coming for dinner tonight, to celebrate their wedding anniversary-that information is communicated by the lead hostess, to the chef-because he might prepare a special appetizer for them. Or a specially prepared dessert plate that they write Happy Anniversary Mr. & Mrs. Smith on, in chocolate in advance, so that it freezes on the plate.

This information will also be shared with the management team-who may want to bless the couple with a complimentary glass of champagne. Of course, that same information is to be communicated to the server who'll be in charge of their table. In fact, oftentimes, this information is printed out on little cards and then distributed to the appropriate parties.

Now, when Mr. and Mrs. Smith arrive, they feel like they are royalty, as everyone is in on the gig. But that doesn't happen without proper planning, preparation, communication and execution by every staff person involved. And usually, it is the lead host, hostess or maître d' that is responsible for the planning and sharing of this vital information. How different is that dining experience for Mr. and Mrs. Smith, than the normal situation at many restaurants, where the server only knows about a celebration when they come to the table and ask the guest, "Are you celebrating anything tonight?"

Now, the hostess, the manager, the kitchen staff, the server and maybe even others, all know who is celebrating what and they give proper recognition and honor to the respective guests.

There are some restaurants that don't have an elaborate reservation data storing system like Open Table, but instead, they do it the old fashioned way. Or at least the servers do-like Sydney Nelson from Next Door Food & Drink in Loveland, Colorado.   She has in the back of her server book-notes, and cards and cheat sheets and lists of regulars with information such as their spouses and children's names and their favorite drinks and when they came in last.

This may not be a very sophisticated system, but Sydney knows both the importance and the effect of doing this. In fact, Jim Edwards, the owner of Next Door, says that Sydney is constantly feeding him information about guests, as they walk in the door because either Sydney has their information written down somewhere, or she has it memorized. That's what getting to know your guests is all about.

A WORD ABOUT VIPS

In the course of writing **Getting to WOW!** I think this is the one topic that there was not really a clear consensus on-Are there VIPs? How do you or do you treat VIPS differently from all your other clientele? I won't reveal who told me what but here's what I heard. "There are no VIPS." "Everybody is a VIP." "Regulars are our VIPs." "VIPs are somebody who knows somebody-the chef, the owner etc." "VIPs shouldn't get special treatment but that's what they expect, so we give it to them."

That is just a small sampling of the various responses I received. So I say, put all that together and that's a good philosophy. Let's try it.

Everybody that comes into your establishment regardless of who they are, want to and hope to be treated like they're special. So, you should treat everyone as if they are a VIP (whatever definition VIP means to you).

At the same time, the people who think they are special-you should treat them that way as well, and in the end, you will have raving, loyal fans that love coming to your establishment, primarily because of the way that you make them feel.

Knowing and reading your guests and understanding what their needs are is foundational to providing WOW! service to them. You have to do things, both as a server, and as an establishment that sets you apart from the others.

One way you can do that is by...

Chapter 12

Getting Beyond "I'll Be Your Server Tonight"

"Good evening, my name is _____ and I'll be your server. I'll be taking care of you tonight."
97% of All Restaurant Servers, Everywhere
"Stop the madness!"
Kevin O' Leary, aka Mr. Wonderful from ABC's Shark Tank

A Personality, Please

Restaurant servers are usually, more often than not, people with big personalities. No, not just personalities but larger than life personalities. And these personalities run the gamut from over the top flamboyant, to flirtatious to loud and boisterous to comedians, entertainers and actors. The service industry has always attracted those with a creative flair.

However, we have all met servers, who seem absolutely put off, that they actually have to engage the public. I find it surprising that there are some who've found their way into this business who truly lack any semblance of a personality whatsoever. And of course, I'm in no way referring to you who are holding this book in your hand. No, this is for your co-worker.

You know the ones-that never seem to be having a good day, or for whatever reason can't seem to find a smile. Or the ones that are so dull, quiet and boring that they really should be working in an office cubicle where they won't be compelled to interact with live human beings. (Please no offense-wonderful office working people)

Hey, the service industry is not for everybody, but please, if you are here, now- please, I beg of you-I implore you-I encourage you-find a way to be interested, interesting and engaging. If you really don't like your job, if you are not thrilled to deal with, communicate with-let alone to serve the public-then, maybe this is not the industry or profession for you (yes, I did say 'profession').

Maybe you're going to school and this is the only job that allows you flexible hours and that was the main attraction for you, so you decided to become a server. Maybe your husband works during the day at a 'real job' (we'll discuss that mentality in a later chapter) and he stays with the baby while you pull the night shift at your local diner.

There's a myriad of reasons why people become servers. But whatever your reason for being here-you are here now. So, embrace it-the fact that you are a server, waitress, waiter-whatever term you prefer. Until you do that, chances are that you will be miserable and your happiness will be on an emotional rollercoaster-based on how well you did. No, let me clarify, how much money you made in tips that day.

The Emotions-Linked-to-Tips-Rollercoaster

Scene:

Kaitlyn: How's it going, Sarah?

Sarah: Oh, okay, I guess. I didn't really make much money today.

Next Day

Kaitlyn: How's it going, Sarah?

Sarah: Oh everything's great. I'm walking with 250 bucks tonight.

Money's up-You're up. Tips are down-you're down.

You cannot let your level of income dictate your emotional state. No matter how long you are in this job, position-profession, it really is important to find within yourself a reason to do what you're doing.

Maybe this is NOT your life's dream-but you are here, now, today.

If you can find joy and satisfaction in the nobleness of what you do and you take pride in providing an exceptional dining experience to your guests, you will not constantly be riding the feast or famine rollercoaster, that so many find themselves on in this business.

I promise that if you do, it will translate to your guests and that translates into higher tips (most of the time), more repeat customers, more requests for you and the cycle continues.

But it has to begin with you. As the saying goes "It really is what you make it."

About ten years or more ago, I read a life changing book by Napoleon Hill- called Think and Grow Rich. In this book the title of the very first chapter is a simple, yet profoundly rich phrase- "Thoughts are things."

Be in Charge of Your Thoughts

"Thoughts Are Things". That little 3 word phrase has become a personal mantra for me. It all begins with me. My thoughts determine how everything around me is going to be. Not the circumstances around me. If I exude an attitude of unhappiness- thinking —"I wish I wasn't here, I hate this job, and I can't wait until these people leave"-it's not just an internal thing-just taking place silently inside your mind. Such thoughts and attitudes will not go unnoticed or be hidden from your guests, no matter how you pretend.

Your thoughts affect your emotions and there is always some physical or outward manifestation of any thought-positive or negative. A fake smile can be detected easily and from a mile away. Both your thoughts and your emotions are energy and your guests can pick up on your true energy you are sending out whether you put on a fake smile or not.

As Napoleon Hill, whom I quoted earlier, said,
"Thoughts are Things". Whatever you think will eventually manifest in some physical form.

Master Your Emotions

There's also the principle that "Whatever you focuses on expands". Although many spiritual and metaphysical authors and teachers teach this, I was first introduced to this principle by Marshall Sylver, in his book Passion, Profit and Power. If you are in an unhappy emotional state-if there is some problem in your mind, whether it's related to your job or not-and you continue to focus and dwell on it- it will not only affect your emotions but also your concentration, your drive, your ambition, your communication with others, and pretty much your whole work. You cannot perform at an exceptional level and provide *WOW!* service if you are not the master of your emotions.

How About Some Creativity?

Hi good evening, my name is Brad and I'll be your server. Hi everybody, I'm Chelsea and I'll be taking care of you.

The above are the two most common, worn out, over-used, tired, unoriginal and b-o-r-i-n-g, goes-without-saying, phrases, that are parroted hundreds and thousands of times in so many restaurants, all across America each and every day.

Why not in keeping with the same mentality, say when people enter your establishment "Welcome to Big Daddy's Cantina, I'm Chuck and I'll be your server and this is the restaurant you'll be eating in."?

Please, please let's have a little originality, a little creativity, a little bit of a personality.

Let's take a moment and examine each of these phrases: "Good evening, I'm Brad and I'll be your server."

Really, Brad? Now, I'm not trying to be facetious here, but let's think about this. Here we are, sitting in a restaurant, the host has already seated us, and you are wearing the same company garb that every other employee in this place is-be it- polo knit shirt and khakis, black shirt and tie or whatever the house uniform may be.

I know that you are not the busser. I know you are not the bartender-Why do I know that? Well, because he is at the bar. I'm sitting here reading the menu in this restaurant and we are not in a self-serve place. So why in the world do you feel compelled to inform me that "You'll be my server"?

If I were sitting at the bar would the bartender approach me and say, "Good evening, my name is Todd and I'll be your bartender"? Of course, not! In that context it sounds absurd. It's obvious that he's the bartender -he's the one making and serving drinks at the bar. So, why then must servers feel compelled to say this phrase? It seems to me that somewhere, way back in the beginning, when the very first restaurants began dotting the landscape, somebody said the phrase "I'm so and so and I'll be your server" and it caught on. First of all, I doubt their actual name was "So and So" Doubtful. Yes, I digress. Back then, it may have been creative and novel. One server said it and then another did and then another and so on and so on. Now, however, everybody who becomes a server anywhere thinks they are required to say it. It is the lead in to their memorized spiel.

You may say "So what? Why does it matter if servers say it?" It matters because everybody is copying everybody else. It sounds robotic. Canned. No creativity. And it's totally unnecessary. One of the traits you brought with you when you were first interviewed for this job was your wonderful, outgoing, dynamic personality-whatever form that took. So, now, why do you not use it and let yourself shine?! Confession-Yes, I've said it myself-in my early years because I-like you, heard others say it and probably thought that I was supposed to. Monkey see, monkey do. But once I actually gave some thought to what I was reciting, repeating, parroting day after day, I never approached a table with that phrase again. And what a relief and release that was for me. When I realized that I can actually be myself and utilize the amazing, charming and fun personality God gave me, when I interact with my guests I was elated! Yes, to me it was a revelation! What I don't get, is why so few servers have yet to come to the same epiphany.

Now please, don't miss my point. I'm not saying don't introduce yourself. Yes, absolutely, you should and you must.
Introducing yourself to your guests is a very important part of **WOW!** service and in fact, of establishing rapport between you and your guests. It is a part of being courteous and it's respectful as well. So what do I mean then? I'm just suggesting that there are a myriad of ways-many, many, many ways to introduce one's self.

Just take yourself out of the context of serving and imagine you are introducing yourself to someone, anyone. What do you say? You simply greet them and say your name, right? 'Hi, my name's Bill. How are you?' There's no need for any "I'll be your " tagline or phrase. You certainly wouldn't say, "Hi, my name is Bill and I'll be your new acquaintance." Sounds silly, doesn't it?

Also, here's a thought, you don't necessarily have to state your name at the very outset. I often will mention my name after I've told them about the specials or after having taken their drink order, right before I step away from the table... "I'll be right back with your drinks. Thank you for being here tonight my friends, by the way, my name is Christoff".

A server friend of mine who also does this, explained to me that it is a better way for your diners to actually remember your name, because if you say your name as soon as you approach the table-your guests are thinking about drinks, what they're going to order etc. Nine times out of ten, the guest will forget your name as soon as you say it. However, if you tell them after taking their order, there's a better chance that they'll remember it. Or you may want to introduce yourself when you first approach the table AND after you've taken their order as well. But if they don't remember your name after their dining experience, maybe it's because you weren't memorable to them. You did nothing to make them remember you or their experience.

My wife and I recently dined at a restaurant in St. Louis, where, in the past, I consistently received excellent service. However, this time the service was about average and one thing that was peculiar, is that since our server did not introduce herself to us we asked her what her name was. She told us but only after saying, "We don't usually tell our names here, because we want it to be about the food, not about us." While, yes it is not about the server, I would say that it is supposed to be about the guests as well as about the food. And as me, being the guest, I do want to know what my server's name is. It's part of being engaging and personal with your guests. I know some people who would say, "I don't care what my server's name is, I just want them to get my order right."

Sometimes using humor is a good icebreaker. Say something like, "By the way my name is Phil, but if you have any problems or complaints my name is Franco"- (mention a co-worker's name that may be standing nearby) "Just kidding."

Servers at Romano's Macaroni Grill are very good, at least at always introducing their name to their guests. They even write it down (usually upside down-but right side up for the guests) on the butcher paper table covering. While I don't necessarily appreciate the over familiarity they often exhibit by sitting down beside their guests or resting their knee on the booth, they absolutely get the introducing one's self to the guest. Now, however, I have heard many of them still say the two dreaded overused phrases. I still give them points for their cheerful, positive and upbeat self-introduction.

The point is, if I'm sitting at a table in a restaurant, you come to my table, you're wearing the company uniform, we talk about the menu, you explain the specials to me, you take my order, you bring me my food, I'm pretty darn sure that -even without you telling me that-YOU ARE MY SERVER and YOU'LL BE SERVING ME!!! Thank you Captain Obvious!

I'm Steve and this is Mary-we'll be your diners.

A simple, yet profound statement I heard once that has stuck with me for many years, is

"What is understood, need not be explained."

You are my server, we are your diners. We all know that, now let's get on with the show.

Now, as for the other phrase that seems to go hand in hand with "I'll be your server." and that is: "I'll be taking care of you."

Similarly with the last statement, I ask you, "Really? You're going to take care of me?" I don't think so. When I think of 'being taken care of', I picture someone waiting on someone hand and foot. Or I think of a patient lying in a hospital bed. The nurses take care of him. Or if you tell me you'll take care of me, I say "Here's a list of my bills that I need paid, I also need a shoe shine and my car washed". That would be 'taking care of me'.

Okay, maybe I'm kidding. Again "What is understood need not be explained". Maybe, there's actually nothing particularly wrong with saying this phrase except for the fact that **EVERY SERVER EVERYWHERE, SAYS IT ALL THE TIME, EVERY SHIFT, TO EVERY GUEST!**

To quote Kevin O' Leary, aka Mr. Wonderful on ABC's show Shark Tank, **"Stop the madness!"**

Why does every server feel compelled to say "I'll be taking care of you"? Why not use a little creativity, or some personality? What about saying something like, "Folks, I don't know if you've dined with us before but I'm going to make sure that tonight you have an exceptional dining experience from start to finish. How does that sound to everyone?" Or "Sir, Ma'am, it is my goal to ensure that you thoroughly enjoy every aspect of your time with us this evening. Are you ready for a great dinner?" That sounds a little more engaging, thought provoking and creative, don't you think?

Am I saying that a server who uses the phrases "I'll be your server" and "I'm going to take care of you" does not provide exceptional service? No, that's not my point. However, if you approach each table, all throughout your shift, with the exact same canned spiel, starting with the same boring, robotic greeting that requires no creativity, then that tells me that you have really put no forethought into this shift. You're just a clone or a drone.

When I'm dining out, all around the entire restaurant, I hear server after server approaching table after table and they're all saying the exact same thing over and over and over again. The only thing that changes is the name of the one speaking...
"Good evening, my name is Cheryl, I'll be your server."
"Hello everyone, my name is Tim and I'll be taking care of you."
"Good afternoon, I am Curtis and I'll be your server."

"Good evening my name is Pam and I'll be your server and I'll be taking care of you." Blah, blah, blah ....

If you make these minor adjustments, and perhaps consider these suggestions, and if you will abandon those two worn out, tired robotic phrases, you can use your gifts to really shine. That's what guests appreciate.

Two ladies come in for a quick lunch and they're stressed because of something that is going on back at the office. You, just by being you, brighten up their day and you may think that all you did was bring them their soup and sandwiches and refill their iced tea a couple of times.

Use your sense of humor, your charm, your charisma to engage and entertain your guests. You probably don't even realize how many times in a day or a week, that you, being your own wonderful self, using your God-given personality, that you have blessed, uplifted, encouraged, cheered up a customer/patron. By being interested and interesting you make your guest's day more often than you're even aware.

It's understood that you are my server, you don't have to say that you'll be taking care of me. Just introduce yourself and provide *WOW!* service. If you give some thought to how you approach each table and use some creativity in your greeting, you will stand out amongst your peers. You will be memorable and your guests will come back to see you and to experience that *WOW!* service, that they know you always provide.

This business is for people with personality and people who are people persons. If that's you, then Smile and be thankful because not everybody was blessed with such a wonderful, upbeat, pleasant personality. Let it Shine.
Isn't it amazing how something so seemingly simple can be transformed into so something that is "*WOW!*"?

Much of what we've been talking about here, is what contributes to the big picture of what *WOW!* Service is all about.
Now it's time that we start...

Chapter 13

GETTING FOCUSED ON THE DETAILS

"Those little things...simple, subtle, tiny things that nobody will see, nobody will applaud, nobody will even notice."
Jeff Olson, The Slight Edge

A faint lipstick stain on a wine glass,
A few bread crumbs on the seat of the booth, A sauce stained menu,
My steak cooked just a little too overdone,
The wrong dressing on my salad- in fact, I said "no dressing" A small stain on the white linen table cloth,
A sticky, unwiped bar,
A table set with all the settings misaligned,
The flatware water-spotted, and chunked with food particles,

Which of the above would you deem to be a more egregious error?
A few crumbs on the seat of the booth where you're about to be seated? Come on-just brush them off. Okay-easy enough.
A faint lipstick stain on your wine glass? Again, it's very simple. Just kindly ask your server or bartender for a clean one. I'm sure he'll gladly bring you one. Okay, you're right. That's not hard to do either.

A sauce stained menu? Give me a break. As before-just ask for a new one. No harm, no foul.
How about this:
You sit down at a bar anticipating a nice refreshing drink and a few relaxing moments. You place your elbows on the beautiful marble bar and ...ugh! It is so sticky and nasty. Yuck! Now you've got sticky elbows-and that's not the name of a new craft cocktail!

Oh, come on now, all you have to do is ask the bartender to wipe it down for you and then go in the bathroom and wash the stickiness off your elbows. So you do and he does. Life goes on. Really, it's not that big of a deal. Granted. It's not.

But think about it. Most of the establishments featured on television shows like Bar Rescue and Restaurant Impossible have problems with poor standards for service, for cleanliness and proper ways of doing things. They have no standards and systems in place. And then here they are calling Robert Irvine or John Taffer or someone to help bail them out or fix their failing bar or restaurant. Those places didn't get that way overnight. Rather, it was the compounded effect of small, seemingly insignificant, details that were overlooked over a period of time.

Maybe each of the little details, in our example above, that were overlooked, in and of themselves, is not that big of a deal. That is, if only one of them was overlooked. But what happens when there is a general, overall, no attention to detail attitude in the whole establishment? Dinner at such a place might go something like this: You take your fiancé and your future in-laws out for dinner at a particular restaurant. When you arrive, you notice that the specials written on the board in the front of the restaurant, has the word tilapia misspelled. It reads "Tillapya". "That's odd"-you think to yourself.

You are greeted by the hostess and escorted to your table. As you pull the chair out for your mother-in-law-to-be, you notice a few bread crumbs on the chair. She doesn't notice-so you just quickly brush them away.

Now, you are all seated. The table is beautifully set, at least upon first glance. But then you notice- a brown spot about the size of a quarter on the table cloth. Dried marinara, you think to yourself. Your guests are all involved in animated conversation and none of them seems to notice. So, you just casually, slyly, push your bread & butter (b & b) plate over to cover the spot. Luckily – it happened to be right in front of your setting. There, done. No one did and no one will notice.

Next, you sit back and take in the elegant surroundings-beautiful chandeliers, nice art on the walls. Then your focus comes back on your table- and now, what you thought was a very beautifully set table-is, actually upon closer inspection, not really that impressive in the least. The flatware is stained with water spots. Your fiancé's place setting has only one fork whereas all the others have two. Of the four bread and butter plates-three match but the fourth one is not only a different size but a different shade of bone as well. To top it all off, the silverware isn't even really nicely arranged on the table but looks like it was just haphazardly thrown there.

You want to focus on the conversation at the table and get your mind off all those details. After all, they really don't matter much anyway, do they? Heck, there's been a whole book written on exactly that. Don't sweat it, we're told. Well, you can be sure that whoever set this table certainly didn't.

Your fiancé passes you the wine list and asks you to choose some wine for the table. You decide to start with a white and move to a red with the entrees. You open the wine list and it has stains on the pages. The waiter comes, you order your wine and mention to him about the stained wine list. His response is a half- hearted, "Well, a lot of people touch the menus".

In a few minutes he returns with the wine you ordered. He really doesn't do much of a presentation. Rather he just mumbles "Sauvignon Blanc" but actually mispronounces it-"Savee-ahn". You're unimpressed.

He pours a taste for you but keeps the cork, rather than presenting it to you. You make no fuss about the cork. The last thing you need is for one of your new in- laws-to-be to make a remark about you being a wine snob. You nod that the bottle is good and motion for him to pour for the other guests. He begins in a clockwise direction. This is good. But then you see that he proceeds to your father-in-law next, *before the ladies* at the table.

And the final, not-so-important- detail that was missed-your mother-in-law, now discovers a nice, big-albeit faint, lipstick stain on her wine glass after her glass was poured! She doesn't tell the waiter because she doesn't want to "cause a scene" and decides she'll just drink from the other side of the glass.

The food has not even come out yet, but in your mind the dinner is already ruined.

Oh come on, now. Aren't you overreacting, just a little? Even if it is just in your mind? Really? Do all those little details really matter? As mentioned previously, haven't you ever heard of the book, Don't Sweat the Small Stuff? Seriously. Do they really matter? And if they don't, then what does matter? Just the quality of the food? What if the chef doesn't care about details either? The correct amount of seasoning. The right time and temperature to cook your steak. Who really cares if it's a little over done, under done. Do details really matter?

As long as the server has a good attitude and a pleasant demeanor-aren't all those other things forgivable? Even forgettable? Many may say yes. But I do not believe so. A nice personality is just that-nice. And although I do expect a nice and pleasant personality from my server, that is not merely enough. And a nice personality but no attention to detail does in no way equal good or great service. And it certainly does not cover over all those missed details-faults. Somebody really dropped the ball here.

It is the server's responsibility (whoever is assigned to the tables in that section) to ensure that everything on that table is in order, clean, neat, polished, wiped and set in a correct manner. No ands, ifs, or buts about it. No questions, no excuses. Period. Over and out. Bartenders are NOT Exempt

The same goes for the bartender. It is his or her responsibility to ensure that those glasses-especially the wine glasses, sparkle and shine-all the time, every time. Yes, sometimes the dishwashing machine doesn't get the lipstick stains out.

Just because a glass runs through the machine does not mean that it's automatically, sufficiently clean. If you're the bartender and you're racking those glasses you better make sure they're clean and sparkling.

You may say "Well it's the busboy or the server assistant that racks the glasses". So what? Whomever is filling those glasses with wine and sending them out to the table better make sure they're clean. If every glass was inspected and polished prior to being racked or placed on a table in front of a guest there would be no question. This often is not the case, and therefore guests, I, myself must examine the stemware in front of them before the wine is poured.

You may think I'm a little harsh in my thinking. Too exacting. A little overboard. I'm not saying there is no room for mistakes for we all make mistakes. We all may miss something once in a while. We all overlook things, but that should be the rare exception not the norm.

Somewhere the bar must be raised and a standard must be set. Take pride in what you do. If you are setting a table and preparing for service, I don't care what kind of restaurant you're working in-be aware. I challenge you to do things in an excellent manner. If this is not your normal practice. Start doing it. I promise you, that not only will you feel better about yourself, you may come to enjoy your job as a server and your guests will notice. Just because no one complains to you, that doesn't mean that they don't notice. It also doesn't mean that they aren't telling someone else about the lack of attention to detail at your establishment.

I have both dined at and worked at some supposedly-so-called, great restaurants where the food was exceptional, the ambience was wonderful but there was no standard set for service, cleanliness and order. Everybody just kind of does their own thing. Each server was somewhat autonomous. Some of us would show up early, polish our glasses and silverware, and arrange everything neatly on every table in our section. While others, would just show up in time to clock in and serve the first table to be seated, paying no attention to the appearance of the tables in their section. Some tables are beautifully set, everything in order, cutlery and glasses shining, and others are just set willy-nilly. No order, no pattern. **NO ATTENTION TO DETAIL.**

Standards Are Set at the Top

Some servers are great at their job and others-well, it doesn't matter because management has set no standards to follow. As I've said before **IT ALL STARTS AT THE TOP**. In an ideal situation, where there is management/owners that are fully aware and engaged in the daily operations of their business-they are the ones that set standards to be met and followed by everyone on the team.

However, at establishments where this is not the case, you, the server, the service professional, must take responsibility and apply some self-discipline. If you care about your guests and desire to provide them with a great dining experience, certainly attention to detail in all aspects is an attitude and a perspective you must adopt.

I've heard many servers say- 'Who notices these things anyway?' Once someone is seated they mess up their table, move the silverware around etc. So why does it really matter?

One of my favorite books is called the The Slight EDGE-Secret to a Successful Life, by Jeff Olson. It is an amazing book but rather than me just explaining, please allow me to share a couple passages:

"The difference between success and failure is not dramatic. In fact, the difference between success and failure is so subtle, most people miss it. The truth is, what you do matters. What you do today matters. What you do everyday matters. "
"A simple, positive action. A simple error in judgment. Either way, it's the Slight Edge at work-working for you or working against you. Invisible results. "
"It's the same with your health, your diet, your exercise, your financial habits, your knowledge, your relationships, your marriage. With anything and everything. With your life."

There is no **Getting to WOW!** in this business, indeed even in life, if you don't get focused on the details. Don't wait for your manager or supervisor to require you to do it. Begin to practice this habit. It may be a challenge at first, if you are not used to doing such things. However, as you develop this attention to detail attitude, you will begin to also exude a pride in your work and it may rub off on your co-workers as well. To be successful in this business of Service requires that you take paying attention to details seriously.

Like Jeff Olson says,
"Those little things that will make you successful in life, that will secure your health, your happiness, your fulfillment, your dreams, are simple, subtle, tiny things that nobody will see, nobody will applaud, nobody will even notice. They are those things that, at the time you do them, often feel like they make absolutely no difference...like they don't matter...THEY DO."

What you do absolutely matters and the details matter as well.
Next, we'll be talking about food, what you're serving, and specifically how to descriptively communicate that to your guests. The best way to do that is by you...

Chapter 14

Getting Enticing

"You can't advertise wow; you can only deliver it."
Grant Cardone-If You're Not First, You're Last

And Tonight's Specials Are...

Perhaps you've been fortunate enough to work at or dine at a restaurant where the chef is the owner or part owner. I find that these independently owned establishments are more apt to have creative chefs who enjoy experimenting to showcase their culinary skills. And that, usually on a daily basis. Hence, 'daily specials'. When it comes to specials of the day, it is not uncommon in such restaurants to feature a special of the day for each course-meaning-an appetizer special, an entrée special and a dessert special. I worked at one restaurant in St. Louis-Vin de Set, where the above mentioned three -appetizer, entrée and dessert specials, were changed daily plus there was also a daily fish, chicken and soup of the day. That is a lot of information to learn in a short period of time and to remember.

As the chapter title implies-you've got to get enticing when you are describing the food that you are serving and selling to your guests. It's not enough to just say what it is; chicken and rice, crab cake, beef tenderloin. Those words don't tell me very much about the dish.

Then there's always the details of each dish to be ascertained-is the sauce a reduction, a gastrique or a demi-glaze? When I worked at said restaurant, the chef would not only tell us about and describe the specials, but we also had the wonderful opportunity to see, smell and taste each one. I realize that not all restaurants do this, but if they do, make sure you take advantage of this learning tool. It is so much easier to describe a dish to a guest after you have actually seen, smelt and tasted it. You can more accurately describe the flavors, the aroma and the textures. The chef may say it has sautéed Anaheim chili peppers in the sauce. Well, are there a lot or a little? Does it burn your tongue or does it just have a little kick to it?

In my experience, at that restaurant, there were also some servers who, seemingly, were just interested in chowing down on some food when the specials were presented to us. They were not truly interested in learning what they were, how they were prepared etc. They'd just grab a fork and stand their salivating, and as soon as the chef finished describing the dish they'd pounce, never even observing the plating or taking in the textures or the taste. To them it was time to eat food-not a time to learn.

I, however, always took this time very seriously. I eagerly looked forward to this time of day-line up. I saw it as an opportunity to equip myself with the tools I needed to be my best and to be knowledgeable about the product I was selling. Maybe it goes without saying, but I find it so much easier to sell or recommend a dish to a guest if I've at least had a chance to see it and to learn how it was prepared. And then it's an added bonus if I've gotten the opportunity to taste it.

The way you describe the specials to your guests will absolutely determine how many of them you sell. And selling more specials, will help increase your guest check average which, hopefully will translate into higher tips for you.

More often than not, chefs create and feature specials because they want to showcase certain fresh ingredients, fresh fish-example- soft shell crabs; specific seasonal produce-heirloom tomatoes, fiddle head ferns etc.

I've dined at many a restaurant where the server runs through the specials, in fact they might even use that phrase, "run through" the specials." So, they proceed with, "Good evening my friends, May I just take a couple minutes to run through the specials for you?"
And 'run through' indeed is what they do. So quickly, repeating what they've memorized and regurgitated to every table throughout   the   evening.
Nopauseseverythingallruntogetherinonecontinuossentencewithno expressionnoenthusiasmandnopassionforwhattheyaretellingyoua ndthosearetonights specials.

At that point the diner, your guest will not even bother to try and understand what it is you just told them. Instead they just order something from the menu that they actually recognize and are comfortable ordering.
Below are some tips to consider that may be helpful when describing the specials to your guests. These are some very specific things you must do to make what you are selling enticing to your guests.

1.   Be Accurate
I worked with a server for a couple of years, whom I always heard say that the sea bass was glazed with olive oil, lemon and garlic.
Well, that may sound very good, the only problem was that the sea bass didn't have a glaze.   It had a sauce-not a glaze.   There is a difference.

You may think I'm being petty or too specific.   I mean, really. What does it matter? And that's exactly my point. Often a server will adopt that attitude of "What does it really matter? A sauce, a glaze. Who's going to know the difference and who cares?" But it does matter. As we just discussed in the previous chapter, details do matter. Please be accurate and tell your guest what it really is.

If you hear a co-worker using certain descriptive words or culinary terms, rather than just parroting them, first make sure that what you are verbally describing, portrays what it actually is. I write down the description of each special on 3 X 5 cards or in a memo notebook and study it. I rehearse and memorize it as if I were preparing for an acting scene.

If there are words or terms that I am unfamiliar with, I'd ask the chef what they mean or consult a reference. The Food Lover's Companion by Sharon Tyler Herbst and Ron Herbst is a fantastic book and an invaluable resource. I've learned many things from the chefs I've worked with over the years, but I have supplemented that learning with wonderful culinary nuggets from this tome.

The point of this is not about trying to impress your guest with how smart you are.   Chef Alex Stratta says that although it is important for a server to be knowledgeable, they need to really know that what they are telling a guest is truly accurate.

"Don't B.S. your guest. Don't say this dish has fresh capers or organic artichokes, on it, for example. Or that the tilapia is wild-caught."

He explains that aside from you being incorrect, you must realize that today's diner, today's consumer is very knowledgeable themselves. Don't tell someone that the tilapia is wild caught because almost all tilapia on the market today and sold in stores and restaurants is farm raised. So don't just make something up-you must know your stuff. However, Alex says, *"It's important that you know the information but don't force feed it to your guests."*

Don't Be a Parrot

On the other hand, it's quite obvious, most of the time, when a server is just repeating what they've heard or have been taught to say, but really have no idea what they're talking about. Take the time to know your product. Your chef has taken much time and care in preparing a wonderful dish for your guests. The least you can do is be correct in conveying to them what they are eating. Your guests will appreciate when you accurately describe the food to them and sound like you at least kind of know what you're saying.

I'm not saying that you will be educating your guests-as we've mentioned, the average diner is quite well read and up on culinary and enological information, especially those guest that would term themselves 'foodies'. In fact, sometimes the situation is reversed, and your guest will be the one imparting some bit of gastronomic insight to you. This has happened to me countless times in my career and each time I express my sincere gratitude to them for teaching me something. They say we learn something new every day and a lot of times that's happened to me in the restaurant when I'm working.

I have also had the privilege many times of passing on interesting tidbits of knowledge to my guests. I don't, however, just repeat terms that I hear another server or even the chef say, unless I understand them myself.

For example, once I was listening to the chef telling us about a special and I thought I heard him say 'pesto' but he was pronouncing it kind of in an odd way. It sounded like he was saying '(pist-ow)' or something to that effect. So do I just mimic him and pronounce pesto in a weird way? Well, I did some research and come to find out, he wasn't saying 'pesto'. He was saying 'pistou'. They are similar but have a distinct difference. Pesto is a common Italian sauce or condiment made by crushing and mixing basil, olive oil, garlic, parmesan and pine nuts. Whereas, a pistou is a French term for a food that traditionally has all the above ingredients, except one-pine nuts. A pistou does not contain pine nuts nor nuts of any kind. That is a very, very important distinction. Many people have nut allergies and therefore would not be able to eat a pesto, but a pistou would be fine for them.

If I didn't find out the difference and just parroted what I thought the chef was saying I would have been uneducated in my product and incorrect or inaccurate in the information I was giving to my guests.

2.)   Be Thorough

When describing the specials or any item on the menu to your guests, in addition to being accurate, you must be thorough. It is very important to communicate the following points.

A.   The name the dish is called

B.   The main ingredients in the dish

C.   The predominant tastes and flavors are, i.e., is it slightly salty, very spicy, is the sauce broth like or creamy? Etc.

D.   How it is prepared- Is it sautéed, is it deep fried, is it baked, grilled etc.

E.   What is the sauce on it?

F.   What accompanies the dish?

Example: Our special tonight is barramundi and it comes with cooked vegetables and lemon sauce.

That's not a very descriptive, informative or enticing rendition of the special.   In fact, does your guest even know what barramundi is?   More importantly, do you? So, let's see if we can do a better job this time. How about saying something like,

"Our special tonight is barramundi, which is sometimes referred to as Australian Seabass. The chef is going to pan fry that with a slightly tangy white wine, lemon and garlic sauce with just a hint of butter. It's going to be served over a bed of fennel and leek quinoa and roasted root vegetables."

We just made that special enticing and appealing. This is how you need to communicate to your guests.

Know your product, know what you are serving and communicate it accurately and completely to your guests.

I don't think you have to tell every single ingredient to them, but if something has meat-for example pancetta or bacon and it's not a meat dish. Tell your guest this information. Your vegetarian guests will be thankful that you did. Also, if the dish has cream or dairy product in it or any kind of nuts, you should disclose that. If the dish is spicy or spicier than most other menu items, be sure to mention that also.

Don't Wait for Your Guest to Ask-Offer the Information

I once served a woman a pasta dish that had marinara on it but it turned out to be too spicy for her. The marinara at the restaurant I worked at was more on the spicy side, whereas some chefs make their marinara on the slightly sweet side. She immediately asked if I could get her a different dish, which of course I did, but I realized I should have told her that our marinara was a bit spicier than most places make it.

Even though she did not ask me, I should have offered her that information.

If you give inaccurate information, it only shows that you didn't take the time to find out what you needed to know. Frankly, it's also a sign that you are lazy and ill-prepared. It's important to realize, if you are a server you are salesperson and you can't accurately and effectively sell your product if you don't know your product. AND YOU MUST KNOW YOUR PRODUCT.

We'll talk more about the sales aspect as it pertains to **Getting to WOW!** in a later chapter.

3.   Be Enthusiastic

What do I mean enthusiastic? You may be saying "Really? Enthusiastic-about specials?   Come on, let's get real".

First, let me tell you what I don't mean. I don't mean being over the top bubbly, saying, like Tony the Tiger, about the specials-"They're GR-R-R-EEAAT!!!!" Ok, I'm sorry if you don't know who Tony the Tiger is. I'm also not talking about being phony. The guest asks what's good on the menu and you, the server say "Everything is absolutely amazing!" That most likely is not true. As Christopher Moore, who's worked for a couple James Beard award winning chefs, told me, *"They themselves (the chefs) will tell you, that no menu is perfect."*

By enthusiastic I mean you must believe in what you're selling.
Here's a perfect example-ME. I'm a vegetarian and I have been for quite a few years now, maybe ten or more, I can't remember exactly how long it's been. In fact, my food choices are more often, closer to vegan. I do not eat meat, no beef, no pork, no poultry-no chicken, no turkey and definitely no turducken. I do eat fish, so on second thought, cancel that idea about almost being a vegan. I eat nothing that has or had feet. Just seafood. Well sometimes shrimp and lobster -they have feet. Okay, so let me rephrase-how about - no land animals. And no air animals. Anyway, you get the point. I am a vegetarian or a pescatarian-and no, I'm not talking about religion here.

Put Your Guests' Enjoyment above Your Personal Preferences
However, at two of the restaurants that I've worked at, while being a vegetarian, I have sold a ton of pork chops at one of the restaurants-Vin de Set and countless, hundreds of stuffed filet mignons at the other-Paul Mineo's Trattoria.
I personally would not and have not ever eaten or even tried them. I sell them because I believe in them for my meat eating guests.

If I know my guests eat meat, I am convinced, without a doubt, that this is the absolute best item that my restaurant has that I can offer them. And part of providing an exceptional dining experience for them, is for me to enthusiastically recommend these specials to them. I know that they will love them and I happily suggest these to them on a daily basis. I, of course, not only recommend them, I accurately describe them to my guests. You could say that I get enticing about the pork chops and stuffed filet mignons.

I know that they are great, because I know how they are prepared. I know the quality of the ingredients that go into them. I have been told repeatedly by countless meat-eaters, both my co-workers and our guests, over the years, who have eaten them, that these are the best that they have ever had. So, although, I would never eat these entrees myself, I can wholeheartedly and enthusiastically-recommend, promote and sell said items to others. I encourage my guests to order the stuffed filet mignon and the bone in pork chop because of the rave reviews that I have heard.

In fact, if I am serving a guest whom I know is a carnivore and I don't offer these items to them just because I personally wouldn't eat them, I believe that I am doing a disservice to them. By not giving them the best possible option available and allowing my personal likes to affect my selling, then I am not providing a *WOW!* experience.

If you have a product that you know is great- push it. Yes, I did say, 'push it'.

Don't Deprive Your Guests of the Best

And yes, it's often true that the specials are usually, somewhat more expensive than other menu items, but if you have a special that you know people consistently enjoy and say is great, don't deprive your guests of the option just because it's more expensive. What is a few dollars more if they are out and wanting to have a great dining experience? Be confident and enthusiastically push it.

It's win-win-win. Your guest is happy in the end and they walk out satisfied and grateful that you made such a wonderful dinner available to them by enthusiastically communicating to them how great the special is.

You are happy because your sales are higher which translates into higher tips, greater income; and the owner is happy because the specials are being sold, guests are leaving happy and will recommend the restaurant and that particular dish to others.

Often, after I've served my guests and have left them to enjoy their meal, I will return to the table after a few minutes and as I approach I will just look at them, catch their eye and watch as a huge SMILE comes across their face. No words need be said.   "What is understood, need not be explained."
I know that they're savoring every bite.
The WOW is clearly expressed on their face!

4.)   Be Clear

I can't count the number of times I've been at a restaurant and the server comes and tells about the specials and after he or she leaves, my dining partner and I, look dumbfounded at each other and say "What?"
We could not understand a word the server just said. Okay, maybe that's an exaggeration, but not much of what was said reached its intended audience-us. Yes, you are right in thinking, "Well, why didn't we, or I, just ask our server to repeat it?" And yes, the guest should, if they've misheard or didn't understand a word or a term mentioned here or there. However, if most of what the server is saying is just mumbling and muttering and garbled sounds, then there is a problem that needs to be addressed. Asking them to repeat it will do no good unless they say it clearly in a way that the guest can understand it.

Enunciate, pronounce your words clearly, project your voice and please speak clearly.

This may seem like I'm beating a dead horse or wasting time on a very basic or remedial subject but I don't think so. This is an important part of communication. After all, what is the point of explaining or telling your guests about the specials if they can't understand what you just said to them? If your guests can't understand what the specials are, there is no way that they will order them anyway, because they still have no clue what they are.

It would be just as effective if the server just stand there in front of his guests and stare blankly at them for a few minutes, not saying a word until they are ready to order. I don't recommend this, but it would have the same outcome.

Make Sure Your Message is Received
One of the main implied components of good communication is making sure that the message is not only delivered but also received by the intended party. We've all heard people say, "Well, I told him. If he didn't hear me that's his problem."

Loud and Clear
Actually, NO, It's YOUR problem. You are the communicator. It is incumbent upon you to clearly communicate your message and that means more than merely mouthing the words. If your guests can not hear you because you are not speaking loudly enough, or they cannot understand you because you are not speaking clearly enough-then, you must make some adjustment to ensure that the message is being received.

A simple statement like, "If you need me to repeat anything", or "If you have any questions about the specials or anything on the menu, please let me know and I'd be happy to answer them," will usually go a long way and open the door for good communication between you and your guests.

5.)   Be Honest

This may be elementary, already assumed, goes without saying- but I feel compelled to state this. Be honest. What do I mean by be honest? This may be a bit tricky on occasion. For example, if the soup of the day is actually made from fish that sat on the buffet table all day yesterday and was not kept chilled at all times prior to it becoming today's soup, I wouldn't mention that detail. If your guests press you to comment on the soup you can be honest without going into specific details.   Simply say,
 "I'm not recommending the soup today."

Nine times out of ten, your guest will take the hint and be grateful to you that you steered them clear of ordering something that they most likely would not enjoy and could cause them an upset stomach later or worse. It doesn't matter if they saw it written on the specials board outside. If you don't think it's good, then I say, don't let them order it.

As a server, you have a responsibility to protect your guests. I just saw this on a recent episode of Restaurant: Impossible with Robert Irvine. He went in to check out the kitchen of the featured restaurant and they had breaded eggplant for eggplant parmesan that was not chilled and was uncovered in an open container, at room temperature, that had been setting there for NINE DAYS! Now, if someone came in to that restaurant and ordered eggplant parmesan, I, as a server, could not in good conscience, let them do so. But the servers at this restaurant were! That's absolutely disgusting and potentially harmful!

If you know something in your restaurant is inedible by your own standards or you even suspect that it may be, immediately mention it to management and do not let your guests order it. If your guests order something that you think is unpalatable and you serve it to them anyway, how will you feel if they are indeed dissatisfied with their choice? Furthermore, how will you feel or how would you respond if they become ill from it?

As a professional server, if your desire is to provide **WOW!** service all the time, everywhere for every guest, it is my strong contention, that you must stop, prevent and prohibit your guest from eating something that you deem inedible.

Caveat-Exception and Clarification

As I mentioned earlier, I am a vegetarian. I do not eat meat, not at all and have not for many years. However, I do not try to influence my guests against eating meat or to try to impose my own personal beliefs on them. Nor do I, except when asked, on a very rare occasion, discuss my food choices with my guest. I do not use my contact or relationship with them as a server in a restaurant or banquet manager or any other role I play in this industry to espouse my views or indoctrinate them into considering my choices and the reasons I hold such perspective.

I do not eat meat, but if I know that what I am serving is high quality, expertly prepared and delicious to those who do enjoy meat, I not only offer and serve it to them, I vigorously and wholeheartedly promote those specials to my carnivorous patrons.

6.)   Own it

One last thought regarding selling specials:-Own it. Buy into what you are selling. Actually believe that what you are offering is 'special'. Make it personal. Your guest may or may not ask you but if you end your spiel on specials by saying something like "These that I mentioned are all excellent and very popular and you can't go wrong with any of them, however, my personal favorite is the sesame encrusted tuna," or whatever your favorite actually is. The point is, your guest may or may not ask for your opinion but if you share it with passion and real enthusiasm they will often trust your judgment or at least seriously consider your opinion.

So, go ahead, and push those specials. You, and your guests will be delighted that you did.

Chapter 15

Getting Clarity, Confirmation & Understanding
(Communication)

"Communication changes everything"
Al Danklefsen, Vice President of Sales & Marketing, STL
Communications

My friend, Al espouses this principle and although he is involved in the IT industry, I believe this aptly applies very much to this business of service as well.

Set up: You're out for dinner with some very close friends who you only see once every year or so when they come to town. So you've decided to take them to which was recently listed as one of the top 5 best new restaurants in your home city. This restaurant has been written up in all the local industry publications. They've been on Show Me St. Louis, on the cover of magazines and have gotten a lot of buzz over the past 12 -14 months. You've never been there but you figure it's the perfect place to enjoy dinner with these special friends.

From the moment you walk in until the moment you leave, you feel like you've been welcomed into the owner's home.
You had a reservation for 7:30 pm, you've arrived about 30 minutes early, so the hostess invites you by name to the bar. The restaurant and the bar are both very busy but there is still an energy of peace not chaos. The hostess escorts you to the bar and she tells you she'll call you when your table is ready.
'What, no paging device with flashing lights for us to hold onto?'

So you settle in at the bar for a drink. As you are greeted by the bartender he not only asks what each of you would like to drink-he also asks if you are the couple meeting friends from out of town- Las Vegas- I think I heard they are from? Apparently you mentioned this when you made the reservation and it was put in the system notes of Open Table.

Open Table is not only an automated reservation system whereby one can make reservations online or by phone but it is also an invaluable resource, a database which a restaurant can use to note guest's likes, dislikes, allergies, birthdays, anniversaries, wine preferences etc. So, in this case, either the manager or the hostess must have read the notes regarding your reservation and communicated it to the bartender.

As the bartender engages you in conversation while making the drinks you find out that you have a certain thing in common. Sure, it's a small thing but how nice does it feel to be acknowledge and communicated with while waiting for your drinks, instead of having a bartender that just says "What can I get ya?" and then he doesn't say another word until he says, "Are you ready for the check?"
When you are nearly finished with your drinks, the bartender addresses you by name and tells you that your table is ready when you are. "Just let me know when you're ready and I'll call Samantha- the hostess, to show you to your seat".

You pay your bar tab and the hostess escorts you to your table.
Now I know that calling someone by their name may not be a big deal and yet isn't it amazing how such a seemingly small thing can set the tone for your evening? Also, it may not be so impressive that the bartender engaged you in conversation, although many bartenders just don't seem to see this as 'part of their job'. However, him remembering and acknowledging that you are meeting friends from out of town and to remember the specific location where they are from, speaks volumes about the place and the mentality of the staff here.

It all begins with communication. As my friend Al, whom I quoted at the top of the chapter says, *"Communication changes everything."* Excellent service-**WOW!** service begins with excellent communication. Your job as a server goes far beyond just greeting the guests, informing them of the night's specials, taking their order and bringing their food to their table. That which I just described is not even the bare minimum -okay, maybe it's the bare minimum but it's often all that one experiences in terms of service. If our goal is to provide a **WOW!** dining experience a key component has to be excellent communication.

What do I mean by excellent communication? What more needs to be communicated? If you tell them about the specials and answer any questions your guests might have -what more is there to communicate?

For one thing, just telling or informing your guests about the specials is not really going to get them interested and excited about ordering them. You have to be creative in not just telling but describing them. But more on that in a minute. Let's consider what communication is. It's so much more than just telling.

Synonyms for Communication:

Tell, Say, Inform, Describe, Explain, Elaborate, Expound, Detail, Impress upon, Imply, Infer, Teach, Train, Discuss, Educate, Influence Proclaim, Declare, Announce, Convey, Transmit, Interact, Relate, Pass on, Put across, Mention

It is incumbent upon you to ensure that your guest knows what's going on in regards to each course. There is nothing more annoying or aggravating for a guest, than being out for dinner and waiting for what seems like an extremely long time for your food and not having anything communicated to you by your server. They're just sitting around and waiting and wondering and waiting and wondering. With no information and no communication.

If there is a delay on a dish, or some kind of hold up in the kitchen, it is not only your responsibility to let your guest know -it is common courtesy to do so. Your guest should never be the one who asks you how much longer it will be. You must be aware and then communicate to them. You must be proactive, rather than reactive in your communication. This goes a long way in alleviating any of their concern. It also preempts any complaint by them at the end of their dinner.

"My friends, I just wanted to let you know that we have a large group of 30 in the other room. The chef is now plating up their entrees and as soon as they are out, he will be finishing your dishes. Thank you so much for your patience."
There. You took preemptive measures. Your guest may still not be happy about the long wait but at least it's now not a wait with wondering. Any complaint is hopefully, now defused.

Communication changes everything
"Sir, I just want you to know that the risotto pescatore does take a little extra time to prepare. Rather than your entrees being ready in 20 minutes or so it will be more like 30 minutes. Is that okay with you?"
You've told them in advance that it will take longer. Now they will not have to ask you what is taking so long. You've been proactive. If a particular menu item has a longer prep/cooking time than other items you are responsible to inform your guests. Do not wait until they are waiting and they then ask you, "What's taking so long?" How would a guest know that risotto will take longer than other menu items to prepare? Do all guests know that soufflés take extra time? Please don't say "Well, they didn't ask."
It's your responsibility to 'offer' the information.

"Sir, Ma'am, I'm certainly not intending to make you feel rushed in making your dinner choices, however, I want you to know that there is a party of 20 being seated right now in the other room and their food is prepared by the same kitchen staff as your dinner and everyone else's in here. So if you have any time constraints- I do recommend we get started. That way, at least we will be able to get your first and maybe even your second course out before that party slows the kitchen down."

Of course your guest did not ask you "Excuse me, do you have any large parties going on tonight?" Or "Is there anything going on that I should know about that might delay you in bringing each dinner course to me in timely manner tonight?"

In fact, many larger restaurants have such a large kitchen that they have a separate chef and kitchen staff dedicated specifically to large parties and banquets, which will in no way affect the other diners. But there are many restaurants where that is not the case. Rather, the rest of the diners' orders take a back seat until they get the large group's table done.

So, a guest could be sitting in a sparsely seated dining room thinking, "It's really not that busy-what is taking so darn long for our order?", having no clue what is going on in the banquet area.
The main point here is -Please, let your guests know. I assure you they will appreciate being 'kept in the loop'. -Hey, that's another synonym for communication.

How many times have you been out for dinner, the server takes your order and it seems all of a sudden, he's a magician, that is, he does a disappearing act? Nowhere to be found. And even his assistant has disappeared as well. Poof. Gone. And then, as if by magic, once your food is ready to be served -Voila! Or, he only reappears after your food is served. He reappears.
Now, while he's disappeared, you're looking around trying to find him. No luck. He's definitely gone.

Or, sometimes, you have a server that didn't disappear, he's just faded out of sight. You're looking, straining your eyes, tilting your head back, and stretching your neck to catch a glimpse of this elusive creature. There! There he is -so far in the distance, he seems to be cavorting with one of his colleagues off in the corner. You try to make eye contact but he never looks your way for more than a fleeting glance.

Without shouting or raising your voice it seems impossible catch his attention.

It seems that many servers feel uncomfortable going back to their table while their guests are waiting for their next course. They often seem uneasy and that's why they disappear. Maybe they don't know what to say to their guests. Some of them don't disappear, they just hide behind the service station peering around the corner, to spy on their guests and see what they are doing while they're waiting.

Waiting is what they are doing. Waiting without knowing. Wondering. Wondering how long it will be before they see you again. Wondering why you won't come back to the table unless you have their food in hand. Wondering with no communication is so disconcerting. It creates a feeling of helplessness. They have no information from you. They see other guests around them being served. They can't go back into the kitchen themselves, so they wait. And their wine glass is empty as is the bread basket. Shame.

Of course, you, the server, can't control what goes on in the kitchen. Yes, that's true, but the situation is not entirely out of your hands. There are many things that you can do.
Here are some suggested action steps:

1. Go to the kitchen & find out what order in line your ticket is. Every restaurant is different in terms of their expediting system.
You may be able to ask the expo person, although, oftentimes they do not want to be interrupted.

2.   You could look on the screen, if the kitchen has a computerized system, or wherever the order tickets are hung and observe what is going on behind the line.
If you know that there are some larger parties in the restaurant that evening you should see, if by chance, that table is being plated ahead of yours.
3.   Ask. Ask the kitchen manager. Ask the expo person. Ask the chef. Find out. Don't just assume.

If it seems that a reasonable amount of time has passed between courses and they are not ready yet-find out what is going on in the kitchen. Of course, each restaurant is different- a high end restaurant in New York City will have longer lag time between courses than a bistro in Topeka, Kansas. You should know your restaurant and what is a normal time between courses.

My friend Adam Gnau, Chef of Acero Restaurant in Maplewood, Missouri aims for 15 minutes between courses. I asked him what about for a table of 12 or 15? He said *"Still the same. Fifteen minutes."* That means that he plans to have guests wait for no more than fifteen minutes from the time they are done with one course until the next one is served.

You must know what is considered normal timing between courses for your restaurant. At the point that it starts to seem like your guests have been waiting too long, you need to be proactive and take action. It is incumbent upon you to be informed and then to inform your guests.

Of course, sometimes there are unusual circumstances. A couple who are sitting at their table waiting for their main course and have not ordered an appetizer, a salad or any sort of first course, will feel like 10 minutes is 30 minutes. The situation will be even more compounded if they have no drinks in front of them. So, imagine, they have no drinks, no first course and they've already devoured all of the bread that you've put in front of them. Waiting fifteen or twenty minutes for their entrée will seem like forever. And of course, they will observe others who were seated after them being served ahead of them but most likely it's a first course or appetizer, which typically takes less time.

Regardless of the situation, it is your job as the server to find out what the status is, communicate it to your guest and set their minds at ease.

If it's going to be a while, don't just disappear. Strike up a conversation with them. Sell them another glass of wine. Talk about your chef, the restaurant or ask them about themselves. Tell a funny story. Humor usually can lighten any situation.

Many people who haven't done it, think that being a server really takes no special skill or talent. That, however is very far from what reality is. I won't say it's easy or difficult. I will say though, that not everybody can do it. And certainly not everybody who does it, does it well.

Being a server takes a variety of aptitudes; one has to be part diplomat, part entertainer, part host. Being able to create and deliver **WOW!** dining experiences for your guests requires that you be a great communicator. You must be informed yourself and then inform your guest what is going on. Don't wait for them to ask. Be proactive. Communication is truly one of the keys to your success as a Service Professional. You hold this key in your hands, use it wisely and use it well.

Developing your communication skills takes practice and commitment to being the best you can be. Once you find yourself becoming proficient in this ability, you will feel more in control of the service you are providing.

Then, you can begin to turn the level of service up a notch by...

Chapter 16

Getting the Right Balance Between TMA & TLA

"Life is a dance between making it happen and letting it happen."
Ariana Huffington

Have you ever heard of or experienced TOO MUCH CUSTOMER CARE or giving guests TOO MUCH ATTENTION?!   Surely   this cannot be possible. "That's absurd!" I hear you say. In my experience, all too often the attention given to dining guest is one extreme or the other- **Too Much Attention (TMA)** or **Too Little Attention (TLA).**   Before you begin your side of the debate, please read on.

Scene: You walk into a beautiful, upscale restaurant. You are greeted cheerfully by the host, who then escorts you and your party to a beautiful table in the corner of the dining room.
Before you're even settled into your seats, here comes the waiter asking if you are ready to order drinks. *WOW!* Now that's prompt service. You order a bottle of Bordeaux. Wine service is performed flawlessly. As the wine is being presented and poured by the Sommelier, the server enthusiastically describes the specials of the evening. He even offers his own recommendations. He rather quickly, yet efficiently, takes everyone's order.

Everything seems to be going great except for one small aspect; all throughout the course of the evening, your server (and his assistant) never-I mean, never, ever leave your presence, with the exception of when they go to bring something- food from the kitchen, wine from the bar etc., or to remove plates from the table.

Then, immediately after each task is performed they return to stand guard, ever vigilant, eyes like a hawk, ready to pounce at the slightest possibility that you may need something. You and your guests are mid-conversation when, for a slight second you look up and you make eye contact with the server. In a flash, he zips to your side, "Yes, sir?"

You're not quite sure what he means. "Pardon, me?" you say.
He says, "Oh, excuse me sir, you looked at me, I thought you needed something."

On the one hand, this is great, because as soon as you take two sips of water someone is there to refill it.   No need to ask.   When the last drop of wine is poured from the bottle, your server is promptly standing beside you with a fresh, clean glass and a new bottle ready to pour if so directed.

So, it sounds like a dream, right? Being treated like a king. So, what is the problem with this kind of focused, attentive service? Well, some people may actually feel uneasy or uncomfortable if a server is constantly standing guard like a gargoyle perched atop an old building gawking at them, following their every move and gesture with his piercing eyes.
I realize that this style and level of service is rare and there are indeed some people- who enjoy, appreciate and seek out restaurants that provide hand and foot catering such as this. But I ask you this:
When is the line of attentiveness crossed over into the realm of annoyance?

A hovering server can really be quite irritating. Once a course is served and wine has been poured and drinks refilled and the initial checking as in "How's your dish," or "Is everything meeting your approval?" or whatever phrase(s) you say, it's time to disappear briefly. Let your guests enjoy their dinner in peace. You don't have to stand there and stare at them, watching them take every single bite. You don't necessarily have to leave the room, but if you did for a few moments at a time, that would be just fine.

I don't believe anybody truly wants to be watched while dining in a restaurant-like they're an animal on display at the zoo. If you happen to be in a food eating contest-then of course, you should expect to be watched and gawked at.   But this is not that.

Your job is to provide exceptional service. Even though each time you approach their table you may be providing some aspect of service, clearing their plates, pouring wine etc., gawking at them and standing ready to pounce at the guest's slightest move or gesture is NOT **WOW!** service.

Yes, my friend, do be attentive and be available but be inconspicuous and unobtrusive. Make an effort to post yourself in a prime location which allows you full view of your tables and yet your guest's view of you is at least partly obscured. That is the ideal to strive for, in my opinion. If you are unable to find a place hidden from view, you might consider not being only 6-10 feet away from them. Go away. Give your guests some room to breathe and eat. I guarantee you that they will think their food taste better. Go fold some napkins for 10 minutes. I'm sure you can find some kind of side work to do.

Unfortunately, the exact opposite extreme of the above scenario is more commonplace in restaurants today. Once the server has taken the order they are nowhere to be found, until they reappear, bearing your food. And then, once the course is served, you're once again hard pressed to even catch a glimpse of said server. That certainly is not **WOW!** service either. It is hardly even passable or acceptable service.

In some restaurants, the server only comes to the table a total of 3 times. Once, to greet the table and take their order for beverage and food. The second time, to deliver the food and once again, to deliver the check. Oh, and a fourth time to return the check. That is not even good service. Even if the food is great and the guests are enjoying everything, and you are observing this from afar, it is still vital that you re-approach the table more than once or twice.

Of course, every diner or guest is different in what their needs and preferences are and this is why learning to read your guests is so important. In order to provide **WOW!** service, you must assess the level of care and attention each of your table's needs and desires.

A while back, my wife and I were having dinner at an upscale restaurant in Caesar's palace (not the real Caesar's palace-as in, Caesar didn't actually live there) in Las Vegas, and while the food was good and the service was good, both of us were a little annoyed and curious as to why our server never once came and asked us if were enjoying our food. He would walk by and look but he never engaged us once our wine was served, and we received our food.

At the end of our dinner as we were about to leave, I decided to ask our server why he didn't inquire as to whether we enjoyed what we were eating and drinking. His reply astounded me. He said, "I've been doing this for a long time and I don't need to ask you if you're enjoying your food. We don't do that here. I saw you eating it so I knew you liked it. And if you didn't like it you would tell me."

That is being a bit arrogant and it goes beyond reading the guest. In fact, it is quite presumptuous. For example, what if we were on a date, (actually we were as we weren't yet married at the time) and one of us didn't like what we were eating but didn't want to draw attention to ourselves by flagging the server down? So, maybe we were just eating our food out of politeness. However, if the server actually had inquired we would have told him that there was something wrong with the food-too salty; too spicy; too overdone or whatever the case may be.

For him to assume, that because we were eating the food, that we enjoyed it, is just plain ignorant. If anyone is a fan of the cooking competition shows-Iron Chef, Top Chef etc., one would know that even professional chefs do not execute their dishes flawlessly every time.

There has to be a balance between overly smothering a guest and this other extreme of being so nonchalant and aloof and unavailable. In order to provide **WOW!** service, you must engage your guests and inquire if everything they are eating and drinking is to their liking. Again, I'm not talking about smothering and being annoying, coming every five minutes and saying "How is everything?"

A good rule of thumb is once any item-whether food or drink has been served, ask your guests how everything looks and how it smells. Then inform them that you will be back in a couple minutes to inquire how their first bites/tastes are. You then return within a couple minutes (2-3) and check on them. Do not wait until they are half way or more, finished with their food. If you can't get back to them within a couple minutes, ask a manager or co-worker to do so for you.

If there is any problem with the food-as in something is not prepared correctly, or they just don't like what they ordered, it is much easier to rectify the situation early into the course, rather than later. It is very frustrating for a diner, who, once they've been served their food and it is not to their liking (regardless of the reason) to sit and wait, and wait and wait until their server reappears. The longer that guest has to wait, the greater the chance that you will not receive a good tip, the restaurant will not get a good review and that guest will tell multiple people about the 'less than excellent service', at said establishment.

The first couple minutes after serving the guests are the most crucial (aside from the first impression) in the guest formulating their opinion of your restaurant. You can greatly influence their perception of you, your restaurant and the overall service there, by being aware, available and timely in your visits to their table.

Providing *WOW!* service is more of an art than a science. Some restaurant managers may be very specific and particular about how many minutes after each course or item is served, that you must return to the table. I don't believe it's that cut and dry and it's not an exact science. Every server is different, and every guest is different. You have to find the balance somewhere between the two extremes we've discussed here-of being a gawking, overbearing, annoying, smothering server and being a nonchalant, aloof, disappearing, inattentive, never-inquiring-because-I've-been-doing-this-for-a-long-time kind of server.

Striking the right balance may take time, but with conscious effort and continual practice, it will come as second nature to you. You'll get to the point where you find the right rhythm of when to return to your tables. It should always be with and for a specific purpose. You'll eventually develop a feel for it and you will be able to intuitively know when each table needs you. You will also be aware of how to adjust your level of care and attention you give to each table. This goes hand in hand with the principles we discussed in the Chapter 11 about Getting to Know/Reading Your Guests.

Another part of this ongoing balancing act, pertains to more than just what is happening with your guests in your own section. It's also important to realize that you are part of a larger performance that is taking place in the restaurant. You have to become perceptive and aware of the show in its entirety.

You must be able to see beyond your own 4 or 6 or 8 table station. You will develop this ability as you become committed to...

Chapter 17

Getting Restaurant Eyes

"There are things known and there are things unknown, and in between are the doors of perception." Aldous Huxley
"Change the way you look at things and the things you look at change."
Wayne W. Dyer

Successful Service and Hospitality professionals have a sixth or seventh sense that the rest of society has no knowledge or awareness of. What is this special ability? My friend, Theo Van Soest, whom I've mentioned previously, taught me about a term he calls "restaurant eyes". Having Restaurant Eyes is expressed in a number of different ways by the adept Hospitality Professional.

First, Restaurant Eyes is not something that just comes automatically and naturally merely because one works in a restaurant. Nor are Restaurant Eyes handed out by the General Manager to each Front of the House staff member along with their apron and employment manual on their first day of employment. On the contrary, Restaurant Eyes is something that is developed over time. But sadly, even people who have been in this industry for many years do not all possess Restaurant Eyes. It certainly takes time and experience to develop them.

While Restaurant Eyes in many aspects is a method of visual perception-as in actually using one's eyes-like many other topics I've discussed here in **Getting to WOW!,** this one also has an internal component to it. In order to develop Restaurant Eyes-one has to have an attitude that I call "Aware and Care". This attitude is simply the opposite of the mentality of "It's not my job, my section, my department".

Those who have an Aware and Care mentality tend to see things, situations, circumstances, potential problems and solutions and ways of doing things that the average person is oblivious to. When you Care about what goes on in the entire restaurant, rather than just your own little section-then you tend to be more Aware. In the same way, when you are Aware of things that your co-workers may not see or choose not to see-you will Care more about that situation or problem. You are an Aware and Care person.

There are so many examples of this that happens on a daily basis in any given restaurant or establishment. For example, most restaurants have area rugs in various walk ways around the restaurant. If you see a piece of paper on the floor, what do you do? Do you stop what you are doing and bend over, pick it up and dispose of it in the trash? Or do you just walk on by? What if your hands are full when you see it? Do you go back when you have nothing in your hand to get it?

Perhaps you are saying a little incredulously, "Come on, now. A piece of paper? I have more important things to take care of than a silly little piece of paper on the floor." And I say, "Absolutely, yes, a piece of paper." Do you know why? Because if you can't be bothered with something small like that, are you going to go out of your way to help your co-server, whom you know is not aware that their guest is complaining about his slow service? Or if you can't be bothered to pick up a piece of trash or paper that's lying on the floor, what do you do if you see a few drops of water on the floor?

In that situation having Restaurant Eyes, or not, could determine the safety of others who might slip and fall because of that water spot. How would that make you feel then? Restaurant Eyes grow out of an Aware and Care attitude. Those that don't have Restaurant Eyes have the opposite. What's that? It's called Tunnel vision. You can only see what is right in front of you. Literally.

So, when your table attempts to catch your attention, if you are not ready for them because you are doing or attending to something else or another table-you ignore them. And if you are relatively new in the business, you have to focus on what you're focusing on. I understand that. But as you become more proficient and competent then you will develop Restaurant Eyes. That is if you are Aware and you Care.

What bothers me is the veterans of the business who are very good at attending to their own tables in their own section but couldn't be bothered with anything else going on in the restaurant. Heck, there could be a fire in the other side of the restaurant and everyone evacuating the building but if it didn't have an immediate effect upon their tables they would probably just go on serving them, saying something like, "The fire's not over here".

It's not just service staff that need to develop Restaurant Eyes, but the owners and management as well. When I worked for Paul Mineo at his restaurant in St. Louis, I was so impressed with his uncanny ability to know everything that was going on in the restaurant. I really don't know how he did it. But he completely epitomized what having Restaurant Eyes is all about. So, many times it seemed as though he had eyes-not just in the back of his head, but everywhere.

Now, at the time Paul was not in the best physical health, so it's not like he was constantly walking the length and breadth of the floor. NO. Instead, he was usually sitting at the bar watching us, servers come in and out of the kitchen. As we would walk by I'd hear him say, "Christy, what happened to that guy's steak on table 42?" Or "Christoff, are you going to sell another bottle of Brunello to John on 31?"

I don't know how he was able to know everything that was going on at all times but I do know that he did have the attitude of Aware and Care. He cared about every one of his guests at all times.

He wanted to make sure that each one had a great dining experience. He also cared about his staff's experience who were working for him.

I, too, when I worked for Paul Mineo developed an Aware and Care mentality. Somehow it is easier for a server to care when you know that your owner does as well. But that's not always the case.

My wife and I have dined at many places where, unfortunately, the owner and management seem very unaware, disengaged and nonchalant about what goes on at their establishment. We used to frequent a relatively upscale Mexican restaurant in Las Vegas, quite often but one time when we went for dinner our food was served on gritty plates.

They obviously had an issue with their dishwasher not cleaning properly. This is not unheard of and a fixable issue. Still, not very pleasant for the guests to know that they are eating off of still-dirty plates. So, I mentioned it to our server and he seemed to be unfazed by it. I, then, went to seek out the manager, found him, showed him the gritty plates and told him about it. The manager barely grunted to me. There was no "I'm sorry, we'll look into it, we'll make it up to you," Nothing like that. He was not aware of the problem and even after I told and showed him, he did not Care. No Restaurant Eyes there. And no restaurant heart.

The Hospitality Professional with Restaurant Eyes sees things before others do. Having Restaurant Eyes gives one the ability to be focused on details, as we discussed in a previous chapter, but also, at the same time, to be able to see the big picture.

Another person I had the great pleasure of working for who demonstrated what Restaurant Eyes is all about, was Chef Ivy Magruder of St. Louis, Missouri. At the time he was executive chef at Vin De Set, a French Bistro with an American twist. His Restaurant Eyes were always open wide and focused.

He was not only aware of what was happening throughout the restaurant, but he led by example. He is and was a true example of servant leadership. The exact opposite of the disengaged, apathetic owner/manager that is all too common in some establishments today.

Although he was executive chef, he was involved in every aspect of the operation. He worked the host stand greeting and seating guests. He often walked the dining room not only to connect with the guests but also to lend a hand to us servers-to open a bottle of wine, bus tables, run appetizers. At the end of the evening he was often seen in the back of the house helping the dishwasher get caught up after a very busy evening service. There was not a job or task that he was unwilling to do. His Restaurant Eyes were wide open and because he led by example; it was pretty easy for a similar Care and Aware attitude to permeate the culture of Vin de Set. It seemed that everyone on staff was following Ivy's lead and developing those Restaurant Eyes.

Restaurant Eyes is using your eyes to scan the room while still paying attention to your guest. Good bussers have this ability. I always would train our bussers at Paul Mineo's to be aware of all the tables around them even as they are clearing one specific one. If you are clearing a table that has been vacated and you see a guest in need of a beverage refill or something else-having Restaurant Eyes enables you to prioritize. Which is more important and requires your more immediate attention? Maybe the hostess is waiting for you to clear that table so she can seat it.

However, that guest has been looking around for their server and is clearly in need. You have to make decisions moment to moment. I can't tell you which you need to do first. But I do know that if you don't develop Restaurant Eyes you will not even be aware of anything beyond the one task you are doing at that moment.

A gentleman who used to work as a busser at one of our favorite restaurants in Summerlin, Las Vegas, is Tulio. His Restaurant Eyes vision was 20/20. He always was aware of what was happening throughout the restaurant, not just in his section. In fact, even though we are friends with the management team and some of the servers at Honey Salt, whenever Michelle and I would go to Honey Salt we would always ask if Tulio was working. Why? Because even though we know we'll get good service there-we know that if Tulio is on that night that we won't really have to ask for anything. The guy really uses his Restaurant Eyes. He'll often let our server know what's happening at our table. Having staff that have Restaurant Eyes and knows how to use them makes for a smooth, seamless flow of service.

Another very simple example which most restaurant patrons are usually unaware of is the non-verbal eye communication that takes place between service staff on the floor. A server may be standing at his table engaged in conversation with his guest and at the same time very surreptitiously he will make an eye motion to his assistant or a teammate-that teammate-if they are aware, will come over and take the plates out of the hand of the server, or bring over a pitcher of water to refill the guests' glasses or retrieve the drinks that are waiting at the bar to be served to that table.

All of this happens throughout the course of the shift and most of the time the non-verbal interaction goes unnoticed by the guest. And that's the way it's meant to be.

Contrast that with a restaurant where no Restaurant Eyes can be found. The service may be decent or ok there but there is certainly no **WOW!** experience delivered, because every staff member is an island. No one is aware or cares about anything but his own tables. And the servers that share the assistance of the same bus person are constantly bickering about whose tables that busser should prioritize.

Having Restaurant Eyes also means the ability to read your guests, to anticipate their needs and to see beyond the present moment. It's something as simple as bringing out a serving spoon for the appetizers you'll be serving. Don't wait until they ask for it. Not everybody wants to use a spoon with the sauce served with their appetizer. So what? Bring it to them anyway. If you do bring it there's a greater chance of them using it. Plus, that small gesture shows that you Care. And that you are Aware.

As I mentioned, working for a manager or owner that truly cares and has Restaurant Eyes himself definitely is what each server hopes for. My assumption is that the reason that Tulio, whom I mentioned earlier, has Restaurant Eyes, is because Kim Canteenwalla, the Chef-Owner of Honey Salt has led by example there. But what do you do if you work at an establishment where that is not the case? Well, since the level of service provided ultimately depends upon you and how you perform, I don't think you have an excuse if your owner doesn't care. That's a sad situation, but we all create our own destiny. So take personal responsibility for your own results.

I read a wonderful book by Shep Hyken entitled, AMAZE EVERY CUSTOMER EVERY TIME. In it he gives great guidance for those who want to provide excellent service. He says that no matter who you are and regardless of what your position is you should:
"Take so much pride in what you do that your customers think you are the owner."

Throughout my career, I have often been mistaken for the owner, especially when I worked at Paul Mineo's. I carried myself in such a way that it was obvious that I cared and that I took pride, not merely in my job, but in the success of the entire operation-even though that wasn't my job. Multiple times a week, new guests would ask me if I was the owner. "No, I'm not," would be my reply. "But thank you for the compliment."

Shep Hyken says, *"If you are the owner, your job is to be so great at what you do that employees aspire to be just like you. If you are the employee, your job is to be so great at what you do that customers mistake you for the owner! Regardless of the size of your company, regardless of who you are or what you do, act like the owner!"*

So my advice, is to follow Shep's advice, whatever your position may be. As you begin to adopt an attitude of taking pride in what you do and caring for the success of the whole restaurant, you will begin to become more aware. With more Care-comes more Awareness. You will start seeing things-both problems and solutions that may have always been there but only now have come to your attention. Use your Restaurant Eyes-strengthen them daily and soon, like Tulio, of Honey Salt, your Restaurant Eyes vision will be 20/20.

As you follow and apply these principles on a daily and weekly basis, you will grow in your position. Others-your colleagues, management, guests and even you, yourself, will soon recognize that you are...

Chapter 18

Getting Competent and Consistent

"I am, as I've said, merely competent. But in an age of incompetence, that makes me extraordinary."
— Billy Joel

The word Competence simply means doing your job right, well, effectively and efficiently. Competence is being good at what you do and achieving the desired results. An amateur is not competent, because they haven't yet developed the skills and ability required for the task, job etc...

As a server, there are a lot of areas that one must gain competence in. A few of those areas are: Traymanship (a word I coined) -is one's ability to use and balance food or drink on a tray. This is not easy to do. It takes manual dexterity, concentration, focus and of course, balance and the other kind of coordination. In basketball, this would be akin to ball handling, in hockey-how you wield your stick to control the puck, etc. You get the picture.

Isn't it interesting that at the root of competence is the word compete? One really can't compete well if they lack competence. I see so many servers that can carry the tray filled with beverages to the table-yet they cannot maneuver and balance the tray as they remove the glasses. Improperly, they set the tray on the table of the guests they are serving, or on an empty table beside them, then they remove the glasses. That would be like a basketball player being proficient at ball handling-able to dribble toward the hoop but having no idea how to actually shoot the ball. This is not acceptable. This person lacks competence in traymanship.

Although there are many, some of the other areas in which competence is needed are: wine presentation and pouring, actual serving of food, how to properly place the plates in front of the guest. Yes, there is actually a proper manner and special knowledge required. The only way to gain competence is through practice and repetition. We've all heard it said that *"Practice makes perfect."*

But that is actually not completely true. I've met servers who have been in this industry for many years and they have been practicing the same thing over and over again. And guess what? They are far from perfect in their manner of serving. Why is that? The problem is that they've never been shown or taught how to do it correctly. So, in actuality, the proper phrase should be:

"Perfect practice makes perfect."

Just as any athlete or musician must continually train, practicing the basics over and over again, so, too, must the service professional, continually practice in order to become more adept and proficient at their craft. A server's competence lends to creating an exceptional dining experience for the guests. And isn't that what it's all about? To have a great experience? If not, then everybody would just be ordering take out all the time. It truly is the service team that makes the guest's meal an experience, an event-a **WOW!** experience.

As a server or hospitality professional you ought to be practicing your craft-your traymanship, your wine bottle opening and pouring. It should be your desire to keep getting better all the time.

Have you ever dined at a restaurant where you've witnessed servers who just seem to have such finesse about the way they move and the manner in which they do everything? This doesn't happen by accident. Those servers have been doing this for a long time and they have now reached a level where it is actually effortless for them.

Conversely, I'll bet you've also witnessed a server, or perhaps it is yourself, someone who just seems to be so stressed, struggling to do everything-from carrying a loaded tray to the way they pour, to everything. If you are one who seems to constantly struggle in opening bottles of wine, or in traymanship or some other element of service, take heart. We all started that way. This is not an easy job, but it does get easier with time and proper practice and with focus and determination. But just like any athlete or musician may have natural ability or talent-you, like them, need to constantly practice to improve your serve.

Whenever anyone approaches learning a new skill, task or discipline there are 4 stages which that person must go through to reach a level of proficiency.

The 4 stages are:

1.   Unconscious Incompetence
"I don't know that I don't know how to do this."
This is described as the stage of blissful ignorance. The individual does not know that they do not know how to do something.
2.   Conscious Incompetence
"I know that I don't know how to do this."
At this stage the individual is very aware that they don't know how to do the specific task, skill etc. This is where learning begins and it is the most difficult of the 4 stages. When one is at this stage, they will often form judgments about themselves. This stage is fraught with much frustration and it is the stage when most people will give up and quit.
3.   Conscious Competence
"I know that I know how to do this."
This stage shows a beginning stage of proficiency in a skill or ability. This stage is much easier than Stage 2, however, it is still uncomfortable for the individual and they must put much conscious effort and attention into it.

4.   Unconscious Competence

"I know how to do this with my eyes closed."

At this stage, the individual is so proficient they've now become an expert in it. There is the rule of 10,000 hours-a person typically has to do something repeatedly for 10,000 hours for them to achieve the expert level in a thing. Working 40 hours a week that would amount to about 5 years. If you have been doing something correctly for 5 years, you can now call yourself an expert. You don't have to have a certificate or a license or a degree to be a master of something.

Learning to drive a car is often cited when giving an example of moving through the 4 stages of learning. When a person is young and has not yet learned to drive, they see their parents driving or other adults and probably never even consider what is involved in driving a motor vehicle. They don't know that they don't know. They are at **unconsciously incompetent.**

Next, the person turns 15 or 16 and they take some classes where they learn the rules of the road and the mechanics of driving but when they actually get behind the wheel of a car they realize that it's not quite as easy as it looks. They are now at stage 2 and they are **consciously incompetent.** They practice and practice. If they're learning to drive a manual transmission, it may even be more difficult, because there's so much more involved. Coordinating the balance of pressing the brake while popping the clutch, just doesn't seem natural. They know that they don't know how to do this and it's very frustrating.

Eventually, after lots of patience and practice they eventually get the hang of it they are at stage 3- **consciously competent.** They know that they know how to drive but they are very cautious and conscious of every aspect of ability and awareness they must employ to accomplish this task.

Finally, after driving to school and to work and on the highway out of town many, many, many times they now know how to drive with ease, they can do a cross country road trip safely and effortlessly because they've been driving for years. They can do this with their eyes closed-**unconsciously competent**. Well maybe not quite, but certainly they can drive with very little or no conscious effort required.

These 4 stages apply to learning any new thing. If you are not very proficient in wine presentation, or tableside flambéing or traymanship or any other task or skill in service you must go through each stage until you reach a level of mastery. And if you persevere and persists you will reach that level. I'm sure of it.

Consistency

If Competence means doing your job right, well and effectively, then just add the two words "every time", and now we have a picture of what Consistency is. Of course, it is possible to be consistently bad at something. That is not the consistency that we are striving for here. Consistency is so important. Does that mean we never make a mistake? No. But your guests don't want it to be a crapshoot every time they come to your establishment.

Yes, I live in Vegas and unfortunately some places that were once my wife and my favorite restaurants have fallen to the less frequently visited category, now due to their inconsistency. Sometimes the food is great. Sometimes it's mediocre. Sometimes the service is spot on, sometimes it seems like nobody really cares. Consistency.

I want to share with you two examples of what consistency is all about. First is my experience at what is one of my favorite restaurants, Next Door Food & Drink in Loveland, Colorado. Michelle and I traveled to Loveland for my brother's wedding this past summer. Loveland is a pretty small town, I think their downtown consists of one main street, and a couple of side streets. While driving around looking for a place for lunch we happened upon Next Door Food & Drink.

We ate lunch there at that time and we were very impressed with the food-all locally sourced, natural, much of it organic and wonderfully, creatively prepared AND the outstanding service.

We met Jim Edwards the owner, whom I've already referred to in **Getting to WOW!** and our server was Sydney Nelson. Sydney's style of service is so refreshing. She has a positive upbeat attitude, a warm and friendly personality. She is very knowledgeable about everything regarding the restaurant-the food sourcing, the preparation, the wine and cocktails, the materials used in the decor of the restaurant-much of it reclaimed and re-purposed. She absolutely knows her stuff!

There are some servers at some restaurants, who have wonderful, pleasant, personalities but they seem to think that that excuses them from actually having service skills and being knowledgeable. Not so, with Sydney. She is a true Hospitality professional in every sense of the word.

I was so impressed with our experience, that the following day I suggested to Michelle that we return to eat at Next Door again, to see if they are consistent. So we did, and they were. We had a different server that day, Jim Edwards, the owner was not, in but everything was excellent, AGAIN. To me, this is a testament to Jim's leadership.

There are many servers who excel at what they do, but they work at restaurants where the leadership is either lacking or non-existent. When one goes to those places-it's really a hit and miss situation. There is no consistency-because no standards are set, management is not engaged and little thought is put into who is hired. Jim Edwards has done a wonderful job at creating a culture of caring Service and Hospitality Professionals. And the food is great as well.

This experience led me to ask both Sydney and Jim if I could interview them for **Getting to *WOW!*** Everybody WINS with 5 Star Service. It was such a pleasure getting their take on what constitutes "WOW!" service and how to achieve it.

Michelle and I returned to Loveland on a cross country tour last month. Although we had to pass through Colorado somewhere along the way, we didn't necessarily have to go through Loveland-but my brother lives there and we wanted to visit Next Door again. And guess what? It was exceptional, once again.

Consistency is the name of the game. This time we had Andy Stephenson as our server, he, too, was outstanding in his affable manner, his knowledge and recommendations and overall excellence in service. And let me just tell you that, unlike Sydney, who says she'll probably always be in the industry in some capacity because she loves it so much, Andy is planning on pursuing other career paths. However, there is no "I'm just doing this until I get a real job" attitude or mentality with him. Andy truly seems to care about his guests and endeavors to give them a great dining experience.

Just as the subtitle of my book states-"Everybody WINS with 5 Star Service", Jim Edwards and his team at Next Door Food and Drink in Loveland, Colorado get it. They are NOT a fine dining establishment. It's a semi casual place, but they prove that 5 Star Service does not necessarily mean white table cloths, tuxedoed servers and fine china. Because they have none of that. What they do have though, is a team of people that pursue excellence on a daily basis and they create **WOW!** dining experiences for their guests. Consistently.

The other example of Consistency that I want to share with you is not from a local, independently owned restaurant. Instead, this example is of a corporate restaurant that has over 50 locations across the county-Fleming's Prime Steakhouse and Bar. We have dined at the Fleming's where we live in Summerlin a few times and each time the food and service were excellent. Recently, our manager friend, Joaquin, was transferred to the other Fleming's in Las Vegas, so, we decided to go there for dinner with friends.

From the way we were greeted and seated by the host team, to the introduction of our server, Brian-guiding us through the wine list and the menu, to the entire dinner-we had a wonderful dining experience. There was no one particular thing that made it special. Rather, it was the entirety of everyone on the team working together in unison that made our dining experience so enjoyable.

None of us had been to this particular Fleming's before. Although, Joaquin, our manager friend, certainly welcomed us and even visited our table a few times, it was the efforts and the hospitality of every team member that really made our evening. The other managers, Leroy and Jay each came to our table as well to check on us. That may seem like a lot but it never felt like we were being bothered or being overly attended to. We enjoyed great conversation, laughed together, ate some wonderful food and partook of some great wines.

Our experience at this new Fleming's was just as remarkable as when we dined at the one in Summerlin. Consistency is obviously something that is highly valued at Fleming's. As is food quality, attention to detail, team mentality, and creating
WOW! dining experiences for their guests. They really do all the above very well.

In this business, there are so many elements that must synchronize in order to achieve success. But consistency is definitely within your control. Like I've mentioned in a previous post on my blog, Soupfly-IT ALL STARTS AT THE TOP. If the owner and management don't care, are not aware and don't show up ready for the game, why would the staff?

Consistency means, treating every guest with respect, care and concern every time. Consistency means that you give your all every time. Your first and main thought is the guests' satisfaction. Consistency is making sure that every plate you bring to every guest is correct, accurate and what they ordered.

When we are consistent in our service, our hospitality and the care we give to each of our guests, then word begins to spread. When your guests know that both you, personally and the restaurant in general, are consistent in both quality of food and service-everyone benefits.

The establishment gets great reviews, it is always busy, it gains a great reputation, (as do you, with your regulars), revenue increases, you receive generous tips, and life is wonderful.
If you are really taking to heart (and mind) this information, then I know that indeed, you are growing and becoming more confident and competent. Hopefully, as your skills and abilities improve, you are also having more fun, and like Greg DaLuz says, you are realizing that this is not really work at all, because you are totally enjoying what you do and you are being paid quite well also.

At this point, you and all your colleagues in the Front of the House are in the flow, working well together, to create and deliver *WOW!* dining experiences for all your guests.
But to be a truly successful operation, you and all the staff, regardless of position, must be...

Chapter 19

Getting the Two 'Houses' in Sync
B.O.H & F.O.H

"The strength of the team is each individual member. The strength of each member is the team."
Phil Jackson

"None of us is as smart as all of us."
Ken Blanchard

The front of the house generally refers to the staff in the restaurant that the guests/customers, patrons, see and interact with. This includes; hostess, receptionist, maître d', the general manager, the assistant manager, supervisors, shift supervisors etc., the floor manager, the servers, bartenders, barbacks, cocktail servers, the bussers and even the coat check person.

The 'Back of the House' refers to those who work mostly behind the scenes-meaning not in the dining areas. These ones often are never seen by the public but are the architects of what goes on in the restaurant. Positions considered as 'Back of the House' include; the chef, sous chef, chef de cuisine, anyone with a title of 'chef', or the cook, head cook, etc., anybody who does kitchen prep, the dishwasher, the expediter-who may also be referred to as the 'expo', or the food runner(s), the kitchen manager-as many/most larger restaurants have a separate manager specifically over the kitchen.

In smaller restaurants there may only be one manager who is in charge of the kitchen and also oversees the front of the house. In many restaurants, these days, the chef often runs the show, being either a partner or owner in the business or functioning as the G.M. as well as Chef. The role of chef is no longer relegated to the kitchen only.

Okay, so now that we've delineated the breakdown of front and back of the house, in general, we now must address the couple positions that cross the line, literally.

There is often crossover of roles between Front of the House and Back of the House. As I just mentioned, often the chef is no longer just a kitchen role. There may be people in your restaurant that bus tables part of the week and wash dishes on other days. In that case, they are both front and back of the house.

Expeditor-The Bridge between Front and Back of the House

Joe Cortes, who's worked for many years for Wolfgang Puck in numerous capacities and recently as Assistant Manager at Honey Salt in Summerlin, Las Vegas, says that the expeditor position is *"The link between the front of the house and the back of the house. This position is so important."*

The expediter or expo person, arguably, may have one of the most difficult and under-appreciated and integral responsibilities of all. For they truly hold the crossover position between front and back of the house. They are stationed in the kitchen. Their role begins there. That is their home base as it were. And they have the task of calling the plays. Telling the kitchen what orders need to be 'fired' and when.

At the same time they have to coordinate with the front of the house, most especially servers and bussers, in order to make sure that each table is ready for the next course. That means plates from the previous course cleared and all required, proper utensils-steak knives, soup spoons, new clean cutlery etc., in place on the table. Communication and attention to detail are of the essence here, for smooth flow of transition to the next course.

An expediter usually makes a minimal hourly wage, certainly more than the minimum wage that a server makes, but not as much as the kitchen staff-sous chef, line cook, chef, etc. He or she also receives a small tip out from each of the servers, usually based on gross sales. A good expediter really keeps the flow of service going from kitchen to dining room. Someone who really knows and takes pride in what they are doing in this role plays a pivotal part in helping to make the whole operation appear seamless.

Becoming an accomplished and competent expeditor takes time. It also requires great attention to detail-for they are the person who says if a dish is ready to be served/brought to the guest. Once a plate has been put in the window by the chef or other kitchen staff, it is the Expeditor's responsibility to make sure that all the plates for that course and that table are also ready to go. A good Expeditor has a great handle on timing. If he does not-food that's cooked and ready to be served may be sitting and dying in the window while waiting for the rest of the items for that same ticket/table to be finished.

This means all the necessary garnishes and finishing touches are done by this person. Does this plate require a lemon wedge, cocktail sauce, a serving spoon to go with the shared appetizer plate? He also must ensure that the plate itself is clean around the edges-no sauce sloppily left on the edges.

An Expeditor really is so vital to the smooth flow of service. Though, he is not seen as often, his effectiveness can contribute greatly to a wonderful dining experience and make the Server look like a star, or he can be a thorn in the side of the server. This is when entrees come out before salads or before the first course is finished or even cleared from the table. Or when the next course for one or some guests at a table comes out, but there is someone still left waiting for their food. This does not make the Server happy and certainly is not pleasing, and is quite frustrating for the guests.

Now, either all the guests refrain from eating and let their food get cold, as they politely wait for their other member to be served. Or, the one that was not served yet, tells the others to "Go ahead and start", as he waits for his meal to be served. Either way, it is an uncomfortable situation for all involved.

Every Restaurant is NOT a Tapas Restaurant

Recently, the proliferation of Tapas style restaurants has flooded the landscape. This style of restaurant came to us from Spain and the manner in which they are served- is not so much as specific courses, but rather they are brought to the table as each one is prepared-in no particular order. Guests will order many different tapas at a time and share and enjoy them as they arrive to the table. Well, it seems to me, that although many restaurants are not technically "tapas bars"-they seem to function that way-meaning not giving care or concern as to what course is to be served when. "I know that you're both still eating your Caesar salad, but your filet is already done, so, I thought I'd bring it out to you now."

Often we may hear comments like, "Well, the food was up and ready." Or "The chef just put it up." Or, "Well, I was just going by the time. They've had their appetizers for 15 minutes. How long does it take to eat an appetizer?"
Really, it doesn't matter how long it takes someone at a table to eat a salad or an appetizer. They are our guests. Your guests. Some people really like to take their time. They are paying customers. Guests. They ought not to feel rushed in their dining. But I digress.

If yours is NOT a tapas style restaurant, please don't treat the service of courses as such. If there's 3 or 4 or 5 people at table-you must bring them all their food at the same time. Or at the very least ladies first. We're talking about providing **WOW!** experiences. Serving some people at a table ahead while others wait for their food to come out is NOT **WOW!** service. Note-I'm not referring to any banquet or large groups here. And if you are serving or running food and you know that the other plates are being brought out by someone else from the kitchen on your heels, please don't just drop the plates and run. Please inform your guests, these are the first two, someone is right behind me with the other plates.

This chapter is about the dynamic between Front and Back of the House. But actually, the above is a great example of the lack of symbiosis between front and back. In this instance the kitchen is only concerned with 'getting the food out'. They can't 'just keep these tickets sitting here on the line'. But this will negatively affect the server's rapport with the guest or at least it potentially could.

Also, an expediter may just want to clear all the tickets and 'call' each ticket to be 'fired', based on their assumption that the guest is ready without having actually been told or seen if the guest is finished or close to being finished with the present course.

The fact of the matter is, that if the food is brought out, most people aren't going to tell the expo person they don't want it or that they are not ready for it. Why? Because they know that it will just sit under a heat lamp until they are ready for it. Or in some restaurants, it will just sit until the guest is finally ready and then it will be reheated in the microwave for them. Yuck! It will not be as hot and fresh as they would like it.

So, when asked by the server, "Why did you bring the entrees out to table 7 so early?" the expo person will say, "They said it was okay. They were ready."
They may have made themselves ready, or rushed, scarfed down their salads, or forewent finishing them because the next course was there. But I guarantee you, most people don't like that, whether they voice it to you or the expediter or not. The role of the expediter is one of bridging the gap between the two 'houses'-front and back.

He is Back of the House as he's in the kitchen interacting with the staff, calling out tickets as they come in, and waiting for orders to come up. Then, once he trays up and if he is also the food runner, which is often common in smaller restaurants, he, then crosses the line to front of the house, as he brings the food to the dining guests. He has a dual role and many times, is under appreciated by both sides, and he still must maintain continuity of service, peace and civility between both.

In any restaurant I dine in, I can usually tell if an expediter takes his role seriously, and if enough emphasis and importance is given to it (his role) by staff and management. If the food is just coming out whenever, sometimes on time, sometimes rushed, sometimes lagging, then I know that that role is really not given the credit and support it deserves.

Another example of a crossover role is, if an establishment may operate with only one manager, who has responsibility for the front of the house, but also has ultimate jurisdiction over the kitchen as well. In this situation, they, too, are a gap-bridger, between front and back. Every establishment has their own unique make-up of personnel and roles. But one thing is clear, most of the time, in most restaurants, regardless of how much of a 'team mentality' may exist- there is definitely a feeling of "We are the Front of the House" and "We are the Back of the House". That mentality can either be very divisive and detrimental to the team or it can forge friendly competition, yet, a sense of shared camaraderie.

I'm sure that we all agree that both front and back are vital to the growth, stability and success of the restaurant, but there seems to be this age old separation between the two. Some places even take it to the point of animosity. It is, unfortunately, not uncommon to hear phrases such as, "You do your job in the dining room and we'll take care of what goes on back here". Or "You wouldn't have anybody to cook for if it weren't for us servers". There's many variations of this mentality but it's real and it does exist. It often may be unspoken but if it's there, it's felt and understood. A clear line between kitchen and dining room staff often is very real and can create untold amounts of stress and tension.

Having said that, allow me now to speak to my server brothers and sisters and management, if I may.

I will quote my friend Joe Cortes again, here, *"If you want to get the WOW! in service, it has to start at the top with management. Management must WOW! their employees first, their own internal customers."*

I really believe that Joe has hit it on the head. We're always talking about the customer is right and pleasing the guest, and while that is important and true, if your own employees don't feel special, appreciated and valued, it's pretty hard for them to give what they themselves don't have and don't experience. Joe is right. If we want our staff to create and deliver **WOW!** experiences, how about we start by taking care of our own internal customers?

This is one area that is so overlooked, when training of service staff takes place. We must all come to an agreement and an understanding and appreciation of the absolute importance of the integral relationship between FOH and BOH. Yes, they are separate, but neither could exist without the other. We need each other. Each enables and equips the other in different ways to shine. You are a great chef. Congratulations. But who's going to enjoy your food if it's not served? Or do you think you'd do better to have your wonderful culinary creations ordered at a walk up counter? I bet not.

You, my friend, are a fantastic, wonderful server. You know your food and wine. You have a great personality. You engage people and make them feel comfortable and at ease. You are a master at creating an exceptional dining experience. Great. But what are you going to serve those wonderful guests of yours, if not the delectable creations so carefully prepared by your back of the house colleagues? Do you want to try creating exceptional dining experiences out of serving boiled hot dogs on paper plates? I'm guessing not.

We obviously need each other. The restaurants that I know that are most successful, like Honey Salt, for example, do not miss or underestimate this point. This is cliché as it may sound or seem- but a team effort. A Team Effort and a true Team Mentality. There's no way around it. If you think it's not important, if people you work with think it's not, if your management acts as if, or exudes the mentality that it is not, then I'll put a wager that that animosity will lead to more than just a lack of symbiotic relationships. Your establishment may be doing ok, but it will never be great.

This all goes back to what we talked about regarding energy. There are some restaurants that I've dined at, where the team energy is palpable, like Flemings Prime Steak House & Bar in Las Vegas, just to name one. You can feel it. It is positively charged and it's invigorating and refreshing just to be around.

Sometimes I think that the Back of the House staff have a feeling of unfairness because they perceive that they do so much more work than the front of the house does. They often view the service staff as lazy, not hard workers. I've heard it been said, "All you do is bring plates to the table. Anybody could do that. You walk, in serve the people, make your tips and leave. That's not real work."

Conversely, many servers have the attitude, whether they say it aloud or not, that, "These kitchen staff couldn't describe, sell a bottle of wine or do a proper wine presentation if their career depended on it. They can cook the food but they don't know the first thing about serving guests."
It's obvious that neither of these attitudes is conducive to harmony between the front and the back of the house. And if there is no harmony, we are missing something very vital that could contribute to the greater success of the restaurant itself, as well as to each individual.

If you desire to be an exceptional server, and you truly care about providing **WOW!** dining experience for your guests, then I believe it is incumbent upon you to foster a peaceful, mutually supportive, relationship with your kitchen peers. I can say honestly, that this is one area that I've had challenges with personally, especially in places that I've worked where 'team mentality' was a foreign concept. Still, it should not be an excuse for me. Or for you.

My experience has taught me that you can apply all the principles in this book and be the most skilled, talented, knowledgeable server, with a wonderful personality, however, if you have less than a friendly or only a cordial or business-like relationship with your kitchen colleagues, then you are really missing something. Not only that, but you will always be at their mercy. Try asking for something 'on the fly', or a special order on an extremely busy night. Your request may be met-because they are professionals, but it will most certainly not be given top priority. It won't be done in the most expedient manner. It will be when they get to it. And that will be whenever they decide to do so.

You may be the most phenomenal server in the world, but if you don't have a real connection with those that prepare the food that you serve, you will not truly be a success, at least in my opinion-regardless of how much you 'walk with' every night.

So, I'm going to offer here, humbly, some ideas of how to build a team mentality between yourself and your Back of the House colleagues, because they actually are the ones who have your back. Be their friend and they will help make you shine. This is all about both houses-Front and Back, getting in sync in order to create greater success for each individual staff member, and the restaurant as a whole.

Fostering a Team Culture

1.   Management should lead the way-Family meal-for everyone-at the same time- daily or at least weekly
2.   Learn your co-worker's names. Each one of them
3.   Stop/Ban the Blame Game-whose fault that an order was messed up or why a mistake in service happened.
4.   Team meeting-once a month-Management share goals, successes/opportunities of the establishment
5.   Team outing-sports event, local, college, semi pro, pro.
6.   Mutual respect for each other's roles-Learn what each other actually does and what their job entails/Shadow for one day to learn what the other side actually does
7.   Volunteer together-Builds unity and creates outward focus instead of thinking of one's self only.
8.   Appreciation and acknowledgement-
9.   Holiday Party-everyone on staff invited, including spouses
10.   Get to know your colleagues outside of work
11.   Start a Restaurant Sponsored Sports team-Softball, Soccer, Darts, Badminton, etc.
12.   Start a juggling club or a sock puppet miming group-online

These are just some suggestions. I don't know which will work best for your restaurant. But I do know that a team mentality is not going to just form automatically by itself, merely because you work in the same restaurant/building. As I've said, the management should take the lead on this. It will take time, commitment and discipline. However, as you move forward applying the above suggestions/principles, you will begin to build a true spirit of camaraderie and that sense of pride that we talked about at the beginning of this book, will grow from being something personal only, into a shared commonality amongst all members, Front and Back of the House.

With that bond established and growing between both "Houses", next, it's time to put your sights on...

Chapter 20

Getting Them to Get Tiramisu

"Dessert is probably the most important stage of the meal, since it will be the last thing your guests remember before they pass out all over the table."
William Powell

At the end of a wonderful meal, now comes the best part, the icing on the cake or the cake, itself, literally. My wife's favorite dessert is tiramisu and she is often disappointed when we are dining out and she learns that the place does not have tiramisu. I tell her, this is a French restaurant-tiramisu is Italian. Still, she thinks they all should serve tiramisu. And I think that every server needs to get their guests to get the tiramisu, in order to properly cap the **WOW!** dining experience.

But this chapter is about more than just selling dessert. This chapter is about selling. Sales is service is sales. You have a captive audience. Guide them, lead them. Don't be afraid to sell. Your income depends upon how well you can sell. You can have all the charm in the world and be the nicest person, but that does not guarantee that you will get the sale or the upsell. What and how much your guests order is directly related to how well you can sell. If you think that sales and service are two different things you are mistaken.

A server who provides **WOW!** service to his guests, gives some thought to his job when he's not at work. Many in the service industry see it merely as a job-a place which allows flexibility with their schedule, a place to have fun, a place to work with some cool (sometimes) people and make some decent money and cash daily, at that.

A Guest Mentality

However, to be one who provides **WOW!** service, requires a different mentality than that stated above. Certainly, there are many mental aspects of this. For one, we have to start thinking of those we serve as more than just customers buying our service or product. Yes, many restaurants parrot the term 'guests' and 'guest mentality' but it seems to be only cliché or a catchphrase. We often hear, "Oh, no, they're not just customers-they're our guests."

Okay, that may be corporate speak on paper and what they parrot, but how does that translate to the staff and how they treat the living, breathing people that come to dine at your establishment. Do the staff at your establishment really consider those that come in to dine as 'guests' or merely 'customers'?

What does a guest mentality really mean?
I believe that it means having an attitude of caring. I can truthfully say that I don't see dollar signs on someone who sits down to be served by me. I do actually care about their experience as a patron of the place where I am working.   I endeavor to treat them the way that I would like to be treated. I say 'endeavor' because I may not always be 100% successful in my task, but at least that is my goal. I treat them the way I would if they were coming to a dinner party at my home-minus the part of me doing the cooking.

If you adopt that kind of attitude or mentality-it's very easy to get beyond seeing them merely as customers.

Service is Sales
A service job is not that different from a sales job. Of course you don't have a list of prospects to call to offer your product to-there really is no prospecting required. But then, on second thought-why not? However, service is definitely a sales job as well. We assume that when someone sits down in our establishment that they actually are going to be buying your product (your food and beverage items)

Once they've been seated they're not just checking out the menu, they pretty much have committed to being a paying customer. But now the question is- how much of a customer? Or, how much are they going to buy? How much of your product are you going to sell to them? What factors influence that person and what determines whether they order simply a sandwich and a soda or a full 3 or 4 course dinner, complete with a glass or two of wine and appetizer and dessert?

Are you merely an order taker? "What'll it be, sir?"

A lot of people think that suggestive selling or up-selling is only for upscale fine dining restaurants. But that's really not true. Whether you work in a diner, a fine dining restaurant or a casual restaurant, you can positively affect your guest check average by the things you say, your energy you project and the rapport you do or don't build with your guest. Your recommendations can directly influence the choices your guest makes for their meal.

You have a captive audience or prospect sitting in front of you. You don't have to ask whether they're interested in your product-they are. That's why they've come in. They are hungry. They are in need of your product. They don't have to ask their wife if they can buy it. They don't have to consult with the board of directors. You have sitting in that table or booth a hot prospect and they are ready to buy!

You've got the product they want (the food and beverage on your menu), they are hungry (ready to buy) and they have your money. A transaction is bound to take place.

Why do some people walk out after having an appetizer for dinner, spending less than 20 dollars and another person has a full 3 or 4 course dinner spending 60 dollars or more? Even 100 dollars?

There's a myriad of factors-but certainly part of it-a large part of it-depends on how the person felt. Did he feel like he was treated as a guest or a customer? Was he-your guest- a person that you genuinely cared about, or at least cared about his dining experience? Or was he just one of the 30 or 40 people you 'had to wait on' that day?

Do you think of your job as 'serving your guests' or 'waiting on customers'? It seems to me that the level of service in some restaurants is often so mediocre that diners have gotten to a point where their expectations are naturally very low. They just don't expect much when they dine out. So, when, on an occasion, they are the recipients of excellent service they are so surprised and taken aback they think it must be a fluke.

Thinking of and treating our guests as indeed guests, rather than just customers, is a great place to start.

Most people want to buy but they don't want to be sold. We've heard that many times before. They don't want to feel like they've been had. Most diners, I presume and there is good evidence to support this thought, don't want to be told what to order. They may not want you to suggest, recommend or guide them in their decision if they don't feel that they're being treated as a guest. They may feel they're being encouraged to order a particular special or menu item solely because it happens to be priced 20% higher than anything else on the menu. Diners want to feel that you are engaging them and that you care about their dining experience. If you only show interest when 'helping them order' something smells fishy and it's probably not yesterday's halibut.

On the other hand, the opposite extreme where a lot of servers tend to be is just order takers. "Are you ready to order? What will you have? And you sir? And you Ma'am?" And so on and so on. If that is the way you go about it, why have a human serving these guests?

Certainly a trained monkey, well, one that spoke and understood English, or a robot, could do that job. That's what I was actually told by someone once.

If your attitude is one of "I really don't care what my customer orders, they're the ones who're going to eat it, not me", then you have a long way in learning what **Getting to WOW!** is all about.

And that's okay, this is a journey. I'm assuming that you are reading this because at the very least, you desire to learn how to become a better server or to be able to glean some bit of information that can help you up your serving game even slightly. So, if this is you, I'm actually glad. I don't think anyone truly wants to just preach to the choir.

I'm writing this book today, after many years in this industry. I pride myself on the fact or at least the perceived assumption by me, that I've reached a certain level of excellence at this thing called the service business in knowledge, insight, understanding, attitude and execution.   I am fully cognizant that I was not always here. I have served many hundreds-no, I'm sure, thousands, of people in my life. And I often remind myself that early on-I was most likely not very memorable to many of those that I served. But I've learned and I've endeavored to be the best at whatever I do-including serving. I know that back when I started, I didn't' provide **WOW!** service.

So take heart, this book is not meant to be an attack or verbal assault on you if you don't currently employ or adopt the attitude, mentality and skills put forth here. I'm only sharing them as a way to raise the bar of what can and should be expected.

You may be at your first, second or third job as a server. Maybe you have very little experience, have never been trained properly and you've pretty much learned everything on your own. So, you most likely have developed some bad habits. Take heart. There is a great saying that makes a lot of sense to me that says,

"You did the best that you could with what you knew and when you knew better, you did better."

Maybe some of this is ringing true for you. It is my hope that this makes sense for you. I pray that my words here are not just blowing in the wind. So, if indeed what I'm putting forth here makes sense to you and you believe that these principles and ideas could make a difference in your service, then ask yourself this understood, implied, rhetorical question, "When would NOW be a good time to start?"

So, I said all of that to say this: Part of **WOW!** service is "Getting them to Get Tiramisu" the Baked Alaska, the Bananas Foster or the Soufflé. Getting them to Get Tiramisu is about upselling but it's so much more than that. Allow me to explain.

As I mentioned above, it is absolutely vital that we see our patrons as truly "guests". Paul Alexander, owner of Vin de Set, where I worked (and a number of other establishments in St. Louis), explained to us that we really have to imagine that these people coming to dine at our restaurant are actually coming to be guests at our home. He said, "Home" not "House". There is a warm and fuzzy feeling when you say, "Welcome to our home" to someone. If you treat your diners as guests, you will want to not only provide them with an exceptional or WOW! dining experience, but you will also want them to experience and enjoy the very best that you have to offer.   True or true?

So, here's my point: **You must get them to get the tiramisu, the soufflé or whatever is your dessert specialty.**

Why? Because say, for example that you work at The Eiffel Tower Restaurant at Paris, Las Vegas, like our friend JP DaLuz does. The food is exquisite and the service is impeccable there. And their Soufflés are AMAZING. Of course, they're a French restaurant. When we dined there JP didn't wait until after we finished dinner to ask, "Did you save any room for dessert?" If he had, the answer would be, "Of course not. We are stuffed." Instead, he mentioned it early in the course of our dinner. I don't remember if it was right at the beginning as he was taking our order, it may have been. What I do know is that at the beginning, he sold us on the soufflé.

Now of course, partially that's because the kitchen needs to know because they need to get the timing right as it takes about 20-30 minutes to make a soufflé. But even if it wasn't something that takes extra time, if it is something-a dessert that is absolutely wonderful-I say that you owe it to your guests to get them to get the soufflé. Why? Because if they don't you have just cheated them out of having a full and complete **WOW!** experience. That's right, you've deprived them of the full experience.

You know how, when someone is traveling to a place that they've never been to before and they ask you, "What should I make sure to get while I'm there?" It may be the hot dog at Coney Island, Gooey Butter Cake in St. Louis, Deep Dish Pizza in Chicago or Beignets in the French Quarter in New Orleans. Whatever it may be-if you don't get it-it's like you've missed something. For me, being from Ottawa, Illinois, its Bianchi's pizza. Anyone who's not from Ottawa, when they go there to visit, they must get Bianchi's pizza.

So I say it is actually your duty, your responsibility as a conscientious server to get your guests to get tiramisu. You will be doing them a favor and they will thank you afterward.

Most restaurants have something that is their signature. It doesn't have to be a dessert. It could be a specialty cocktail or even an appetizer.   There's a couple Italian restaurants in St. Louis that serve flash fried spinach.   You have to get it.   You'll love it.

So, this goes way beyond just upselling. But that is a side benefit of having this mentality. Rather than only thinking "What can I upsell to increase my guest check average?" Ask yourself, "What do we serve here that my guests absolutely must try?" When you put your focus on the guest first, then naturally you will sell more.

Isn't it interesting that at every restaurant the server who sells the most wine, most desserts and has the highest guest check average is ALWAYS the person who cares the most about their guests' dining experience and NOT the person who is the pushiest sales person? Don't get me wrong, you are in the sales business but the way you go about it will determine whether you are successful or just seen as a very pushy server. Of course, the caveat is, as we mentioned earlier, you must always read your
guests. Even though you have a plan in mind-that of getting them to get tiramisu-you have to be willing to adjust and modify according to the needs and wants of your guests.

Many restaurants do some type of tableside flambé presentation-bananas foster, baked Alaska, flambéed bread pudding, etc. If you have the opportunity when dining out to order such thing, do it. You will enjoy the experience.

Oh and the soufflé at The Eiffel Tower Restaurant? I ate a few bites of my wife's even though I rarely eat dairy, but I knew that I didn't want to miss out. And it was d-e-l-i-c-i-o-u-s! Now if we had not ordered the soufflé and we talked to others who know The Eiffel Tower Restaurant very well and they ask, "Did you get the soufflé?" And we responded with, "No, but our dinner was great." We would feel as though we didn't get the total experience.   "You didn't get the soufflé? That's too bad."

This is not about pressuring your guests or causing them to overspend or to get something that they don't want. People don't know what they don't know. If one has never experienced or tasted it-they cannot know if they want it or not. It is up to you guide them. So, please if you do care about your guests, don't hold back. Do them a favor and go for the upsell and get them to get the tiramisu. That is 5 star service and we all know that **Everybody WINS with 5 Star Service!**

After such an amazing dining experience, your guests will feel happy and utterly satisfied. Thanks to you and your team. What a wonderful feeling for both you and your guests.
And now, well, it just may be time for...

Chapter 21

Getting Them Where They Need to Go
Show Me the Way

"A leader is one who knows the way, goes the way, and shows the way."
John C. Maxwell

Here's a **WOW!** experience that's simple and easy to execute with multiple opportunities to practice it on a daily basis. This will make a lasting impression on your dining guests. And I'm not talking about calling them a taxi.

Scene:
Guest: Excuse me, sir, where is the lady's room?

Server: Go down the hallway, take a left, when you see the kitchen, go around the corner and take two steps down. If you see the elevator, then you've gone too far. Back track about 15 feet and take a right. You can't miss it.   But if you get lost, just come back and I'll explain it to you again.

Does that sound familiar? At so many restaurants, something to that effect seems to be the norm. And I suppose most people don't think twice about it. But really, there's not a whole lot of service involved there.

Okay, here's a simple **WOW!** idea taught to me by Mandy, who was the GM of J. Bucks in St. Louis, when I worked there. What do they do that is so amazing? Well for starters, they never tell people where the restrooms are located.   And I mean never.

"What?!" you say, "That's not very courteous or nice or good service." They also don't ever even direct guests to the restroom. Instead, they simply SHOW them. That's right. They take the time and they walk their guests to the restroom. They show them and then there is no getting lost. There's no mistaking did she say left or right at the end of the long hallway?

Maybe it's because St. Louis is in Missouri, which is known as the 'Show Me' state. I'm not sure. Certainly not all restaurants in St. Louis do this. Maybe it's because the people at J. Buck's in St. Louis, know how much of an impact something seemingly so insignificant, can actually have upon their guests.

If a guest happens to ask a bartender behind the bar who is very busy, or someone who has a tray of food in their hand, and if that staff member is not able at that moment to actually walk the guest, they will say to the guest, "Just a moment, please, Ma'am." Then they will request a nearby colleague to escort the guest to the restroom. Yes it may seem like a very small thing, but the impression is lasting. Think about it. If the people at an establishment think that something so insignificant as showing where the restroom is, is important, it's more than likely that they take pride in other seemingly, small things as well. Like, the cleanliness of said restroom.

So, next time your guest asks you where the restroom is, take the few extra seconds and walk them to where it is located. Or at least close enough that you can then stretch out your hand and say- "right there, sir, ma'am, up that step."

Yes, it's simple. It's just walking them to the restroom. Yes, it will take a few seconds of your time, but I guarantee it will definitely make a lasting, positive impression on them. I'm also willing to bet you that more than a couple of them will comment either to their companions, or to you how impressed they are.

And their comment will be "Wow, now that is service." Imagine if they haven't even begun their dining experience yet. You have just set the tone of, helpfulness, courtesy and friendliness. They already have a good first impression of you and your establishment.

They say going the extra mile is important in establishing rapport with a customer and in showing that you care. Well, I say, how about just going the extra 30 feet?
I rest my case.

Chapter 22

Getting Past the Soupfly

Waiter, what's this fly doing in my soup?
Um, looks to me to be the backstroke, sir
...Oldest Restaurant Joke in the Book

"...Isn't it ironic?"
Alannis Morissette

*Note-The beginning of this chapter first appeared as the inaugural post of my blog-entitled Soupfly. You will notice the subtitle has changed since this post, it is now: **Getting to WOW! Everybody WINS with 5 Star Service.**

WHEN THE WORLD BRINGS YOU SOUP AND THERE'S A FLY IN IT

I'm in the process of writing-well, actually, finishing a book about restaurant service entitled, **Getting to WOW!** First Class Restaurant Service
So, why wouldn't my blog be the same title as my book? Good question. For one, I think it's catchy-"Soupfly". But beyond that, since my book is about Service-and First Class Restaurant Service- I wanted a title that would be memorable. Of course, I could call my blog-"Excellent Restaurant Service". But then you'd be compelled to remember-wait, was it "Restaurant Service Excellence"? Or "Excellence in Restaurant Service"? Or... you get the idea.

So... -yep, Soupfly, it is. Yes, I've made it a compound noun. That's right-Soupfly.   No, it's not in the dictionary.   But someday it may be.

Now to be forthright-I hate when people say-"to be honest with you". Well, what have you been until now? Less than honest? But I digest. Digress.

Actually, in all my years of working in the service industry-I have never actually seen a fly in someone's soup, ever. We've all heard Alannis Morisette sing of "a black fly in your Chardonnay". And that may make more sense and be more realistic, perhaps, but it certainly is not quick and easy to type. Nor is it short and sweet and a great name for a blog. A BLACK FLY IN YOUR CHARDONNAY. More likely, it would be a fruitfly in your Chardonnay.   But this is my blog and I like my title so, hence it is now and ever shall be called SOUPFLY.   Unless I decide to change it.

Aside from all the above drivel, (or is it drivvel?), let's be serious for a moment. The concept of Soupfly is actually the antithesis of Excellent Restaurant Service and it presents an opportunity to respond in a way that allows you to provide exceptional customer service. Now, granted, I am currently not working as a server today but if I were, I would not necessarily hope for but I am quite certain that I would welcome a Soupfly. For such an event is rich with possibilities.

So, let's consider: If there were a fly in my guest's soup, how would I respond?

First, I believe it's important to clarify-Is the fly floating visibly on top of the soup or does our diner discover it as he spoons a bit and is about to bring it to his mouth?

If indeed, the fly is floating on top of the soup as if it were enjoying a mid-afternoon summer day on an inflatable raft, sunning itself and enjoying an adult beverage while in the soup, then shame on me, the server, for not paying closer attention while picking up said bowl.

In this case the lesson of the Soupfly is: we must pay attention to details. If you as a server walk into the kitchen, chef says order up and you grab the bowl of soup and don't really look at it, inspect it before you leave the kitchen, then I would say you're not really a very conscientious server.

There is a principle that states:
"You can't expect what you don't inspect.'"

You must be aware of and know what you are bringing to your guest. Is it what they ordered?   Is it prepared correctly?-Any requested modifications,
i.e. sauce on the side, no bacon etc., done as ordered? Do not blame the kitchen or your chef if a Soupfly is just floating comfortably on the surface of the soup and you don't notice it until after you've served it to your guest. If it's visible, then you my friend are responsible.   You may have not placed it there but it's on you if you bring it to your guest.

Next scenario-
You serve your guest the soup, no visible Soupfly.   You've carefully perused the surface of the soup, nothing visible but the soup itself and steam coming off of it.   A few moments later, however, your guest flags you over to witness that indeed there is a fly in their soup, or a hair in their pasta or a fingernail in their gumbo or even a Band-Aid in their chili.

Side note-in my opinion, none of the above are very catchy blog titles-"Gumbo fingernail", "Pasta hair", etc.
The difference, however, is that though a Soupfly would most likely be visible on top of soup, a hair in the pasta or the other two examples would not be. So, if said foreign object is immersed, hidden, folded in or tossed together and not visible in the food, then of course you cannot be held responsible for unknowingly bringing it to your guest. At this point, it really is irrelevant how it got there, the only thing that matters is how will you respond?

I have seen servers actually stand there and argue with the guest as to whether the foreign object came from the kitchen or whether it was planted there. They say things like, "Sir, there was no fly in your soup when I brought it out to you. I know your type, always trying to get something for free.   Well, I'm not buying it."
Others might say something to the effect of, "Look sir, I didn't make your soup, I can't control what goes on back in that kitchen. I'm just a server. Do you want me to get you something else?"
Others will completely shirk any responsibility and simply say, "Do you want to talk to a manager?"

So, back to the title-"Soupfly". Soupfly brings out in a person whatever is already intrinsically there. If I served a guest soup and they told me there was a Soupfly in it, my response would be very different from any of the above.   Rather, I would first apologize profusely.

Second, I would ensure them that this Has Never Happened Before. And if it were now clearly visible on the surface of the soup, I would say, "Shame on me. I thought I looked. It is absolutely my fault and I am so very sorry that I missed it. We are going to remedy this situation immediately."

Now, if what you ordered was your absolute favorite, say, an amazing bouillabaisse-if you are like most people, you probably don't want a new, freshly made, clean bowl of the same sans the Soupfly. Just the sight of the same dish still conjures up repulsive memories and an emotional gut response that certainly doesn't entice one to attempt it again. You've lost your appetite (and your faith in humanity) well, maybe not the latter. If it were me all I could think of doing is cringeing and saying "G-r-r-o-s-s."

Welcome back to another serving of Soupfly

As we discussed previously, the Soupfly, as well as being an actual literal event, (the soup with a fly in it) it more often is a metaphor for what could go wrong in restaurant service.

The restaurant business is filled with so many variables and unforeseen and oftentimes uncontrollable circumstances. Circumstances that the server often feels powerless to have any effect over. The Restaurant Business/Food and Beverage industry seems to be unlike any other. You're not selling a car, a tailored suit, a Starbucks coffee or even a set of Encyclopedias. In any one of those examples, you, the seller and they, the buyer, pretty much know what to expect. If you sell someone a Honda Accord-that's what they'll get. And they get to actually test drive the vehicle and see the actual product before taking ownership of it. They don't have to wonder if they'll get a Honda with an Anaconda in it. Unless they're buying one in the Republic of Myanmar (Burma).

If you are in retail, same situation-your customers actually see and even try on what they're buying as they select it. There's no mystery in what they're going to get- well maybe in online shopping. Yes, I know this is all very basic. We all know this. I'm just saying this to make my point.   In this business, however, your guests at the restaurant do not get to try it before they buy it. Nor do they have the privilege of test driving a bunch of different samples.

"I'll try some of the nachos, the fried calamari and the sliders. They all sound very good. Let me just taste of few of each, then I'll let you know which one I'm actually going to decide to buy."

Of course that's not gonna happen. That would be ludicrous. My point? Sometimes, there's going to be a Soupfly-steak not done to guest's specifications; risotto is waaaay too salty; the server brings you soup and there's no fly in it but he does spill it all over your lap.   Ow!

There's a myriad of things that can happen and do happen. Mishaps, accidents and mistakes.   Human error and otherwise. Circumstances that are less than pleasant. Some avoidable, some maybe not. Some even painful.

The question is how do you respond when a Soupfly happens? Do you fly off the handle? (Ok maybe a bit of a pun there. Sorry.) Do you blame the kitchen staff or look for others to point at? Do you become defensive and make it about you? Do you empathize with your guest and show true care and concern? Or do you argue with the guest or someone else about who really is at fault?   Do you ignore the guest complaint and just act as if it didn't even happen? Do you suddenly go on a smoke break and disappear so you don't have to "deal with it"?

Unfortunately, I've either witnessed or personally have experienced co-workers, managers and even owners respond to Soupflies in all of the above ways. Perhaps sometimes when something as unpleasant as a Soupfly happens, the server may think that now this guest's dining experience is ruined and that they're bound to leave here-the restaurant-upset, angry and bad-mouthing the establishment. It's a foregone conclusion.

Well, I don't believe that. Why? Because it has also been my experience that the exact opposite is absolutely possible. Any Soupfly incident, I believe, can be turned around and the end result the guest leaves having had a *WOW!* dining experience. Is it easy to do? No, but it is entirely possible. You may think that the odds are not in your favor but I actually believe that they are.

Guest: Excuse me, Sir, I have a complaint. Server: Oh? What seems to be the problem?

Guest: I ordered my steak medium rare and this steak is well done.
OR
Guest: I thought I was getting a baked potato with my dinner but you gave me mashed- I hate mashed potatoes.
OR
Guest: This coffee is not even lukewarm.   It's disgusting.
OR

Guest: This fish tastes like it's turned and now I feel like my stomach is going to turn.
OR
Guest: We've been sitting here for 15 minutes and we don't even have a drink yet. How long will we have to wait for our food?

And the list goes on and on and on and on. Guests complain not only about the food but also about the poor or slow service that they receive, about dirty seats or utensils or about something that a server may have said to them or their not very pleasant attitude.
There is no limit to the number and types of things people will and do complain about in restaurants.
Guests will complain. It is to be expected. Some people complain because they didn't get what they ordered, hoped for or expected.

Some complaints are legitimate and justified. Other times their complaints may seem unreasonable, even ridiculous to you. Some people complain because they want their meal the way they want it. Some people are not easily satisfied and have very specific requirements and very exacting standards.   Others are just complainers by nature.

Since we know that complaints will come -my question is - How do you respond?

Do you tell the guest, "I'm sorry Sir, there's nothing I can do about that." Do you tell the manager and leave it up to them?

Do you take their dinner back to the kitchen, fix it or replace it with a new one?

Do you walk away and pretend that you didn't even hear them? What is the best way to respond and to deal with complaints?

Getting Your Guests to Complain

Well before we even talk about how to respond to complaints, let's make sure that we are getting them in a timely manner. You should want your guests to complain.

What do I mean by this? Well, oftentimes guests don't complain until after they've left the building.

Jim Edwards of Next Door Food & Drink says,

"I wish they would just tell their server if something is not right. I hate getting the complaint after the fact. If they would just let me know, I could fix that problem in 10 seconds."

How does one make sure that a guest is actually conveying what they truly feel about their experience? It starts, as we mentioned earlier, in the first 5 minutes.

The guest must be made to feel comfortable from the very outset. Edwards explains,

"It comes from a genuineness in the server. If you're really genuine with your guests at the table and they feel that, the attention you're giving, making eye contact, showing that you're really listening and that you really want to take care of them in this dining experience, when they feel that, then if something isn't quite right, they'll tell you about it."

So, taking a cue from Jim Edwards, let's assume that indeed that you're guest has no problem voicing their dissatisfaction-that is complaining to you, what do we do?

First, one thing we must realize is that no matter how absurd or seemingly petty the guest's complaint may appear to you, it appears absolutely reasonable and makes complete and logical sense in the mind of the one doing the complaining.

In my experience, I've found that it all begins with a positive attitude on the part of the server. Remember our MAP from Chapter 1? If you show genuine care and concern, that is, if you can convey to the guest that you actually want them to be happy and satisfied then, that is a good first step forward. Many times a guest will become more upset if they believe or feel that you are trying to appease them rather than addressing and fixing the problem.

It is my belief, that no matter how big the problem-how seemingly grave the situation is-it is always still somehow redeemable. I would even go so far as to say that if a guest has a complaint that providing a **WOW!** experience is still possible and not a foregone conclusion. If the guest is willing, then I believe there is still an opportunity to turn around any situation. But it will take a concerted effort, not just by you, but most likely, by yourself and many others of your team.

How should we handle/respond to complaints?

1.   Acknowledge the complaint, the problem, the perceived wrong done.

Dr. Phil is famous for espousing this principle.   It's simple but profound.
"You can't fix what you don't acknowledge."

Agree with the guest that something (even if in their mind) was not done properly, to their liking or the way that they expected it to be. This does not mean that they are correct but at least you acknowledging their dissatisfaction is the important part.

"Sir, I understand that you told the server/me that you wanted your steak to be cooked medium rare, I agree with you that steak you have is clearly not medium rare."

Jim Edwards calls it *"Validating their concern"*

2.   Apologize -Two Very Powerful Words - "I'm Sorry"

I don't think it matters who made the mistake at this point. There is no value in saying "It wasn't my fault."
Any number of things could have transpired. You, the server could have written down one thing- 'medium rare' and then typed in or hit the wrong button on the POS system- 'medium well'. You could have typed in 'medium rare' and the chef cooked it medium rare but the expo person sent out the wrong steak to your table. You could have taken this guest's steak to the right or wrong table but given it to the wrong person. Stuff happens.

At this point it really doesn't matter who messed up. And the guest certainly doesn't care who did it. They are dealing with you. You are the representative of the restaurant to them.   Figuring out whose fault it is, is something to be dealt with internally between you and the staff and management at a later time.
But the issue at hand is the situation with your guest.

Acknowledge and then apologize to your guest. If you know you made the mistake then, by all means, say you are sorry.

I have known managers and have even interviewed some who state outright to me that they Do NOT Ever apologize to the guests. Rather, they just seek to find a solution to the problem without actually admitting fault or wrongdoing. I'm not sure if it's because we live in such an overly litigious society that they fear actually admitting fault would make them fodder for being sued. I, however, DO NOT agree with this mentality. If you've made a mistake, done wrong-admit it. **Take responsibility and move on to making it right.**

If it wasn't your fault-still, do not point the finger at someone else. That is very small of you as a person. That is not going to build rapport with your guest. So please don't say "I rang it in right but the kitchen messed up."   Or anything to that effect. Instead, own it.

They are your guests. They don't know anybody in the kitchen. The manager is not the one waiting on them. You are.

If you know for a fact that it wasn't you specifically that screwed up, it doesn't really matter. Just make it plural, say "I am so sorry, We messed up but We are going to make it right."

By apologizing and acknowledging fault you will, most of the time begin to defuse the situation. Your guest may still be upset or not happy but you are now on the road to turning the situation around. I will put odds in your favor that by taking ownership of the situation you can begin to earn some respect in the eyes of your guests.

Let them feel that you are on their side.

3.   Be Humble and Do Not be Argumentative

By following the first two steps alone, oftentimes the intensity of the situation can be diffused. It's like opening the valve and letting the steam out. If you say to your guest, "Sir, Ma'am, I am so very sorry that this happened. It is my fault. Please forgive me. We are going to fix this right away." They most likely are going to forgive you. How can the guest argue with someone who is offering no resistance? They really can't.

Chef Adam Gnau of Acero Restaurant, cautions servers against doing what some in the business do and that's taking a passive aggressive approach. They agree with the guest but in a condescending or sarcastic way.

He says, *"It's never okay to tell a guest that they are wrong or to argue with them. The customer IS always right, even if they're not."* Adam says the only way is to, *"Kill them with kindness."*

On the contrary, what I see that often happens, instead, is that the server, or the manager offer a half-hearted, feebly spoken, "I'm sorry". But that's never followed with "please forgive me". "I'm sorry" is just the first half of an apology." Without saying "Please forgive me", it's incomplete in my opinion.

4.   Communicate to your Manager/Supervisor

This is of vital importance. It's not important how seemingly small and relatively insignificant the problem may or may not be-in your eyes. You really don't know how your guest is looking at it. It doesn't matter how quickly and easily you were able to remedy the problem-you must inform your supervisor/manager. After all, it is not your restaurant and management needs to be apprised of any complaints just in case the guest brings it up as they are leaving or if they call a couple of days later.

It's important for the manager to know and be aware of any potential backlash. It also gives them an opportunity to apologize again to the guest or to offer some compensation or to authorize you to do something more than just fixing the problem. If for no other reason than for information sake then it is important for you to do so. So you can be rest assured that you've covered all your bases.

Don't think- "Well I told the chef- he knows". Unless the chef is part owner or considered part of the management team, you still MUST go the next step and tell someone in management who is interacting or at least overseeing what is going on in the dining room.

You can't expect your manager to have your back if a guest springs a surprise on him as they are leaving if he has no knowledge of what occurred and this is the first time that he is hearing of it. But if they are aware they can back you up and also participate in turning the situation around.

You might have fixed the problem in your eyes but some guests don't like the fact that a manager wasn't told. To them it may seem like you're attempting to make light of the situation and then whatever you've done to remedy the situation would be for naught because the guests are upset that management was unaware of the grievous error that was committed.   So, I implore you -Please tell your manager!

5.   Fix the Problem immediately

And I do mean *immediately*.
Whatever else you have going on-this now needs to become priority Number 1. If you have food that needs to go out to another table, enlist the assistance of a team mate or manager or someone. As you head back to the kitchen you should pass by any table along your way that may be waiting or expecting something from you and tell them that it may take a couple minutes longer than you expected because you have to go fix a problem. Do this quickly. A little communication will go a long way.

Go back to the kitchen and make it right. Do not engage in an argument with the chef, the kitchen manager, the expo person. If you made a mistake acknowledge it and apologize. If it wasn't your fault just be humble and ask them, the chef, whomever to please fix it.
Now is not the time to place blame. Telling the chef he screwed up is not going to motivate him to want to expedite fixing the problem. Chefs are known, as many creatives are, to have huge egos and short fuses-not all, but many. So, please do not engage them in a discussion of whose fault it was.

So often at this point, it becomes a long drawn out conversation or argument between the manager, the server, the kitchen staff, or the chef. "Well, why did you ring it in that way?"
"I told you he didn't want any garlic." "I thought you said 'no added garlic'." "No I said 'no garlic'"
"yada, yada, yada."
All the while, the guest is still waiting for their order to be done right. That IS NOT WHAT YOU WANT.

Also, as Chef Gnau mentioned to me that he has witnessed, as I'm sure many of us have, servers in the kitchen, not arguing with the kitchen staff, but instead bad-mouthing the guest who made the complaint. This, too, is absolutely not acceptable and should not be tolerated in any restaurant. What would happen if as you are standing there either arguing or bad mouthing the guest, and they actually either walk into your kitchen or poke their head in and hear what has just been said? That would not be a very good situation and that's putting it lightly.

Right now the focus and energy should be on one thing and one thing only-Getting it Right.
The clock is ticking and the guest is fuming.   No conversation in the kitchen will make the guest happy.

Now, I know that there are times when a manager wants to know who screwed up. If he's going to have the chef put another steak on the grill he's got to account for it.   Filet mignon is not cheap.
True but an angry unpleased customer will tell more people, write a negative review and the damage will be many times greater than the cost of one steak.

I do understand the manager's perspective. However, I, as the server, would just ask the manager if we could continue the discussion later, once the problem has been fixed.

For now, let's just focus on getting the man his food the way he wants it and we can re-visit and discuss who dropped the ball later.

If possible, try to ascertain a reasonable estimated time that the fixed proper dish will be ready to take out to the guest.
And then...

6.   Return to your Guest and Communicate with them

"Sir, I just talked with the chef and he has another steak already on the grill. He says it will be about another 13 minutes or so. Again, I do apologize and thank you for your patience."

7.   Offer them something to eat or drink while they are waiting for the item being re-made to be brought out

Of, course every restaurant is different as to what their policies of what you are authorized to do in such situation. If possible, maybe you can bring a small plate of pasta out to your guest to eat while waiting for his steak.   That way he is not the only one at the table not dining.   If that is not possible or allowed where you work, certainly something as simple as a free glass of wine or another cocktail on the house would be in order. If that's not allowed, then certainly your manager will not prevent you from actually buying a cocktail, glass of wine, or whatever for your guest.

If that is the case, I highly recommend that you do it and bring it to your guest saying "This is on me." Your guest may readily accept it, hoping that you would've done something like that or they may be a bit uncomfortable accepting something that they didn't order or pay for. Either way, I believe you are now on track to winning your guest over.

8.   The Manager Should Always, Be the One to Bring the New, Freshly Cooked, Properly Prepared Item, to the Guest

I realize that you may work at a restaurant where a manager is not available, for whatever reason. If that be the case, then of course, you, the server must bring the item to your guest and apologize once again and thank them for their patience.

It is quite unfortunate that many owners and managers are more concerned with their bottom line than the ultimate experience of their guests. They feel that if one of their staff messes up, they should not have to underwrite the cost of appeasing the displeased customer. You often hear them say things like "We can't be giving away the store every time one of you messes up."
"We're not in business to give food away." Etc, etc.

If you find yourself in such an environment maybe you ought to consider finding an establishment that values the guest's experience above the company's bottom line.

Complaints will happen. But if you can defuse the situation quickly, if you communicate with your manager immediately, if you let the guest know that you truly care and that you are sorry for the mistake and that your number one priority right now is making it right, then I truly believe with all my heart, that you still have an opportunity for your guest to walk away from their dinner having been "Wowed" by you. This is not just theory, I know this to be true because I've seen it happen and have been a part of it many, many times.

So what is the determining factor in all of this? Your demeanor, your care and concern, your attitude under pressure and the way you handled the situation. Because, ultimately, that's the only thing you have absolute control over- you, what you do and how you respond.

I am personally not fazed by complaints. I see them as opportunities. Some guests don't voice their complaints until they are heading out the door, after the opportunity to fix it, make a new dish or change it, is gone. So then what does one do? If they are still inside your establishment, there are still so many things that can be done or offered to make it right.

Certainly, addressing the situation and asking them to come back and give us another chance is one thing at the very minimum that should be done.

Depending on what the problem or complaint is a free after dinner drink, a free dessert, a gift certificate for next time, all are small things that could be offered. But oftentimes if the guest is on the way out the door, just a sincere "I'm sorry and please give us an opportunity to do better next time," may soften their heart enough to consider a return visit.

Or perhaps, you just may say to them, "Soupflies are bound to happen once in a while, and the fact that it happened to you, well, isn't it ironic?"

I'm kidding, I hope you realize that.
In all seriousness, your next goal now has to be...

Chapter 23

Getting the Recovery

"... the end result has to be more than just a fixed problem. It is about restoring confidence. You want the customer to say this: "I love doing business with them. Even when there is a problem, I can count on them."
Shep Hyken, Amaze Every Customer Every Time

"I tell my staff all the time, Every restaurant has problems. How you deal with them is what sets you apart. How you handle a situation yields more money in the long run because now the manager or owner gets involved, the situation is not only fixed but turned around. All of a sudden that guest now leaves a 25% tip."
Jim Edwards, Owner Next Door Food & Drink, Loveland, Colorado

This is now where the opportunity to woo your guest back and **WOW!** them takes center focus and full effect. How do you do this? There's really no cut and dry method, but I believe it begins with maintaining that humble attitude and communicating your desire to still make this an excellent dining experience for your guest.

You may even state that to them, saying something to the effect of: "Sir, Ma'am, Mr. So and So, My friends, (however you address them) I know we dropped the ball at the beginning but it's still my desire to make sure you leave here happy that you came to dine here with us tonight."
Don't ever ask your guest what they want you to do to make up for the Soupfly. You must offer and make suggestions. If their food was prepared improperly or it's too salty or cold or whatever the case may be you-the server (and sometimes the manager) must make decisions and take the proper action that will make the situation right.

Do not put your guest in the uncomfortable situation of them having to decide what should be done. They are the guest. Make them feel welcome and put them at ease. And get it right for them. They are here to dine, to have a pleasant experience. It is your job to make sure that happens. Find a way.

Next, it's time for action. Fix the problem. Re-fire the proper food. Help clean up a spill. Tell them the restaurant will take care of the dry-cleaning bill, etc. One other reason it's so important that you communicate with your manager about the Fly in the Soup is that now you can enlist them and the kitchen's help to win your guest back. A special appetizer, another specialty cocktail or bottle of champagne. There are so many things that can be done to let your guests feel special. Accidents happen. People make mistakes. Even chefs. Now we move on.

They are the guest. Make them feel welcome and put them at ease. And get it right for them. They are here to dine, to have a pleasant experience. It is your job to make sure that happens. Find a way.
I wouldn't recommend reiterating or commenting on the Soupfly incident repeatedly over the course of the rest of the evening. What's done is done. Now you focus on providing exceptional service and you have the opportunity to **WOW!** them. Be Creative.
Don't just say "We'll just take it off the bill." This happens all too often and that is Definitely NOT providing excellent service. That is the absolute bare minimum that should be done.

A Soupfly is an Opportunity. They will happen. Be ready, be prepared and believe that you can turn the situation around.
In fact, some guests become lifelong regulars of restaurants because a Soupfly –a potential disaster, was turned around and that guest, that customer was won over. They can become your raving, diehard fans if you take the time and put in the effort to make it right.

Complaints will happen. But if you can defuse the situation quickly, if you communicate with your manager immediately, if you let the guest know that you truly care and that you are sorry for the mistake and that your number one priority right now is making it right, then I truly believe with all my heart, that you still have an opportunity for your guest to walk away from their dinner having been "**WOWed**" by you. This is not just theory, I know this to be true because I've seen it happen and have been a part of it many, many times.

So what is the determining factor in all of this? Your demeanor, your care and concern, your attitude under pressure and the way you handled the situation. Because, ultimately, that's the only thing you have absolute control over- you, what you do and how you respond.

When I was interviewing my friend, Greg DaLuz for this book he said something that I thought at first was a little audacious. He said:
"Its something that I can't teach. I have a smoothness, an intrinsic charm that, I have the ability, if your entrée was 45 minutes late, you hated your cocktail, you found gum under your table- even after all that, I have the ability to, still, after all that, to smooth out dinner and show you a good time. And keep you from complaining and telling ten of your friends that you hated us. I am thankful that I have this ability. I thank God that I have it. I feel blessed to have it. People perceive me very calmly and I'm able to build a nice following from it."

Truth be told, Greg's statement is completely accurate and not boastful in the least. And I know this because Michelle and I experienced it first hand when we first dined where Greg was managing at the now defunct, Pizza Lounge at Tivoli Village in Summerlin (Las Vegas).

We waited for a very long time for a server to come to our table once we were seated. Next, our appetizers took nearly 20 minutes-for a hummus plate. The pizzas that we ordered were both wrong. Nothing seemed to be going right and yet-Greg being Greg, indeed smoothed it over. I don't know what he said. But I do know that we became regulars at the Pizza Lounge. The place had many inconsistencies, and yet we kept going back because we knew that if Greg was there, that ultimately everything was going to be great.

So, maybe it's not something that Greg can teach, but it should be something that others can emulate from him. He may have a special gift, but I believe that with the right attitude and humility, we can all learn how to turn unfortunate Soupflies around and get the recovery. In fact, some guests become lifelong regulars of restaurants, because a Soupfly –a potential disaster was turned around and that guest, that customer, was won over. They can become your raving, diehard fans if you take the time and put in the effort to make it right.

One last thought-First impressions are so important in every business. But maybe even more so in the restaurant business. How a guest is greeted and seated, how the server approaches a table, and a host of other factors, all work together in setting the tone for a guest's dining experience. If the right tone is set from the beginning and later a Soupfly does unfortunately, occur-it is much easier to get to a successful Recovery.

A Short Word Regarding Online Reviews and Complaints

Yelp, Trip Advisor, Open Table, Chow Hound, And Urban Spoon. There is no limit to the online review sites and more seem to be cropping up all the time. These sites allow the diner to rate and review and rant and complain in a public online forum.

While there is definitely some positive value of these sites, as many diners actually do use them to praise a restaurant's good points. However, many of the managers and owners that I spoke with, tell me that although they know they must be responsible and monitor these reviews on a daily basis-they are also the bane of their existence as restaurant managers.

Joe Cortes, of Honey Salt in Las Vegas, says that he and his management team spend a considerable amount of time every day searching the sites-not so much to find the praises to pass onto their staff but more specifically to be the first to see any negative reviews or dissatisfaction expressed by a guest. I'm pretty sure that they actually get alerts each time a new review is posted. It's a reality that most everyone with a smart phone or a pc can now be a self-ordained restaurant critic.

I know that while most of the owners and managers that I spoke with do not relish these reviews, they know the power of the internet. And it's no longer just word of mouth-because in the old days-true word of mouth was one person telling another person that they know, and another and another-one at a time. We all know that bad news travels ten times faster than good news. Well compound that by about 1000, now with the power of the internet. Is this fair? Probably not all the time. But it is reality.

That is why Joe Cortes and others, like Mitchell Sjevern of Bouchon of Santa Barbara all say, *"If you, as a guest have a complaint, please tell us. Give us the opportunity to know about it while you are still within the walls of our establishment."*

Once a guest is gone from the restaurant, the server, the manager or the owner are all now powerless to make your experience right. They will never again have the opportunity to make that visit-that particular experience, right.

And the chances of that guest returning to give them a second chance-if the manager sees the negative review and invites the guest to return-are extremely slim. Why? Because most people live in cities or towns where there's a myriad of options of restaurants to choose from. They would rather just go to a place where they know what to expect in service and food quality, or try another new place, rather than give another shot to a place that has already failed them once.

I do not envy this predicament that restaurant owners and managers find themselves in. I do agree with them completely that if a guest is dissatisfied-they should tell their server, or ask for a manager while they are still at the restaurant.
It costs so much to acquire new clients in this business, and it is our responsibility, your responsibility to provide them with a great dining experience and multiple reasons that they will not only want to come back, but will want to tell their friends about the place as well.
So, are all reviews on these online sites accurate? No. Sometimes a person may not understand what they are eating. If a guest has never eaten caviar before- and they order it and complain that it is too salty-that's not a well-informed complaint. But of course that guest is entitled to their opinion.

Sjevern explained to me that he prefers Open Table as a review site because the reviewer is required to actually make a reservation through the Open Table site and have a confirmed dining reservation in order to post a review of said restaurant. Meaning, that if they didn't actually make a reservation and keep the reservation they can't just go online to Open Table and write a bogus review. So, the date, the time, the serving staff, all of it can be checked out and verified. Unlike other sites, like Yelp, where one only need open an account and they can write a review of any place they want, whether they've been there or not.

What I did find very interesting in my conversation with Joe Cortes, even though he stated how much their management can dislike review sites like Yelp, he did admit to using them himself when seeking out new establishments for him to patronize.

A few last thoughts: If you are one who uses these sites and writes reviews, please, I encourage you to also verbally share your praise and your complaints to the management BEFORE you leave the restaurant. Give them a chance to do right for you. If you are a server or bartender and you read reviews online-please do not engage the reviewer in an online argument as Jon Favreau's character did with the food critic in the movie Chef. It was not a pretty scene and it led to him, the Chef, losing his job.

I know it hurts to read negative reviews about you, whether they have truth in them or not. I would advise you to take it with a grain of salt. Examine yourself and see if there might be some area that you can improve upon in your service and make adjustments. We are all works in progress.

And finally, if you are an owner or manager and you monitor the online reviews of your establishment, I implore you, please, remember to share with your staff the positive reviews with your team, and NOT just the negative ones. In fact, make it a point to make a bigger deal out of the positive ones than the negative ones. Use the negative ones to coach individuals, one on one. But broadcast the positive ones to the entire staff. Even post them where they are visible for everyone to see them and watch it foster greater teamwork, uplift their spirits and inspire them to repeat the same. Catch them doing right.

The recovery is definitely possible and once you've got that- or, if there was no complaint and the guest just had a very gratifying, wonderful experience at your establishment, you will now want to solidify that positive experience in their mind.
This may be the perfect opportunity for...

Chapter 24

Getting Anchored
(The Power of Touch)

"Anchoring can be utilized in a customer service situation by reinforcing a positive state, for instance, the happy satisfied feeling a person feels after a good dining experience….If you do that the next time you see them, they will experience this same happy feeling again and may soon find that your restaurant is their favorite place to eat."
Marlo Shay Boutte', Hypnotherapist / NLP Practioner

Now I'm about to broach a subject which may be controversial to some-to others, it may seem like no big deal. Some of you may be thinking 'Why even waste time and paper on the subject?" Others of you may be saying, "What?!   The power of touch?   Are we getting sexual here?"

Well, actually, sexual energy and sales energy are almost the same thing. Have you ever known someone who was a great salesperson? Any kind of sales-people who excel at sales- 90% or more are very sexual individuals.

NO, I'm not talking about people who are rude and crude, making verbal sexual innuendos. What I am talking about here is energy, and sales and sexual energy to me are one and the same.

Now when I say the power of touch-I'm not talking about a sexy, scantily clad cocktail waitress bending over, dangling her breasts in front of you and putting her hand on your knee, asking if you're ready for another margarita. That's obviously overt and crossing the line.

I'm talking about a handshake, a hand on the shoulder-a physical non-overtly sexual connection with someone as you ask them a question related to their dining experience. Of course, one has to be adept to some degree at reading people-as not everyone welcomes or enjoys being touched at all by strangers apart from a handshake.

However, there is something about this business that opens people up.

Consider this, they-your guests-are at your establishment to enjoy good food, wine perhaps, music and good company-it is natural to offer a gesture of welcoming. A touch on the person's shoulder, or even a hug as they're leaving may not be out of line.

The most successful restaurant owners, managers and maître d's seem very comfortable and adept at this. They generally tend to be very out-going and people persons. If you've ever had the privilege of dining at Spago or any of the other Wolfgang Puck restaurants while he was in house, you would have most likely at least viewed this, if not actually experienced it as well.

If you are a regular guest at his establishments and he comes to your table, the first thing Wolfgang will do is place a hand on your shoulder as he shakes your other hand. When he lets go of the hand he is shaking, he will keep the other one resting on your shoulder while he is engaging you and your dinner party. Certainly what he says is important and special but that is not the focus here.

This simple gesture accomplishes so many powerful things. For one, it obviously makes the person who is the focus of his attention feel wonderful. Why? Because we all enjoy being made to feel special. Even though you may see Wolfgang go to a myriad of other tables in the restaurant and perform this same ritual-it does in no way lessen the impact and the positive effect it has upon you, when you are the recipient of it. By him doing this, in the eyes of your dinner guests, you are a king. Special.   A friend of Wolfgang.   That's pretty amazing.

Think of certain ethnic groups-Greeks, Italians, Spanish- others that talk with their hands a lot and hug and kiss everyone.   Greeks, Italians, people from Latin America, actually, many cultures except Americans. Well, and the British. Most cultures of the world seem to understand the power of touch. It's not uncommon if someone is thanking me for the dinner they just had at the restaurant that I'm working at, for me to give them a hug and thank them or vice versa.

I don't do it unless it feels natural and I perceive that it would be welcomed by the other individual.   I am sure that it somehow subconsciously seals the deal or anchors in their mind a good feeling that they associate either with me or the restaurant or both. They enjoyed their dinner, the food, the wine and the service and they are experiencing a feeling of well-being, and verbally acknowledging it out loud-by thanking you-using the power of touch, the hug, the handshake, the hand on the shoulder reinforces that feeling. And I'm quite sure that they will be back. These expressions of touch will impress upon them that they must be back.

In fact, if you understand anything about NLP-neurolinguistic programming-it's actually a very good example of anchoring. A physical connection, a handshake, a hug during a high emotional state helps impress upon the person's psyche that that place-your restaurant(hopefully) was a great place and a great experience for them and a memorable event.

And that, my friend is what **Getting WOW!-**comes down to, a memorable event, a wonderful experience, an expression of happiness and joy.

Two of my friends happen to be experts on the subject, Marlo Boutte, and Hanna Redi are both NLP practitioners and licensed Hypnotherapists. Here's what they have to say:

"NLP offers a variety of communication skills based on successful peoples thought processes. We all have a strategy for arriving at an emotion. It reveals the connections between our perceptions of situations, the pictures we run in our minds creating our language to ourselves and how this affects our neurology, affecting our behavior thus affecting our communication with others and ourselves. My personal interpretation of NLP in laymans terms is, it's a method to stop being a victim of your negative emotions. It's about owning your inner world.

The beauty of Neuro-Linguistic Programming is that you don't have to believe it for it to work for you and most exercises can take seconds or minutes. Anchoring can be utilized in a customer service situation by anchoring a positive state, for instance, the happy satisfied feeling a person feels after a good dining experience. If you can catch someone while they are laughing or smiling, even better so. Just by giving a different kind of hand shake where maybe you shake their hand and then touch the same arm with your other hand, a double hand shake, or you touch them on the shoulder at the opportune time, during a smile or laugh, then you will be anchoring in that "good" feeling. If you do that the next time you see them, they will experience this happy feeling again and may soon find that your restaurant is their favorite place to eat.

NLP is now scientifically proven and can assist in not only changing your association with others but also change your entire perception on how you feel about yourself, about others or certain triggering situations. You will exude a positive energy because your views will change.

Your behavior in your customer service position will act as a springboard towards making you a more pleasurable employee who receives more tips, gets more promotions and has a better sense of self. An overall feeling of well-being will spill into your life by being in command of your emotions."   Marlo Shay Boutte', Hypnotherapist / NLP Practioner

My friend, Hanna Redi, who has worked in the service industry and is a licensed hypnotherapist explains it like this:

"NLP NeuroLinguisticPrograming is a method of influencing brain behavior.

ANCHORING is a NLP technique, where an internal state of mind is connected to an, often, external STIMULUS. Once the two are associated with each other, the simple external STIMULUS, when later performed, has the power to bring upon recall, and the more complex, and desired, state of mind.

A STIMULUS is brought upon by our SENSES. As you likely are familiar with, we commonly refer to 5 SENSES. #1 Seeing (VISUAL), #2 Hearing (AUDITORY), #3 Taste (GUSTATORY), #4 Smell (OLFACTORY) and #5 TOUCH (KINESTHETIC).

At least 1 of 5 SENSES must be involved in the ANCHORING.

The internal, state of mind, in this case is likely to be CONTENT. CONTENT by the physical wellbeing that comes with a good meal, CONTENT by the effortless communication, while being heard and served, by a great server, etc.

NOW, at the height of this sense of CONTENT, it is time to ANCHOR this internal sense of wellbeing, with the outside stimulus, which is brought upon by and through 1 of our 5 SENSES - often a firm TOUCH will suffice.

The more of your customers SENSES that are involved, the more likely is a well ANCHORED experience, and the more likely your Customer, will think of your restaurant, for no apparent reason to him, (but you know better) and with an urge, to visit again, to experience what feels good to him.

We assume that your Customer already did enjoy the decor of your establishment and the presentation on their plate #1(VISUAL). Many restaurants play soothing, relaxing or otherwise stimulating music in the background #2 (AUDITORY). Of course the food is hopefully not only tasting amazing #3 (GUSTATORY) but also smelling great. #4 (OLFACTORY)
...So now, GIVE ME 5, and let's seal the deal, and ANCHOR with your finishing T O U C H #5 (KINESTHETIC)"
Hanna Redi, Certified Clinical Hypnotherapist C.Ht.

I would say that both, Marlo and Hanna, have described it quite simply and clearly. By employing these techniques, we can actually reinforce a positive mental state in an individual through a simple handshake, touch or a high five. If you work at a sports bar and you perceive that your guests have had an enjoyable time and you would like to anchor that feeling of well-being that they have to your establishment, a simple high five may be appropriate.

Of course, we must be aware of and respectful of the guest's demeanor and if they are hesitant in any way **PLEASE DO NOT DO THIS.**
As Marlo explained, the beauty of it is that you don't have to understand it or believe it for it to work.   NLP is scientifically proven.   If it's of interest to you and you wish to explore it further, there's a myriad of books and teachers you can find on the topic.

If it's not for you, then just foggedabotit!

Now we are at the point where you have brought your guests from a warm and pleasant welcome to a *WOW!* dining experience. You've not only served them, but you've actually hosted them as if they were a guest in your home. You and your team working in unison, in sync, have put on an amazing, expectation-shattering performance.
You and your guests are in a positive state of mind and although the dinner may be over, now it's time to be...

Chapter 25

Getting the Encore

en•core /ˈänkôr/
NOUN
A repeated or additional performance of an item at the end of a
concert, as called for by an audience.
EXCLAMATION
Called out by an audience at the end of a concert to request an
additional performance

"As a spectator I witnessed the applause given to the performer,
so I decided to be the performer."
Amit Kalantri

Just as any performer wants to know that they have connected with their audience, that their performance captured the heart and emotions of the viewer, so too, it is with us, in our industry. We as service professionals desire to know that we did more than enough to not only please our guests, and deliver **WOW!** service to them, but hopefully, we will have anchored, either consciously or unconsciously (or both) in their mind that ours is the place to come to in order to receive wonderful service.

Getting the Encore, then, goes beyond just the applause-so to speak, beyond the wonderful tip but also to the point that the guest's dining experience was so great that they cannot wait to come back. I remember the very first week that I was working at Paul Mineo's Trattoria-soon after they had opened. I had a guest, John-we'll call him, who came in for dinner by himself and he was so happy with his dining experience in its entirety, that at the end of his meal, then and there-he called his friends that he had reservations to have dinner with for New Year's Eve and he told them, "I'm cancelling our reservations at XYZ Restaurant, we're coming here to Paul MIneo's for New Year's."

That was a really great feeling, knowing that we had executed so perfectly that dinner service that it motivated our guest to not only decide to come back but he multiplied our clientele with that one phone call. John became not only a valued guest but a loyal customer of that restaurant.

Once a guest has walked into our restaurant, it should be our goal, always to do such a fantastic job of delivering excellent service that not only is the guest happy and satisfied but that now they become your marketer. Word of mouth advertisement is still the strongest advertisement there is. And now with the internet, a person's word of mouth is multiplied very quickly.

However, we don't ever want merely satisfied customers. As Shep Hyken explains in his book, Amaze Every Customer, Every Time,

"Satisfaction is just a rating-and an average rating at that. Whenever a customer checks off a "Yes" answer to the questions, "Were you satisfied with this purchase, experience, whatever?" all that really proves is that we've fulfilled the minimum requirement to avoid a complaint. We've delivered an average experience, a Moment of Mediocrity-nothing more. We've done nothing to create loyalty."

So, obviously we don't want to just create moments of mediocrity for our guests. We want to perform so amazingly every time that we know that that guest is not only returning but they'll be returning with others-new customers for your business. The compounding effect of this is quite astounding.

We have to learn to have a long term view of our relationship with our guests/customers. Every one of the Service Professionals that I interviewed for this book, regardless of their position in the industry, in one way or another, talked about what a customer's business is worth to an establishment over time.

If you have two businessmen that come to your restaurant for lunch and they have a very positive dining experience, imagine what those two guests could amount to in revenue, say over 5 years. Let's just consider an example of only 2 years. Let's assume that they come in for lunch about once a week. Although, realistically, if your establishment is ideally located for your business clientele-it's not unheard of for some of the same clientele to come 3, 4 or even 5 times a week.

But for example sake, let's say they come in once a week. Now although there's two of them, we'll just do this equation for one of them. So, once a week for a year would be 52 but we'll cut that to 44 to allow for holidays, vacation etc. Each time our patron, let's call him Mike, comes for lunch he spends about 18.00. That amounts to $792.00 for lunch over the course of 44 weeks. Okay, you may think that that's not that much, but let's continue.

Mike is married and once a month his wife and her group of friends get together for happy hour. There's 6 of them. Sometimes only 4 show up but usually at least 5 do. They used to have their favorite place to go for happy hour but since Mike has become such a loyal customer, he mentions to his wife, Barbara that she and her group should consider your restaurant. So they do and they are so warmly welcomed by the staff and treated like queens because they all know Mike and now this becomes their monthly place to go. On average their bill for happy hour is $150.00.   Again, not that much but it all begins to add up.

Let's calculate:
$150/monthly happy hour x 12 months = $1800

Let's consider, each of these women have families, and from time to time they may take the family out for dinner. How often? Let's just say each one with their family dines at the restaurant about once every 3 months.

The 6 families vary in size, so let's just say a family of 4 on average. Now we all know that dinner is going to cost considerably more than lunch. Lunch is usually a soft drink or iced tea, a salad and an entrée. At dinner they may order appetizers, salads, entrees, wine, they may even get tiramisu.

A family of 4 having dinner here could easily spend $200 or more. Multiply that times 4 times a year and 6 families and here's how our calculation now looks:

$18.00/lunch x 44 weeks------------------------------=$ 792.00
$150/monthly happy hour x 12 months----------=$1,800.00
$200/family dinner x 4 times a year x 6 families $4,800.00

$7,392.00

So far, in this example, our one businessman, Mike has generated through the people that he knows, over $7000.00 in revenue for your establishment.

This is not to mention when he decides to have his company Christmas party at your restaurant. Thirty employees, set menu-4 course dinner. What do you think that might be worth? Well, at a price of $45.00 per person not including wine or alcohol-we could be talking about another $2000.

If Mike tips 20% then he's actually contributing over $11,000.00 in one year to your business and your staff. This example is not unrealistic. In fact it is based upon actual clientele at a restaurant that I worked at. So, how important is executing Service and Hospitality on a very high level, all the time for every guest? I would say, extremely high. Would you agree?

In your current place of business, how many Mikes do you have? Seeing the long term picture will help you understand that what you do matters. What happens today will have a lasting impact upon your business' future. Does everybody fit the picture of Mike? No, but many do.

We live in community. We like to hang out with, dine with, watch sports with and drink with people we know. Most people will invite or recommend at least one person to an establishment that they are fond of. You need to know that your guests, your customers wield so much influence and that's without even considering review sites and social media.

Seeing the long term view also helps put any problems or small issues in perspective. If every manager and owner would embrace this vision and mentality, putting a fresh steak on the grill to fix a mistake would not even be given a second thought. Just do it. Get it right, make that guest know that you care, earn their trust and loyalty and you've got them. They'll tell their wife, and their golfing buddies and their colleagues. And guess what? You don't even have to pay them for all that marketing that they are doing for you. Direct, targeted and effective marketing.

Olivier de Roany, of MiX Restaurant in Las Vegas, whom I've referred to many times throughout, t **Getting to WOW!** tells me that so many owners and managers are so mistaken when they say they're concerned about the bottom line. When they say bottom line they are maybe thinking about cost for that day or maybe that month but they should be looking at the lifetime of the guest.

He says it's important to be generous and sometimes giving something away to the guest, (he says to say "Complimentary" rather than "Free"), will benefit you so much in the long run. For example, even if a server goes crazy and 'abuses' this discretion to be able to give something to a guest and he gives away 30 desserts in one night, is that the end of the world? No, not at all. What did it cost to give away those 30 desserts? $100.00 in food costs, maybe?   But look, you were able to bless 30 guests who, now, are one step closer or maybe they already are a loyal customer. Now, how much revenue could those 30 customers be worth to you over the next year or two?

There are restaurants that have loyalty programs in which guests are rewarded for continued patronage. For example after 10 visits you receive a free entrée or dessert or something of that nature. While I have nothing against these 'loyalty programs' per se, I think that there needs to be way more than a card with some holes punched in it in order to build loyalty amongst clientele. Many of these places don't really exhibit that they know anything about customer care, service or hospitality, they just want to know if I have a loyalty card that I want to have punched.

Let's get our focus on the right thing. Please understand me, I think it's great to give frequent flier/diner discounts but let's make sure that everyone on staff knows what excellent service is all about and loyalty card or not, when your guests feel at home and welcomed at your establishment they'll be coming back regularly and with friends.

We must remember, every time you walk on that floor as a server, bartender, hostess or whatever FOH position, this is a Show, you are a Performer and your guest is the Audience. They will usually give you immediate feedback if you are giving a stellar performance or not.

The encore comes with them returning through that front door to your establishment to be welcomed like an old friend or family member into your home and them applauding you saying, "Bravo, bravo! We're back and we can't wait to have that same magical experience one more time. Encore!"

Chapter 26

WELCOME to WOW!

"One's destination is never a place but a new way of looking at things"
Henry Miller

Congratulations! You made it. Actually, we made it here, together. I appreciate you trusting me and taking this journey with me. We have arrived at our destination, our goal, of **Getting to WOW!**

So, now what? What does that actually mean? From the outset, I have shared with you that this was not merely to be a set of rules or simply a "Service Manual". I think most every restaurant, or at least the majority of them, have a Service Manual. But does anybody ever read it beyond the date when they first got hired? My observation is, that no, they don't. While Service Manuals may play a role in the function of an establishment, you can do everything properly and correctly according to their manual and yet still NOT provide **WOW!** service, because your attitude and your energy are all wrong.

Getting to WOW!, as we've learned, starts with the internal, what's going on in our hearts and minds. No matter how great your technique or your personality or ability to sell might be, if you don't always have that MAP with you, of a positive Mindset, good Attitude and a Passion for the business or for service, you will always be missing the mark.

After getting our MAP, we considered the importance and the amazing power the Energy of our thoughts carry. As vibrational, or energetic beings, we send out vibrations through our thoughts and feelings which have either a positive or negative effect upon the people around us, including those that we serve-our guests.

When we realize and daily remember that "Thoughts are Things", we can choose to use our thoughts to positively influence those around us. Taking control of our thoughts leads to us taking responsibility for the results we experience.

No longer should you be riding the emotions-linked-to-tips rollercoaster. Your peers may be constantly allowing themselves to float on the wind of up days and down days, but not you. You now approach each day, each shift, with an upbeat, positive attitude, which emanates out to your guests, and they in turn, respond positively to what you are sending out.

And even on the rare occasion, when your guests don't respond positively to you, you still take responsibility for what happens because you know that even though the (E) Event, may not be what you hoped for, you know that the (O) Outcome is largely due to the (R), which is your response-and that is one thing that you can control.

It is my sincere, hope that you have now made a choice to have a sense of pride in your work. Remember, that no matter what you do in this business-your role is vital to the success of the overall operation. Having that sense of personal pride, and a servant heart, will truly help you move forward and upward, not only in this industry, but in life as well. It is so important to realize that every day that you come to work, you must be prepared, knowledgeable, focused on the details and understand that you are giving a performance. Your guests are expecting a *WOW!* dining experience and you and your team, are the ones who can make that happen.

I'm sure that by now, you understand the value and effect that ongoing, continuous education and training can have upon your success. I encourage you to be committed to continual self-improvement. Please refer to the Author's Resources guide at the back of the book to find some books and authors you may want to start learning from.

Although I said, "Congratulations and welcome", and yes, you have arrived here at our destination, our goal of **Getting to *WOW!*** -I want you to think of this as just the beginning. Now you have the mindset, the understanding, the skillset and the knowledge, that you need to always treat your guests as if they were coming to your own home to dine. You have what it takes to be an Exceptional Service and Hospitality Professional-a **Deliverer of the *WOW!*** if you will.

Perhaps, over the course of this journey, you have begun to really develop a passion for the business, for service and you not only have a desire to serve, but you also want to bring your peers along on this same journey. I expect that, in that case, you will be sharing this book, **Getting to *WOW!*** with them, as well.

If, however, the fire is still not yet in you, but you want it to be, I strongly encourage you to seek out other like-minded individuals-people with a love for food and wine and for creating **WOW!** service experiences for their guests. Find yourself a mentor that you can learn from and catch that passion from. Seek out a chef or restaurateur in your area, who cares about the quality of service and hospitality provided, as much, or more, than they care about the food.
If you seek, you will find. Look for a mentor who is committed to elevating the level and standard of service and hospitality in your community. When you find someone like that, go and ask if you can work for him.

I do know this-now that you are focused on applying the principles you've learned in **Getting to *WOW!*,** you are well on your way to great success in this industry and in every other area of your life.

There is a saying-"When the Student is ready...The Master shall appear"
You are ready. Welcome to **WOW!**
Congratulations and Cheers!

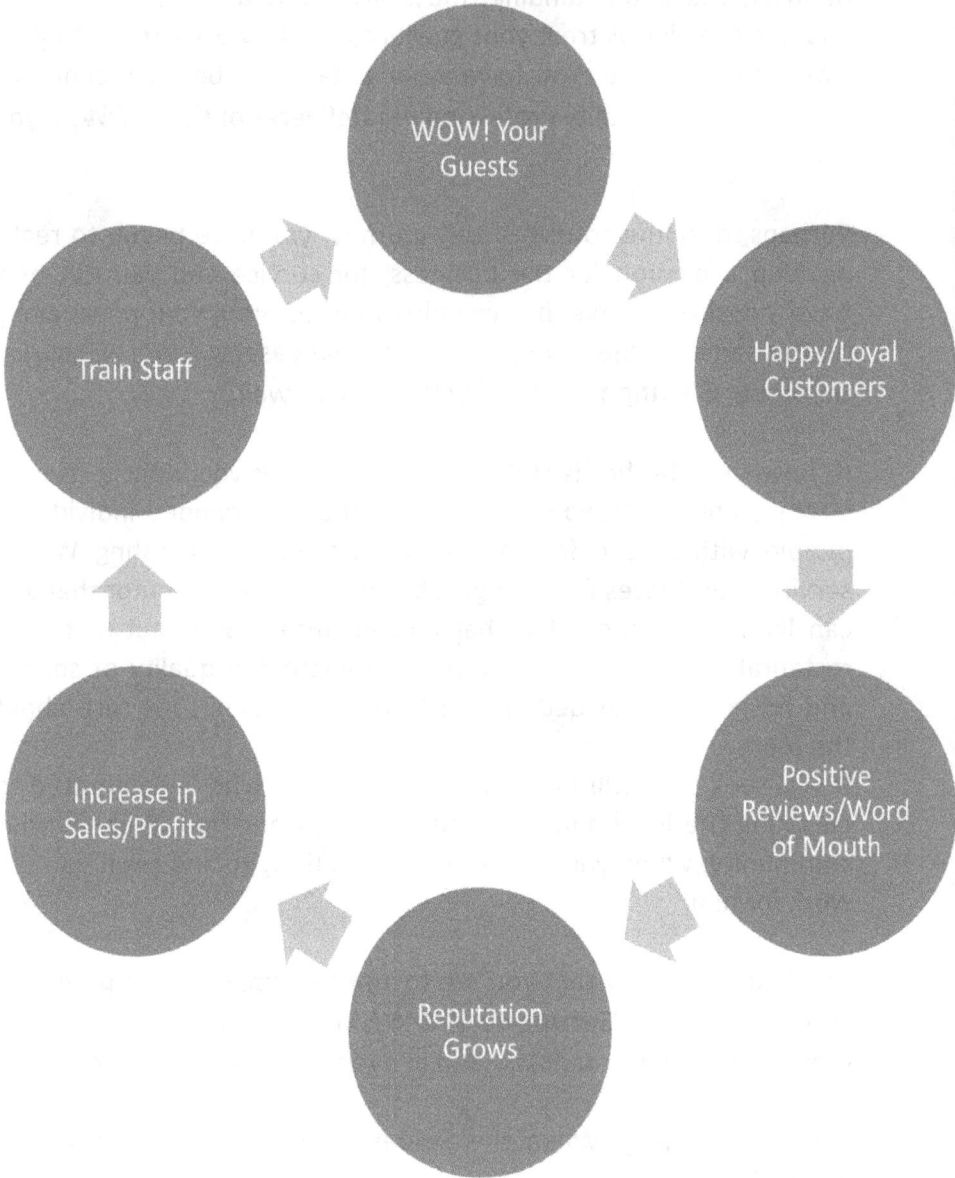

WOW! Your Guests

Happy/Loyal Customers

Positive Reviews/Word of Mouth

Reputation Grows

Increase in Sales/Profits

Train Staff

Author's Resources

The following are books and other authors and experts that have influenced me in some positive way. I have referred to them or quoted them in **Getting to WOW!** Or I just highly recommend them to you:

Aspire- Kevin Hall
Amaze Every Customer, Every Time- Shep Hyken
ATTRACT MONEY NOW- Dr. Joe Vitale
Awaken the Giant Within, & anything by- Anthony Robbins
Change Your Thoughts-Change Your Life- Dr. Wayne W. Dyer
Eating Vegan in Vegas- Paul Graham
Extra Dry with a Twist, An Insider's Guide to Bartending...Shaun Daugherty
IF YOU'RE NOT FIRST, YOU'RE LAST- Grant Cardone
Passion, Profit & Power- Marshall Sylver
Secrets of the Millionaire Mind-T. Harv Eker
Smarter, Faster, Cheaper- David Siteman Garland
The 21 Irrefutable Laws of Leadership- John Maxwell The Advantage- Patrick Lencioni
The Little Red Book of Selling- Jeffrey Gitomer
The One Minute Millionaire- Mark Victor Hansen
The Secret- Rhonda Byrne
The Answer- John Assaraf
The Slight Edge- Jeff Olson
The Success Principles- Jack Canfield
Think and Grow Rich- Napoleon Hill
You Can, You Will, Joel Osteen